Flash Facebook Cookbook

Over 60 recipes for integrating Flash applications with the
Graph API and Facebook

James Ford

PUBLISHING

BIRMINGHAM - MUMBAI

Flash Facebook Cookbook

Copyright © 2011 Packt Publishing

First published: August 2011

Production Reference: 1170811

Published by Packt Publishing Ltd.
Livery Place
35 Livery Street
Birmingham B3 2PB, UK

ISBN 978-1-849690-72-0

www.packtpub.com

Cover Image by Charwak A. (charwak86@gmail.com)

Credits

Author

James Ford

Reviewers

Emanuele Feronato

Paulius Uza

Acquisition Editor

Steven Wilding

Development Editor

Hyacintha D'Souza

Technical Editors

Prashant Macha

Gauri Iyer

Sakina Kaydawala

Project Coordinator

Leena Purkait

Proofreader

Lynda Silwoski

Indexer

Monica Ajmera Mehta

Production Coordinator

Shantanu Zhagade

Cover Work

Shantanu Zhagade

About the Author

James Ford lives and works in the relatively sedate Midlands of England, and is constantly thankful that he doesn't have to contend with public transport or large volumes of traffic on a regular basis. Occasionally being stuck behind a tractor for several miles is a small price to pay for that!

Macromedia Flash 8 represented his first serious interaction with a programming language, an epiphany whereupon his BA in Design for Interactive Media became far more focused on the Programming side of things than the Art (although it turned out okay).

He considers himself to be fortunate to have encountered the Flash Platform when he did, as during that time between first contact and today, the Flash Platform has evolved at just the right pace to enable him to keep up with the latest shiny new features.

In addition to developing Facebook-integrated Flash Player applications, James has also developed a few AIR applications, built a couple of Apps for iOS and Android devices, helped develop a load of websites, and blogs about all of this on his website: `http://www.psyked.co.uk/`.

Acknowledgement

So much of what seems original in the world of programming can be achieved by simply learning to use the tools that others have already developed, and the code that we use in this cookbook does a lot of just that. With this in mind, we should acknowledge the authors of the two main Facebook ActionScript libraries:

Jason Christ, the team from `http://gskinner.com/` and the teams at both Adobe and Facebook, who have collaborated to produce the Official Facebook ActionScript 3 SDK.

Mark Walters, a.k.a. yourpalmark, who almost singlehandedly extended the Official SDK into the unofficial community-supported SDK, introducing a more frequent update schedule and a range of helpful new ActionScript classes. It's his version of the SDK that we use in this cookbook, and I'm very grateful for it.

Thanks also to my technical reviewers, Emanuele and Paul, whose comments have been invaluable—keeping my propensity for bad coding practice in check as much as everything else, I hope it wasn't too harrowing a task for you guys.

And of course, the team at Packt Publishing—particulary Steven, Hyacintha, and Leena—and everyone else who's been involved. No doubt that I could not have done it without you.

About the Reviewers

Emanuele Feronato has been studying programming languages since the early eighties, with a particular interest in web and game development. He taught online programming for the European Social Fund and now owns a web development company in Italy where he also works as a lead programmer.

As a writer, he has worked as technical reviewer for Packt Publishing and he's actually writing a book about Flash game development.

His blog, www.emanueleferonato.com, is one of the most visited blogs about indie programming.

> I would like to thank Leena Purkait at Packt Publishing for the opportunity to review this book, and my little daughter Kimora for making my life happy.

Paulius Uza is an award winning Interactive Producer and Managing Partner at InRuntime Inc. Over the last nine years, Paulius has gained significant experience in various fields of digital advertising and technology by working with a world renowned brands such as MTV, Nokia, ZuluTrade, AAAFx, and Donzi Marine to name a few. Being an artist and a technology expert, Paulius combines best of both worlds by creating and delivering engaging digital advertising and interactive media experiences.

Paulius is a major contributor to open source community, with his software featured in hundreds of open source and commercial software projects such as Adobe Captivate.

During his free time he writes a blog about interactive design and programming topics at: http://www.uza.lt

www.PacktPub.com

Support files, eBooks, discount offers, and more

You might want to visit www.PacktPub.com for support files and downloads related to your book.

Did you know that Packt offers eBook versions of every book published, with PDF and ePub files available? You can upgrade to the eBook version at www.PacktPub.com and as a print book customer, you are entitled to a discount on the eBook copy. Get in touch with us at service@packtpub.com for more details.

At www.PacktPub.com, you can also read a collection of free technical articles, sign up for a range of free newsletters and receive exclusive discounts and offers on Packt books and eBooks.

http://PacktLib.PacktPub.com

Do you need instant solutions to your IT questions? PacktLib is Packt's online digital book library. Here, you can access, read, and search across Packt's entire library of books.

Why Subscribe?

- Fully searchable across every book published by Packt
- Copy and paste, print and bookmark content
- On demand and accessible via web browser

Free Access for Packt account holders

If you have an account with Packt at www.PacktPub.com, you can use this to access PacktLib today and view nine entirely free books. Simply use your login credentials for immediate access.

This book is dedicated to Leonie; my soulmate, my better half. She's been infinitely patient and supportive, both before and during the writing of this cookbook. Couldn't have done it without you, you know.

Family and friends deserve credit also—encouragement and support is very warmly received. I apologize profoundly for being distant and unreachable for so long while I've been writing.

Table of Contents

Preface

Flash applications are popular and becoming increasingly social. With Flash applications for Facebook you can tap into a potential audience of half a billion existing users, their connections and affiliations, their uploaded images, posts, comments, and more.

The Flash Facebook Cookbook is packed with recipes for the Graph API and FQL, used for reading and writing data as well as interacting with Facebook anonymously or on behalf of an authorized Facebook User.

The topics covered by the recipes in this cookbook include working with News Feeds, uploading Photos, searching for and plotting Places on a Map and much more. The cookbook has recipes ranging from those that work without any authentication with Facebook to those that do, and act on behalf of a user. Packed with recipes that yield practical demonstrations of the Graph API functionality, the Flash Facebook Cookbook is an essential tool for Flash Platform developers.

What this book covers

Chapter 1, Getting Started with Flash and Facebook: This chapter deals with downloading the Facebook ActionScript 3 SDK, registering a new Application on Facebook.com, getting your Flash Builder development environment set up, and getting ready to start working with the Facebook APIs.

Chapter 2, Authenticating with Facebook: Our application can't do much unless it's first authenticated with Facebook, so this chapter covers logging in, logging out, and tapping into existing Facebook sessions, for both Flash Player and AIR-based projects.

Chapter 3, Working with Facebook Permissions: Even authenticated, our application can't do much without the correct permissions, so this chapter covers processes, tactics, and strategies for working with and requesting those Extended Permissions for Facebook users.

Chapter 4, Reading and Writing Data with the Graph API: A generalized introduction to working with the core Graph API, including retrieving specific objects, multiple objects, and object connections; searching for data, limiting and paging results; and an introduction to creating and managing data with the Graph API.

Chapter 5, Loading Data with FQL: FQL is the SQL-like syntax for retrieving data from Facebook, and with it we can retrieve far more specific data than we can with the Graph API, including data that is unavailable via the Graph API.

Chapter 6, Facebook News Feeds and Status Updates: In this chapter, we look at loading Facebook News and Profile Feeds, creating new Status updates and Links, and adding custom actions to links to help promote your Facebook application.

Chapter 7, Comments and "Like this": Following on from the previous chapter, we look at loading, creating, and deleting Comments for Graph API objects, and the same for 'Likes', with both Graph API objects and web URLs.

Chapter 8, Working with Photos, Albums, and Tags: In this chapter, we'll load Photos from the Graph API—both photos of the current user, and photos from the current user. We display these images and overlay Facebook tagging information, and use the Flash Player to upload new images on the user's behalf.

Chapter 9, Working with Groups and Events: In this chapter, we retrieve Facebook Group and Event information, locate them on a Map, create new Events, and respond to Event invitations on the user's behalf.

Chapter 10, Checkins with Facebook Places: In this chapter, we download and integrate the Google Maps components and use them to plot Checkins and Facebook Places. We work with the Geolocation capabilities of HTML5, and use them to search for nearby Facebook Places and create new Checkins.

Chapter 11, Bridging the Flash and Application Gap: Finally, we'll look to improve the integration between your application and Facebook—imitate the Facebook.com website interface, use native dialogs to bypass the need for Extended Permissions, and develop a new class to simplify the authentication and permissions management for our application.

What you need for this book

- Software:
    - Adobe Flash Builder 4 (or greater), with the Flex 4 SDK and AIR libraries
    - A web browser (obviously)
- Additional hardware/software:
    - (Access to) an HTTP web server, either online or local

Who this book is for

This cookbook is targeted towards those with at least a basic understanding of the Flash Builder IDE and the Flex framework. No prior knowledge of the Facebook APIs is assumed or required. If you want to start building Flash Facebook apps quickly and effectively this is the book for you.

Conventions

In this book, you will find a number of styles of text that distinguish between different kinds of information. Here are some examples of these styles, and an explanation of their meaning.

Code words in text are shown as follows: "Our user interface should include two `Button` components—`login_btn` and `logout_btn`."

A block of code is set as follows:

```
function tryRequest():void
{
    var data:Object = new Object();
    data.message = "Hello world!";
    Facebook.postData("/me/feed", onPostStatusCallback, data);
}
```

When we wish to draw your attention to a particular part of a code block, the relevant lines or items are set in bold:

```
<s:Button buttonMode="true"
          click="requestThePermissions()"
          enabled="false" height="32" id="request_btn"
          label="Request Permissions" width="100%" />
```

Any command-line input or output is written as follows:

```
SELECT x
    FROM page
    WHERE page_id = 19292868552
```

New terms and **important words** are shown in bold. Words that you see on the screen, in menus or dialog boxes for example, appear in the text like this: "We should update the user interface to initially disable the **Request Permissions** and **Post status message** buttons".

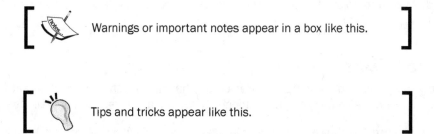

> Warnings or important notes appear in a box like this.

> Tips and tricks appear like this.

Reader feedback

Feedback from our readers is always welcome. Let us know what you think about this book—what you liked or may have disliked. Reader feedback is important for us to develop titles that you really get the most out of.

To send us general feedback, simply send an e-mail to feedback@packtpub.com, and mention the book title via the subject of your message.

If there is a book that you need and would like to see us publish, please send us a note in the **SUGGEST A TITLE** form on www.packtpub.com or e-mail suggest@packtpub.com.

If there is a topic that you have expertise in and you are interested in either writing or contributing to a book, see our author guide on www.packtpub.com/authors.

Customer support

Now that you are the proud owner of a Packt book, we have a number of things to help you to get the most from your purchase.

Downloading the example code for this book

You can download the example code files for all Packt books you have purchased from your account at http://www.PacktPub.com. If you purchased this book elsewhere, you can visit http://www.PacktPub.com/support and register to have the files e-mailed directly to you.

Errata

Although we have taken every care to ensure the accuracy of our content, mistakes do happen. If you find a mistake in one of our books—maybe a mistake in the text or the code—we would be grateful if you would report this to us. By doing so, you can save other readers from frustration and help us improve subsequent versions of this book. If you find any errata, please report them by visiting http://www.packtpub.com/support, selecting your book, clicking on the **errata submission form** link, and entering the details of your errata. Once your errata are verified, your submission will be accepted and the errata will be uploaded on our website, or added to any list of existing errata, under the Errata section of that title. Any existing errata can be viewed by selecting your title from http://www.packtpub.com/support.

Piracy

Piracy of copyright material on the Internet is an ongoing problem across all media. At Packt, we take the protection of our copyright and licenses very seriously. If you come across any illegal copies of our works, in any form, on the Internet, please provide us with the location address or website name immediately so that we can pursue a remedy.

Please contact us at copyright@packtpub.com with a link to the suspected pirated material.

We appreciate your help in protecting our authors, and our ability to bring you valuable content.

Questions

You can contact us at questions@packtpub.com if you are having a problem with any aspect of the book, and we will do our best to address it.

1
Getting Started with Flash and Facebook

In this chapter, we will cover:

- ▶ Setting up a new application on Facebook
- ▶ Downloading the Facebook ActionScript 3 SDK
- ▶ Including the Facebook ActionScript 3 SDK in a Flash Builder project
- ▶ Including the Facebook ActionScript 3 SDK as a Flash Builder library project
- ▶ Preparing your Flash Player application's HTML template for Facebook integration

Introduction

All third-party systems that work with data from Facebook do so through the Facebook API, which is a combination of REST-style techniques, OAuth 2.0, and an ever-evolving combination of web technologies, collectively titled by Facebook as the Graph API.

Facebook provides developers with a number of different code libraries through its developer portal, and of these the only one that's completely client-side is the JavaScript SDK. But anything that JavaScript can do can be done by both ActionScript 3 and the Flash Platform, more or less.

You might think, having looked at the SDKs officially listed by Facebook in their developer portal, that you'd need to build a code library yourself but luckily for us, there's already an existing, officially supported, ActionScript 3 library for working with the Graph API. This library, the **Facebook ActionScript 3 SDK**, is supported by both Adobe and Facebook, so you can be assured that it will be kept up-to-date and fully functional, even if there is a significant overhaul of the Facebook APIs—after all, who better to support this SDK than Adobe and Facebook themselves?

There's no sense in recreating the wheel, as they say, so the examples in this cookbook will be using the existing Facebook ActionScript 3 SDK almost exclusively for its recipes. We'll also be using the Flex SDK 4.0 for our examples, as it's a quick and easy way to construct user interfaces and put together working prototypes for our recipes. However, using Flex isn't a requirement for the Facebook ActionScript 3 SDK to work—it's just for the examples in this Cookbook. Integrating the Facebook SDK with a normal ActionScript-only project or a Flash Professional-based project is entirely possible—it will just inevitably require a little more time creating the interface, but the ActionScript 3 code behind it all will work pretty much the same.

In this chapter we'll be getting ready to start developing with Facebook—we'll download the Facebook ActionScript 3 SDK, integrate that SDK with our Flash Builder workspace, set up our application on **Facebook.com**, and generally get everything set up that we need to before we can start communicating with the Facebook APIs.

Setting up a new application on Facebook

To access the full range of data available from the Facebook API, you need an API key, and for that, you need to set up an application on Facebook itself. To do this you need to set up an account on Facebook, and use that account to join the Facebook developer program.

Every Facebook application, whether it's based on server-side languages (like PHP), or client-side technologies (like JavaScript or ActionScript), needs an API key to send and receive data through the Facebook API. Alongside the API key, the application also gets a unique Application ID that makes it possible for Facebook to keep track of what actions a user has allowed your application to perform with their data, and an Application Secret, which is used for authentication.

As well as giving you the ability to use more features of the API, setting up your Flash project as an application and promoting it through Facebook greatly improves the chance that users will discover your application organically through the social network. For example, status updates created by your application will all link back to the application's *Fan Page*.

In this section, we're going to go through the necessary steps to register a new application on Facebook, and what we actually need is the API Key, Application ID, and an Application Secret for Flash.

Getting ready

You can set up your application as soon as you're registered as a developer with Facebook. To register as a developer you first need a Facebook profile. You've probably already got one, but you'll probably want to create at least one other Facebook account for development or testing purposes. I'm sure your existing Facebook friends won't appreciate a wave of "test message" spam in the near future.

Once you've logged in with the Facebook account you want to use for development, go to URL: `http://www.facebook.com/developers/` to add the Facebook Developer application to your profile.

From the Facebook Developer center you can see the latest news from the Facebook developer blog, as well as useful links for developers (Documentation, Privacy Polices, Rules, and so on).

Click on the link **+ Set Up New App** or go to the following website address: `http://www.facebook.com/developers/createapp.php` to start the application setup process.

How to do it...

If you just want to get up and run as fast as possible, the minimal amount of data that's needed to register a new application is its name.

Your application name does not need to be unique—even for yourself. It's acceptable to name two (or more!) of your applications exactly the same, as Facebook assigns every application its own unique **Application ID**. Good thing to, really—otherwise all the good names would likely be taken in a frantic bout of application name-squatting.

There's far more information you can add, such as application icons, description, contact e-mail addresses, and support URLs—all pretty simple stuff, and you can always return to the settings screen to change or update things later on.

Once you've entered your application name (and any other information you wish) save your changes and you'll get a screen containing the following information:

Now that we've got ourselves an **API Key**, we can start using it in requests to the Facebook Graph API. We'll also need the **Application ID**, so make a note of that, but the **Application Secret** is something we don't actually need for any of the recipes covered in this cookbook.

How it works...

All applications that integrate with Facebook aren't actually part of Facebook; they're an external application, and that's true for every third-party application that you might have seen appear within the Facebook interface (these are known as Canvas or Tab applications, depending on whether they're on their own page, or a Tab on another page). Technically, they are external websites that are loaded into the Facebook interface using an iframe element in HTML.

Without the **API Key** an application can't do anything other than retrieve the information that is publicly available. All other actions—such as requesting news feeds or publishing information to Facebook—require the end user to give your application the explicit permission to perform that action, with the **API Key** being what the Graph API relies upon when generating access tokens and authorizing requests.

Our application can request new permissions at any point, and similarly the end user can modify or reject our application permissions at any point, so generating an access token and passing it in all data requests is an easy way for Facebook to maintain the user's control over their data access.

There's more...

To get a broader overview of the settings that can be changed for a Facebook application, the best place to look is the Developer Documentation, which is available online on the Facebook Developer center: `http://developers.facebook.com/docs/`.

There's no single page which gives a description of the settings, but rather the information is distributed around the pages where it's actually relevant.

When we set up an application on Facebook, it also sets up a Profile Page specifically for that application—similar to a Facebook page (but not exactly the same)—and devoted to our new application.

See also

▶ *Preparing your Flash Player application's HTML template for Facebook integration* recipe in this chapter

Downloading the Facebook ActionScript 3 SDK

There are two ways to get the source code for the Facebook ActionScript SDK—one is simply download a precompiled version of the source code, and for that all you need is an Internet connection.

The other way to obtain the source code is to download the very latest version directly from a source control repository.

There are in fact two main versions of the Facebook ActionScript 3 SDK. One is the 'Official' version of the SDK, hosted in a **Subversion** repository on Google code, maintained and updated by teams associated with Adobe and Facebook; and the other is more of a community-driven effort, stored in a **Git** repository and hosted on GitHub.

In this recipe and all of the recipes in this Cookbook, we will be working with a branch of the community-driven version of the Facebook ActionScript 3 SDK, rather than the 'Official' version of the SDK.

Getting ready

To download the SDK from Git, we need to have Git installed on your computer, which can be downloaded and installed from the URL: `http://git-scm.com/`.

How to do it...

1. If you have no desire to work with code which includes version-control information, both the precompiled SWC files and the raw ActionScript source code for the Facebook ActionScript 3 SDK can be downloaded from the following URLs:

   - `https://github.com/psyked/facebook-actionscript-api`
   - `https://github.com/psyked/facebook-air-api`

2. Within the pages at these URLs, select the **Downloads** button that appears in the top-left of the page, and you'll get popup containing the download options:

3. To download the raw ActionScript files, select the **Download .zip** option—listed under the **DOWNLOAD SOURCE** heading—or to download the precompiled SWC file, select the **Facebook Web SDK.swc** (or the **Facebook Desktop SDK.swc**) file—listed under the **DOWNLOAD PACKAGES** heading.

4. Alternatively, if you have **Git** installed, you can clone the entire repository, including its past history and references to its original source location, with the following command-line statement:

```
git clone git@github.com:psyked/facebook-actionscript-api.git
```

or

```
git clone git@github.com:psyked/facebook-air-api.git
```

This command will create a new folder with the name **'facebook-actionscript-api'** and within that, create three key folders—**docs**, **examples**, and **src**. Unsurprisingly, these folders contain the source code for the library, the documentation for the library, and several sample applications, respectively.

How it works...

The download locations for this recipe, and the source code for the Facebook SDKs which form the backbone of the recipes in this cookbook, point to Git repositories which are hosted by **GitHub**.

The source code for this repository is itself originally based on the official version of the SDK which is hosted on Google code, but it has been extended and expanded by other developers, (primarily Mark Walters, of `http://yourpalmark.com/`). The advantage of using our community-driven version of the SDK over the official one is that the source code is traditionally updated much more frequently, and includes a wide array of value-object classes, which the official version of the SDK does not yet include.

There's more

Not sure which version of the SDK is best for your project?

The Flash Player version, or the AIR version of the SDK?

In addition to the different download options, there are also two different versions of the Facebook ActionScript 3 SDK, and the one which we will use depends on whether we're building desktop applications that run in Adobe AIR, or browser-based applications that use the Flash Player.

Both versions of the SDK are available for download from GitHub, but you can only use the Adobe AIR libraries with an Adobe AIR project, and the web-based libraries will only work properly with a web-based Flash Builder project that has the Facebook JavaScript SDK included in the HTML template, which is what we'll look at in the next recipe, *Preparing your Flash Player application's HTML template for Facebook integration*.

What if I want to build my own Facebook library?

There's nothing 'magical' about this Facebook ActionScript API—everything it can do is built on standard capabilities of ActionScript 3 and the Flash Player. If you wanted to, it's entirely possible to write your own code that works with Facebook without using this library, but why, as mentioned in the introduction, should you re-invent the wheel?

That doesn't mean that the official API isn't subject to an occasional change—the move by Facebook to the 'Open Graph' in 2010 is evidence of that—but it does mean that there's always going to be someone maintaining the project and making sure it works with the latest version of the Facebook API.

See also

> ▶ *Including the Facebook ActionScript 3 SDK in a Flash Builder project*
> ▶ *Preparing your Flash Player application's HTML template for Facebook integration*

Including the Facebook ActionScript 3 SDK in a Flash Builder project

Your situation, experience, personal preferences and the complexity of your final project dictate exactly how you'll integrate the Facebook ActionScript 3 SDK into your project. In this recipe we're going to use the precompiled SWC files that we've downloaded in our earlier recipe, *Downloading the Facebook ActionScript 3 SDK,* and integrate them with a new Flash Builder project.

How to do it...

Within your project structure you will, by default, have a `libs` folder. Copy your downloaded SWC file into that folder, and at a basic level, that's all there is to it.

The classes from the Facebook ActionScript 3 SDK will now be available to your project—you should get auto-complete code suggestions as you type, and more importantly, be able to compile your code!

How it works...

An SWC file is a compiled set of source files—which could be ActionScript source code or symbols and images—and is a useful way of making your source code available for others to use, while still protecting the actual original code. Anyone with the SWC can get access to the classes it contains and all their properties and methods, but can't actually see the code behind those methods. Of course, protecting the code isn't a huge concern for the Facebook ActionScript 3 SDK, as we can get all of the source code from other sources anyway.

The great thing about using a SWC file is that it minimizes the clutter of source files in your project—you don't need to include anything more than the SWC, whereas if you wanted to use the actual source files, you'd need to add 20-odd additional ActionScript files. That might not sound bad, but when you start using the source-code versions of multiple ActionScript libraries, you can easily end up with 10, 20, 50, or more ActionScript files that aren't actually written by you for this project.

Another little plus with SWC files are that they're precompiled, which theoretically means lower compile times for your project. I don't think it actually makes much of a difference for this SDK, but every little bit helps I guess!

There's more...

What about the downsides of SWC files? Well, the main downside of a SWC file is also partially the reason it exists—that you can't see the actual source code. If you want to browse through the source code, but still get the advantages of using a SWC file in your project, follow the next recipe *Including the Facebook ActionScript 3 SDK as a Flash Builder library project*.

If you're using a SWC exclusively then you'll be flying blind if you should trigger errors on the classes you don't have the source code for, and will be presented with a dialog similar to this:

Informative, but really not helpful when you're trying to find out where your code is breaking down. Luckily there's a solution for that, and it is by linking source files to an included SWC.

Of course, when it comes to Runtime Errors, it's more likely that the error is in your code, rather than the Facebook ActionScript 3 SDK. Linking to the source is more about helping you find and debug your own errors, rather than searching for errors in the SWC.

Linking source files to an included SWC

Before we start out, it's important to note that linking source files to an included SWC file doesn't actually have any effect on the SWC itself. Instead, what we're doing is giving Flash Builder the location of the SWC's source files.

When Flash Builder tries to open your project in debug mode it will use this information, but it won't magically enable Flash Builder to recreate the SWC file for you—for that you need to set up the code as a Flash Builder library project (which is, coincidentally, the subject of the next recipe).

Once you've downloaded the Facebook ActionScript 3 SDK source files, place them in a sensible location somewhere on your computer—it doesn't matter where exactly, only that you remember the location.

Open your project preferences screen, and switch to the tab **Flex Build Path** and within that, **Library path**:

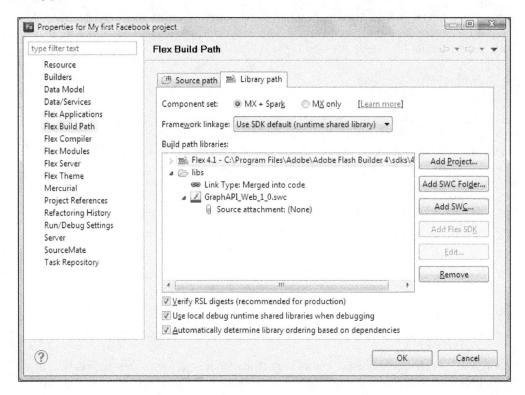

In the preceding screenshot, you can see the **GraphAPI_Web_1_0.swc** file, and underneath that you can see there is a **Source attachment** option—double-click on that to open a new window, labeled **Edit Folder Path**:

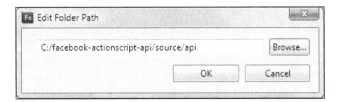

From this dialog you can select the location of the source files for the SWC. There won't be any visual confirmation whether the location you've selected is correct or not, but when you start coding or debugging, you should be able to explore the source code of the classes in the SWC, and see far less of the *Code Navigation Error* dialog.

See also

▶ *Including the Facebook ActionScript 3 SDK as a Flash Builder library project*

Including the Facebook ActionScript 3 SDK as a Flash Builder library project

An alternative to including the Facebook AS3 SDK in its precompiled SWC form is to set up the SDK as a Flash Builder library project.

The end result, as far as the compiler and the user are concerned, is no different, but our own way of developing, reusing, and exploring the code is a little simpler. And unlike the precompiled SWC files that can be downloaded from the GitHub repositories, by using a Flash Builder library project, we can make modifications to the source code.

Using a Flash Builder library project makes it easy to reuse the code in the library in multiple other projects, and for the remaining recipes in this cookbook we're going to be linking to the library projects that we set up in this recipe.

There are two versions of the Facebook ActionScript 3 SDK, and just as there are two versions of the precompiled SWC to download, we will also need to create two Flash Builder library projects. In this recipe we're going to cover setting both of these library projects up and linking to these library projects from other projects.

How to do it...

1. Create a new library project in Flash Builder, using the basic Flex SDK only (don't include the Adobe AIR libraries), and call it **Facebook Web SDK**.

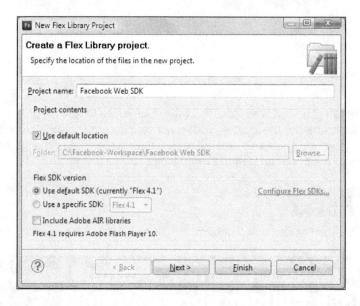

2. Copy the files and folders from the downloaded **facebook-actionscript-api** folder to the **root folder** of our project, setting up the following folder structure:

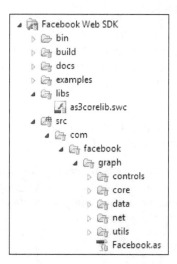

That will create a library project which we can use in basic Flash Player-based web projects. Next, we'll create a project that gives us the Adobe AIR version of the SDK.

3. Keep the **Facebook SDK Web** project open, and create a new Flash Builder library project; call it the **'Facebook Desktop SDK'**, only this time, be sure to include the Adobe AIR libraries in your project.

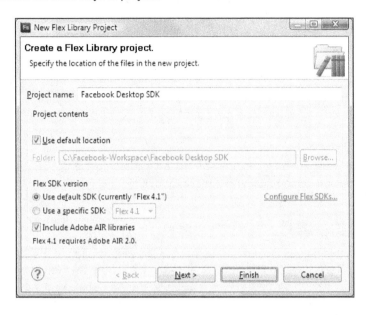

4. As with the web version of the SDK, copy the files you've downloaded from the **facebook-air-api** folder into our new library project, creating the following folder structure:

Not much to see in terms of source code, is there? Unlike the web version of the SDK, the desktop version isn't completely standalone; it relies on core classes from the web project—so what we need to do now is add the web project to the desktop project as a linked library.

5. Open your project preferences, go to the **Flex Library Build Path** and then the **Library path'** tab, then click **Add Project...** and select the **Facebook Web SDK** project.

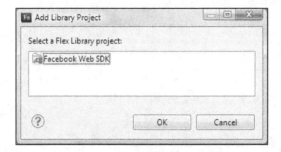

Once the web project is added as a library for the desktop library project, both of those projects should be able to compile, and that's it for this recipe.

How it works...

The complexity in this setup is just realizing that the Desktop version of the SDK is not a standalone library, and does, in fact, require all of the code from the web version. The source code files aren't duplicated for both versions because that would make things more complex to manage, and rather than merging the two sets into a single library project, we have to set things up in a way that keeps all of the AIR-specific source code in its own project.

Both versions of the Facebook ActionScript 3 SDK—Web and Desktop—rely on a core set of classes. The source code for the web version of the library contains all of these classes, whereas the desktop version of the library contains only the classes that require the AIR libraries, which is why it needs to be set up like this—to inherit those core files from the web project.

There's more...

The original release version of the Graph API—version 1.0—included an additional JavaScript file—the `FBJSBridge.js` file. Since version 1.5 of the SDK there's no need for this additional JavaScript file—the Facebook ActionScript 3 SDK works to inject the original contents of that file into the containing HTML page, removing the necessity for those additional files, leaving only the ActionScript SDK as a requirement.

> ▸ *Including the Facebook ActionScript 3 SDK in a Flash Builder project*

Preparing your Flash Player application's HTML template for Facebook integration

Before our web-based application will be able to work with the Facebook Graph API, it will need the Facebook JavaScript SDK to be included in the host HTML page, and it will have to be hosted on a domain or subdomain specified in our Facebook Application settings.

The Facebook JavaScript SDK is what makes it possible for our Flash Player application to obtain details of any active Facebook sessions, and it allows our application to perform actions such as prompting for authentication or requesting additional permissions.

In this recipe we will be extending our web project's default HTML template file to include the Facebook JavaScript SDK. In addition, we also have some more settings to change for our application in the Facebook Developer center—setting up the online Canvas or Tab page URLs, as well as the domains and subdomains which are allowed to access the Graph API.

Getting ready

For our Flash Player application to integrate with Facebook, we will need some form of HTTP server, so that we can run our application from an `http://`-based URL, rather than simply launching a file from a local folder on your computer. Ideally we need a live, publicly-accessible domain under our control, and we'll configure our Facebook Application to use pages on that domain as the basis for our Canvas and Tab applications.

In addition, if we can, it would be most efficient (but not essential) to have an HTTP server set up on our local machine—allowing us to test and debug our Flash Player applications locally, without having to re-upload files to a remote site every time we need to test new functionality.

How to do it...

1   The first thing we'll need is a web-based Flash Player application, which we can get by specifying **Web (runs in Adobe Flash Player)** when we create our Flex project:

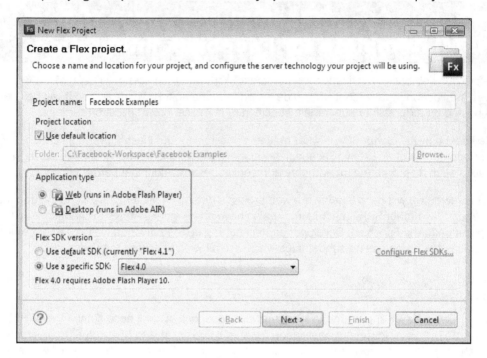

2. Open the folder in your project named **html-template**. If that folder doesn't exist, open your project settings, and make sure that the option **Generate HTML wrapper file** under the **Flex compiler** section is checked.

Downloading the example code for this book

You can download the example code files for all Packt books you have purchased from your account at http://www.PacktPub.com. If you purchased this book elsewhere, you can visit http://www.PacktPub.com/support and register to have the files e-mailed directly to you.

3. The first change we're going to make to our file is to import the Facebook JavaScript SDK. Into the head section of the HTML page (between the opening `<head>` and closing `</head>` tags) add the following code:

```
<script type="text/javascript" src="http://connect.facebook.net/
en_US/all.js"></script>
```

4. This script tag imports the JavaScript SDK into our HTML page, but to activate it we need to add a specific HTML element—a div element with a specific ID. Jump to the bottom of the page, before the penultimate closing tag, `</body>`, and add a new DIV element, with the ID of **fb-root**:

```
<div id="fb-root"></div>
```

5. With these additions, our final HTML code for the entire page template should be similar to this (with our additions to the HTML highlighted):

```
<!DOCTYPE html PUBLIC "-//W3C//DTD XHTML 1.0 Transitional//EN"
"http://www.w3.org/TR/xhtml1/DTD/xhtml1-transitional.dtd">
<!-- saved from url=(0014)about:internet -->
<html xmlns="http://www.w3.org/1999/xhtml" lang="en" xml:
lang="en">
    <head>
        <title>${title}</title>
        <style type="text/css" media="screen">
                html, body    { height:100%; }
                body { margin:0; padding:0; overflow:auto;
text-align:center; background-color: ${bgcolor}; }
                #flashContent { display:none; }
        </style>
        <script type="text/javascript" src="swfobject.js"></
script>
        <script type="text/javascript">
            var swfVersionStr = "${version_major}.${version_
minor}.${version_revision}";
            var xiSwfUrlStr = "${expressInstallSwf}";
            var flashvars = {};
            var params = {};
            params.quality = "high";
            params.bgcolor = "${bgcolor}";
            params.allowscriptaccess = "sameDomain";
            params.allowfullscreen = "true";
            var attributes = {};
            attributes.id = "${application}";
            attributes.name = "${application}";
            attributes.align = "middle";
            swfobject.embedSWF(
                "${swf}.swf", "flashContent",
                "${width}", "${height}",
                swfVersionStr, xiSwfUrlStr,
                flashvars, params, attributes);
                swfobject.createCSS("#flashContent",
                "display:block;text-align:left;");
        </script>
        <script type="text/javascript"
         src="http://connect.facebook.net/en_US/all.js"></script>
    </head>
    <body>
        <div id="flashContent">
```

```
            <p>To view this page ensure that Adobe Flash
    Player version ${version_major}.${version_minor}.
    ${version_revision} or greater is installed.</p>
            </div>
            <div id="fb-root">
            </div>
        </body>
    </html>
```

6. These additions are all we need to attempt communication with the Graph API from a technical point of view, but before our API requests are successful, we must make sure that our application is configured correctly on Facebook.com.

7. Open the Facebook Developer center, from the URL:

   `http://www.facebook.com/developers/apps.php`

8. Edit our existing application, and switch the **Web Site** tab, which contains two key fields—**Site URL** and **Site Domain**:

9. Our **Site URL** will be the location of our application when we upload it to a publicly-accessible HTTP server, and should be expressed as an URL (starting with `http://`).

10. The **Site Domain** (expressed *without* the `http://` prefix) allows us to control the domain and subdomains that are allowed to access the Graph API, while identifying as our application. Once this property is set, only requests that appear to come from that specified URL (or part URL) will be allowed to make requests, and all others will be summarily rejected by the Graph API with the error message:

    Given URL is not allowed by the Application configuration.

11. Change the **Site URL** property to point at our Flash application's live location, such as: `http://facebook.psyked.co.uk/packt/`.

12. Change the **Site Domain** property so that it lists the main domain of our application's live location, for example: `psyked.co.uk`.

13. Now, with the Site's URL and Domain settings established, our next step should be to upload our application and its HTML files to the location we've specified in the Site URL field. Once those files are uploaded and available from the domain we specified in the Site Domain field, we should see no more of those **Given URL is not allowed...** errors.

14. Finally, to test our application we will need to upload our HTML and SWF files to a live web server—one that is able to serve up our application's HTML file from within the domain that we specified in the **Site Domain** setting in the Facebook Developer center. For example, `http://psyked.co.uk/packt/Facebook.html`.

How it works...

The web-based version of the Facebook ActionScript 3 SDK has been developed with a reliance on the Facebook JavaScript SDK being included in the containing HTML page—hence the requirement for us to extend our HTML template to incorporate this SDK.

When we add the **script** tag to our HTML template—using the URL `http://connect.facebook.net/en_US/all.js` as the source location—we are importing the Facebook JavaScript SDK from the **Facebook.com** servers. There are a few fringe benefits to loading the JavaScript SDK in this way—it keeps the SDK up-to-date and it helps with caching resources, but the primary reason for loading the SDK from the **Facebook.com** domain, rather than downloading it and packaging it alongside the HTML and SWF files on our own servers, is that this avoids a lot of potential for cross-domain scripting issues, and makes domain-restricted information such as cookies available to our application.

The addition of an HTML element with an ID of `fb-root` is part of the basic requirements for the JavaScript SDK, which are also discussed in more detail in the Facebook Developer documentation:

`http://developers.facebook.com/docs/reference/javascript/`

In short, the JavaScript SDK needs an actual element on the HTML page to hook into, and that element is one with an ID of `fb-root`—which is hardcoded into the SDK itself.

There's more

What we've done is in this recipe is simply to set up our project so that it will be able to work with the Facebook APIs, when it's uploaded to the domain that we've specified for our application, in the applications' settings, in the Facebook Developer center.

Testing and debugging our Flash Builder project locally

The Graph API automatically rejects requests that use our Application's API Key if those requests come from a domain other than the domain specified by the **Site URL** and **Site Domain** settings—which means that if we try to test our code using URLS like:

```
C:\Workspace\Facebook Example\bin-debug\Facebook.html
```

or

```
file://Users/Admin/Workspace/Facebook Example/bin-debug/Facebook.html
```

the Graph API would automatically reject requests originating from those URLs, because they're not on the domain specified in our Facebook Application settings.

In actual fact, trying to work with these URLs would likely throw a **Security Sandbox Error** from the Flash Player before things even got to the point of communicating with the Graph API. The ideal setup to avoid this is instead to have a HTTP server running locally that can deliver these same HTML files, but from an `http://` protocol, such as:

```
http://localhost/Facebook%20Example/bin-debug/Facebook.html
```

This would avoid any Flash Player security issues, but requests to the Graph API would still be rejected, because the domain, `localhost`, is not the same as the domain specified in our application settings (in my case, `psyked.co.uk`).

To develop efficiently for Facebook, we should expect to be able to code and test frequently, without the constant need to upload and re-upload our Flash application to a remote domain, yet still have everything work as if our application were online at the domain outlined in the **Site Domain** setting we previously specified.

> To test our application locally, we must have an HTTP server installed and running on our computer, something like the Apache HTTP Server, which is available from: `http://httpd.apache.org/`.
>
> Support for server-side languages isn't important for our needs—all we require is the ability to launch our Flash Player application from an `http://`-based URL, rather than a local or network path.

There are two approaches we can take to get a Project that we have running locally to work with the Graph API:

1. Adjust the **Site Domain** project setting to work exclusively with the domain `localhost`.

   or

2. Use setup a subdomain (such as `localhost.psyked.co.uk`) on our live website domain that points at our local machine.

Either of these solutions is valid—they both conspire to ensure that the **Site Domain** in our Facebook Application settings and the current URL that we're viewing match up.

If we choose the first option—adjusting our **Site Domain** property to say `localhost`—it should allow our local machine to work with Facebook, but at the cost of our live, publicly-accessible website not being able to communicate with the Graph API. Of course, that doesn't preclude us from setting up more than one Facebook application—a local development and live deployment application, if necessary.

The other alternative—using a subdomain—assumes that we can manage our top-level domain and create entries for new subdomains. All that is actually required for domain validation with the Graph API is that the computer on which the code is running *believes* that it is running on a specific domain—not that the domain is actually valid, or even that the domain even exists.

Thus we could create a new subdomain on our live website, such as `localhost.psyked.co.uk`, and have it point at the IP Address `127.0.0.1`. For users without an HTTP server installed, they'll see nothing, and for developers like us, we'll see our own local HTTP server.

With our allowed domain effectively being `*.psyked.co.uk` the requests from `localhost.psyked.co.uk` will be accepted by the Graph API, and we can test our code much faster.

Where can users access our Facebook application from?

There are (currently) three main kinds of Facebook-enabled applications. These are:

1. Facebook Canvas applications
2. Facebook Page Tab applications
3. Websites with Facebook integration

This categorization represents the route by which users discover our application, as much as anything else. From a technical perspective, our application is always an HTML page, with a Flash Player application nested inside.

Canvas and Page Tab applications are actually HTML iframe elements on the Facebook.com website—they appear within the normal Facebook website interface, but the content that's being displayed comes from your own web server, and the same content is technically available from outside those iframe elements, if you have a direct link.

For example, we can have a Canvas application accessible from the URL:

```
http://apps.facebook.com/packt_facebook/
```

But the HTML source for this Canvas application is actually located at the URL:

```
http://facebook.psyked.co.uk/packt/
```

The integration of these two separate websites is seamless for the end user, but the context of each places different constraints on our application in terms of the dimensions of the application.

Setting up a Canvas or Tab application on Facebook.com

To set up our application so that it appears within the Facebook.com website as a Canvas or Page Tab we need to visit the Facebook Developer center and edit the settings of our Facebook Application, which we can do via the URL:

```
http://www.facebook.com/developers/apps.php
```

Select an application, click **Edit settings**, and then go to the **Facebook Integration** section, where you can make specific entries for the **Canvas URL** and **Tab URL** parameters—choosing exact URLs that point to an HTML page that would be formatted correctly for the dimensions of the iframes. Canvas applications are 760 pixels wide and Tab applications are only 520 pixels wide.

Not every application has to be a Canvas or Page Tab application, however. It doesn't even have to be an application on Facebook—it can just be one that interacts with Facebook, so long as our Flash application remains within the **Site Domain** boundaries we've specified in the Facebook Developer center.

Working without the JavaScript SDK?

If you are adding Flash elements to a Facebook application you've already developed in a server-side language, then you may find that you don't need to worry about adding additional JavaScript files to the mix.

Say for example you've already developed a Facebook login process; using Facebook's own PHP SDK, you could simply forget about including the JavaScript SDK and instead use FlashVars to pass in the session data and authorization tokens at the point the page is generated. Not only would you not need to load an additional JavaScript file, but you'd also not have to make duplicate session requests with Facebook, which should speed things up a little.

The key point is that Facebook cannot always know—and doesn't really care—how you're making requests to its APIs, only that you do so with valid authorization tokens and request parameters.

See also

▶   *Setting up a new Application on Facebook*

2
Authenticating with Facebook

In this chapter, we will cover:

- ▶ Authentication with the Web SDK, for Flash Player applications
- ▶ Authentication with the Desktop SDK, for AIR applications
- ▶ Logging out of Facebook
- ▶ Retrieving information about the current session and active Facebook user
- ▶ Reacting to Facebook session changes that occur outside our Flash movie

Introduction

Before we can load any data through the Facebook APIs, we will need to authenticate our application, and we'll need to do this each time our Flash movie is displayed in the HTML page (or each time our AIR application is launched).

The authentication process is fairly complex, based as it is on the OAuth 2.0 protocol, but it is thankfully wrapped up nicely and neatly by the Facebook ActionScript 3 SDK, so our actual setup in ActionScript isn't too complex.

This next image outlines the major layers involved when communicating with Facebook, through the Facebook ActionScript 3 SDK, from a Flash Platform application. It doesn't comprehensively outline every interaction or capability of the platforms, but it should give you an overview of the elements involved.

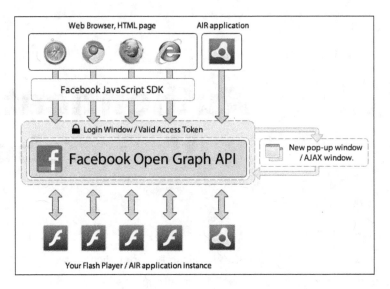

Facebook authentication is built around the OAuth 2.0 protocol, which in conceptual terms means that instead of having the user enter their login credentials to our third-party applications, they'll always be entering those credentials directly into Facebook itself, and that will then give our application an access token to use for authentication.

This means that at no point does our application have access to the user's login credentials (which keeps things far more secure for the user), and so all that our application needs to keep track of is the access token, which the Facebook API makes available when the user logs in.

 More details about authentication with the Facebook API can be found online, in the Facebook Developer documentation pages at:

`http://developers.facebook.com/docs/authentication/`

It's all about Access tokens

The first step for any Facebook application—regardless of whether or not it's based in the Flash Platform—is to authenticate with Facebook and obtain a valid access token for the Graph API, which is then used to authorize subsequent API requests.

Unlike the more common server-driven Facebook Apps, the Facebook ActionScript 3 SDK authenticates as a specific Facebook user, rather than as an Application. Authenticating as an application is a task more oriented towards server-side, persistently-online technologies than the client-side Flash Platform.

 The **Access Token** is the *key* to authentication with Facebook—it's what a successful login on the Facebook pop-up window returns to our application, and it's what identifies the authenticated session to the Facebook API.

For as long as an access token is valid, requests to the Facebook APIs will be authorized. The length of time that an access key is valid depends primarily on what else the user does in Facebook. Simply leaving the Facebook-enabled web page isn't sufficient to log the user out anymore!

We can use the **Facebook.com** website to view information about the user's active logins, under the `Account security | Account activity` section of the `My account` page, which is available from the URL: `https://www.facebook.com/editaccount.php` and will look a little like this:

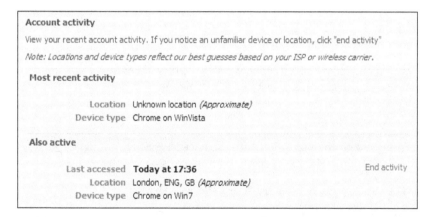

Both the Web and the Desktop versions of the ActionScript 3 SDK have the ability to request new access tokens from Facebook, which they obtain via launching a new login dialog, and they both also have the ability to use existing, valid access tokens that they've been supplied during the initialization process.

In the recipes in this chapter, we'll be exploring the initialization, login, and logout methods of the Web and Desktop versions of the Facebook ActionScript 3 SDK. In addition to these basic methods, we can also set our applications up to authenticate automatically, and we'll see how that works for both versions of the SDK.

Authentication with the Web SDK, for Flash Player applications

There are two main steps to the authentication process, when working with Facebook and its ActionScript 3 SDK:

1. The first step is to initialize the library, passing in a few application settings, such as the API Key, which will then be used to find any active Facebook sessions that our application can use.

2. The next step is manually logging in to Facebook and creating a new session, although this is optional, depending on whether or not the previous initialization was successful.

In this recipe, we're going to explore the simple tasks of initializing the Facebook ActionScript 3 SDK and logging in to Facebook, for a web-based Flash Player application.

Getting ready

Before we can start working with the Facebook APIs, we'll need the **API Key** for the application that we set up on the Facebook Developer Portal, in the recipe *Setting up a new Application on Facebook* from the previous chapter.

Create a new web project in Flash Builder, which will in turn generate a new instance of the Flex framework's `Application` class as an MXML file. To that class we should add two `Button` components and a `Label` component, with IDs of `initialize_btn`, `login_btn`, and `status_lbl` respectively.

The buttons are going to be used to initialize the Facebook SDK and trigger the login process, and the label component we'll use to display status messages to the end user.

The layout of our application need only be very simple, like this:

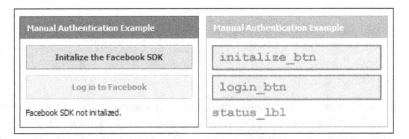

In the recipes in this cookbook we won't list the MXML needed for each example in explicit detail, we'll just list the appropriate IDs and event handler properties—the placement of components and additional user interface elements remains up to you. In addition, including readable MXML code for each recipe would lead to pages and pages of unhelpful layout and styling code!

If you're not familiar with MXML, then for the most part, the interfaces can be constructed with the drag-and-drop design view of Flash Builder.

How to do it...

In our interface we have two buttons, and only one of those buttons should be enabled at any one time. After all, we can't initialize the Facebook SDK when it's already been initialized, and we can't log in to Facebook without the SDK first being initialized. In addition to the Facebook-specific ActionScript code, as we work through this recipe we'll also be enabling and disabling these buttons to reflect the actions which are supported at that point.

The first thing we need to do is to create and attach a click event handler to our `initialize_btn` Button component, and inside that handler function we would initialize the Facebook ActionScript 3 SDK, passing it the **API Key** property that we retrieved from the Facebook Developer Portal.

The format of the code needed to initialize the Facebook SDK looks like this:

```
Facebook.init("api key", callback function[, options, "access token"]);
```

The first parameter for this method is the application's API Key; the second parameter is the callback function (the function that is executed when a response is received from the Facebook API). The third and fourth parameters—options and access token—are optional, and we won't be using them in this recipe.

1. If our `Application` file does not already have one, create an `fx:Script` tag, which allows us to insert raw ActionScript 3 code in the MXML file.

2. Into that `Script` tag, create a click handler function which would execute the `Facebook.init` method, like this (but replace the `[YOUR_API_KEY]` with your own, of course):

```
<fx:Script>
    <![CDATA[
        import com.facebook.graph.Facebook;
        function initializeClickHandler(e:Event):void
        {
            var apiKey:String = "[YOUR_API_KEY]";
            Facebook.init(apiKey, onFacebookInit);
        }
    ]]>
</fx:Script>
```

3. To associate this click handler function with our `initialize_btn` Button component we should add an MXML attribute of `click`, and enter the name of our ActionScript 3 function, as shown here (with the all-important attribute highlighted):

```
<s:Button buttonMode="true"
        click="initializeClickHandler(event)"
        height="32" id="initialize_btn"
        label="Initialize the Facebook SDK"
        width="100%" />
```

Once the SDK has been initialized it will run the callback function that we specified in the `Facebook.init` method. This callback function should accept two objects as its parameters, and the signature for the function looks like this:

```
function callbackFunction(session:FacebookSession, error:Object):
void {};
```

The first parameter is all that matters for the initialization process, and will return a `FacebookSession` instance if one is available. The second parameter is in fact hardcoded to always return a null value (but because of the way the SDK is developed, the function needs to accept two parameters).

It's easy to check whether an API call has been successful—simply check to see if the value of the first parameter is null, and react accordingly—which in this case means displaying a status message and enabling the `login_btn` component.

4. With this in mind, create the response handler function for the initialization process, which should look like this:

```
function onFacebookInit(session:FacebookSession, error:Object):
void {
    initialize_btn.enabled = false;
    if (session) {
        login_btn.enabled = false;
        status_lbl.text = "User is logged in.";
    } else {
        login_btn.enabled = true;
        status_lbl.text = "No available user logged in.";
    }
}
```

If our user is already logged in to Facebook, and has also already authorized our application, then simply calling this initialize function will return us the active session information as an instance of the `FacebookSession` class, and means that we don't actually have to try and log the user in manually—they already are logged in!

If we assume however, that initializing the Facebook class in our code was not enough to obtain a session, we will need to add a way for our users to call the `Facebook.login` method, which will open a new window and wait for a response.

Launching a `Facebook` / `OAuth` login window from ActionScript 3 is as simple as writing:

`Facebook.login( callback function [, options] );`

The login function requires one parameter—the callback function, but also accepts an optional second parameter, which is where you would supply an array of the required Facebook Extended Permissions to customize to login window (which are covered in the next chapter, *Chapter 2, Working with Facebook Permissions*).

5. To allow our users to interact and initiate the login process manually, create a click handler function for the `login_btn` component, which should look like this:

```
function loginClickHandler(e:Event):void {
    Facebook.login(onFacebookLogin);
}
```

6. To associate this function with our `login_btn` component add the (highlighted) `click` property to the button's MXML:

```
<s:Button buttonMode="true"
          click="loginClickHandler(event)"
          height="32" id="login_btn"
          label="Log in to Facebook" width="100%" />
```

Calling the `Facebook.login` method will open a pop-up window, and once that window is closed, our application will receive the response.

As with the response handler for the initialization method, the callback function for this login method should accept two parameters—one Object for successful calls, and a second Object for failed calls. Unlike the initialize method however, both of these parameters could be populated, but the logic for handling the response is much the same.

7. Finally, add the following response handler function to handle the response that comes from closing the login dialog window:

```
function onFacebookLogin(success:Object, fail:Object):void {
    if (success) {
        login_btn.enabled = false;
        status_lbl.text = "User is logged in.";
    } else {
        login_btn.enabled = true;
        status_lbl.text = "User failed to log in.";
    }
}
```

That's all for this recipe. We've created a simple user interface which we can use to authenticate our users on demand. Clicking the **Initialize the Facebook SDK** button starts our application communicating with Facebook, and it attempts to retrieve a valid access token that it can work with. If this request is not successful, and the user is unable to log in automatically, they can then use our **Log in to Facebook** button to log in and allow our application to access their Facebook information.

How it works...

If the current user is already logged in to Facebook, and has already authorized our application, then their session is automatically passed into our application when the SDK is initialized, making any further authentication unnecessary.

In this situation we should see that, after we click the **Initialize the Facebook SDK** button, both of the onscreen buttons will be disabled and the status message will read **User is logged in**.

Alternatively, if the user hasn't authorized our application before, or doesn't have an active Facebook session, then we have to go through the login process to obtain a valid Facebook session.

In this situation we should see that, after we click the **Initialize the Facebook SDK** button, the first button is disabled, with the status message reading **No available user logged in**.

The **Log in to Facebook** button is enabled at this point, so clicking it will launch the dialog window, which for a new user should look like this:

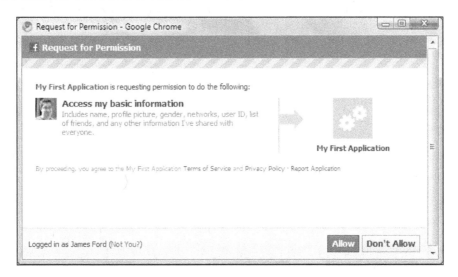

In short, the authentication process with Facebook *may* always require manual interaction from the user. If it's the first time they've used our application, it certainly will require a manual login. If not, there's a chance that our user could be authenticated without any further interaction from them.

Under the hood, what the Facebook ActionScript 3 SDK does is initialize the JavaScript SDK in the containing HTML page, and sets up two-way communication with the JavaScript and ActionScript code through use of the ExternalInterface classes built-in to the Flash Player. The various Facebook SDKs in this instance are simply forwarding the values passed in from ActionScript 3 to the external JavaScript SDK and vice-versa.

There's more...

That was a basic, albeit verbose, introduction to authenticating users with the Facebook API. There are a couple more concepts you might want to know before moving on, however.

Automatic authentication with Facebook

You may be thinking that the user experience in this recipe isn't terribly good—after all, on our user's initial visit, they'll have to click twice in our Flash Player application—once to initialize the SDK, and then again to log in and authorize our application.

There are two major things we can do about this. The first is to sidestep the need for the user to interact with our Flash Player application before it initializes the SDK. There's no real reason why we can't do this; the `Facebook.init` method doesn't actually try to open any pop-up windows or dialogs, it just picks up any existing valid sessions, and this makes it safe to use at any point in our application, such as the point just after our Flex application is initialized. To do that, we need to:

1. Remove the `initialize_btn` component, and all references to it in our code, and have our interface look like this:

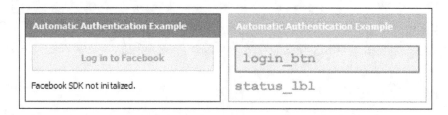

2. Add an event listener for the Flex framework's `ApplicationComplete` event:

```
<s:Application height="400"width="758"
        applicationComplete="applicationCompleteHandler(event)"
        xmlns:fx="http://ns.adobe.com/mxml/2009"
        xmlns:s="library://ns.adobe.com/flex/spark">
```

3. And add move our initialization code into a newly created `applicationCompleteHandler` function:

```
function applicationCompleteHandler(e:Event):void {
    var apiKey:String = "[YOUR_API_KEY]";
    Facebook.init(apiKey, onFacebookInit);
}
```

That's one major step towards automatic authentication. The other is to be aware that our Flash Player application might not be the only element onscreen that can connect to, and authenticate with, the Facebook API. The ActionScript SDK runs on top of the JavaScript SDK after all, so it's possible that, after initializing the SDK, the user might log in via the JavaScript SDK.

The recipe *Reacting to external session changes and JavaScript events* later in this chapter covers this scenario in more detail, so refer to that for a more robust and in-depth solution to automatic authentication.

When should we launch the Login Dialog?

Logging in to Facebook can only be done through the Facebook.com HTML login pages, which either means launching a new native browser window or opening an iframe-based dialog, both of which contain a separate web page from the live Facebook website.

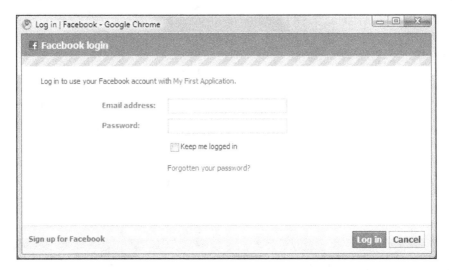

Unfortunately, launching a new native browser window is a bit of a problem if you don't do it properly—pop-up blockers have a bit of a thing about JavaScript launching new windows. The only (generally) reliable way of avoiding pop-up blockers is to only trigger them from a user interaction, meaning a mouse click or (for touch-screen devices) a touch event. If we do this, then because we're initiating the login popup as a direct result of user interaction—which the popup blockers will be aware of—they shouldn't intervene.

This login dialog contains a page from the Facebook website, and it's into this that the user enters their login credentials. Once they've entered their details the dialog window returns either the Facebook session information or an Error message to our Flash Player instance, before closing the pop-up window or iframe element that it opened.

If it returns a Facebook session object, that contains a valid OAuth 2.0 style access token, which the SDK then uses in all subsequent API requests, which is what makes it possible for everything to work over the API.

Desktop projects, built on the AIR platform, follow more or less the same process, but do so without the underlying JavaScript SDK. The embedded WebKit browser is instead used in a new Native window, and launches in the same fashion as the JavaScript popup, before closing itself when the authentication process is complete.

The "options" parameter

When we initialize the Facebook SDK in ActionScript, we are given the option to provide an `Object` instance, containing options for the initialization process, which allows us to slightly change the behavior of the JavaScript SDK's initialization.

The options are passed in as the third parameter for the `Facebook.init` method, and are actually transformed as-is from our ActionScript to the initialization of the external JavaScript. With the options parameter, we can signal if we want the SDK to initialize with cookies support, or to not refresh the login status automatically, or do anything else listed in the JavaScript SDK's `FB.init` method documentation, which is available online at: `http://developers.facebook.com/docs/reference/javascript/FB.init`.

In all honesty though, the situations where a primarily Flash Platform-based application would have to make use of the options object are pretty slim.

See also

► *Reacting to external sessions changes and JavaScript events*

Authentication with the Desktop SDK, for AIR applications

The technology that powers the authentication for the Facebook APIs in an AIR-based application is a little different to its equivalent Flash Player-based web application.

As we mentioned in the introduction, the Web version of the Facebook ActionScript 3 SDK relies on the underlying JavaScript SDK. The Desktop version however doesn't have the same luxury—everything that it has to do, such as launching pop-up windows or maintaining user sessions, must be done through ActionScript 3 and the enhanced capabilities of the AIR runtime alone. Fortunately for us however, this functionality has already been built into the Facebook ActionScript 3 SDK.

The methods that we use to work with the Facebook are much the same in the Desktop SDK as those of the web-based SDK, but there are a few important variations in the parameters you pass that means it's not just a case of swapping the root class of **Facebook** for **FacebookDesktop**.

In this recipe we're going to go through the same automatic initialization and login process as the previous recipes, only using this time the Desktop version of the SDK for AIR applications.

Getting ready

Create a new Desktop | AIR application in Flash Builder, and add the desktop version of the library project as a linked library. We'll initialize the Facebook SDK automatically, so the only user interface that we need to include is one button for logging in, and another for logging out. Our user interface should include two `Button` components—`login_btn` and `logout_btn`.

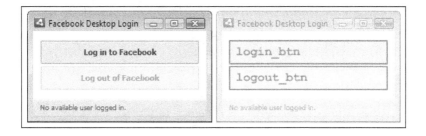

Unlike the previous recipes, the `WindowedApplication` component that is the root class of an AIR application has a built-in status bar, so we won't need to add additional `Label` components to the interface just to provide feedback to the end user.

How to do it...

To distinguish the web-based SDK and the Desktop SDK, the basic class for the Desktop SDK is named `FacebookDesktop` class, as opposed to the `Facebook` class.

The first step for our application is to initialize the SDK with our API Key, callback function and, if we've got it, a session token (more on that in a moment). The format of the initialization function for the Desktop SDK looks like this:

```
FacebookDesktop.init("api key", callback function [, access token]);
```

Similar to the Web SDK's `init` method, this method can take up to three parameters, but whereas in the Web version the third parameter is an Object of login options, in the Desktop version the third parameter should be an access token.

In the Web version of the SDK the access token is retained automatically by the JavaScript, using mechanisms such as browser cookies. The Desktop version of the SDK obviously doesn't have access to these mechanisms, but it does have its own storage system for maintaining access tokens between the times our application is running. This comes in the form of the `manageSession` property:

```
FacebookDesktop.manageSession = true;
```

The option is not enabled by default, but once enabled, the Desktop SDK saves and reloads the session key in-between sessions automatically.

1. Add the following code to our application to initialize the Facebook ActionScript 3 SDK and add the response handler:

```
function applicationCompleteHandler(e:Event):void {
    var apiKey:String = "API_KEY";
    FacebookDesktop.manageSession = true;
    FacebookDesktop.init(apiKey, onFacebookInit);
}
```

```
function onFacebookInit(success:Object, fail:Object):void {
    if (success) {
        login_btn.enabled = false;
        logout_btn.enabled = true;
        status = "User is logged in.";
    } else {
        login_btn.enabled = true;
        logout_btn.enabled = false;
        status = "No available user logged in.";
    }
}
```

As with our other recipes, if the user can't be authenticated automatically, we should allow them to login manually. For the Desktop SDK, the format of the login method looks like this:

FacebookDesktop.login(callback function [, permissions, "access token"]);

The difference between the Web and Desktop SDK here is the permissions object that you pass to the login window. In the Web version we pass an Object, with the parameter `perms`, containing a single comma-delimited string of Extended Permission names. In the Desktop SDK this value is instead an Array of those Extended Permission names. It's essentially the same content, just in a slightly different format. (We'll look at permissions in more detail in the next chapter.)

2. Add the following code to our application, which creates the click handler functions for our two `Button` components, calls the `FacebookDesktop.login` and `FacebookDesktop.logout` methods, updates the Button's enabled state appropriately and changes the window status message:

```
function loginClickHandler(e:Event):void {
    FacebookDesktop.login(onFacebookLogin);
    status = "Launching login dialog...";
}
function logoutClickHandler(e:Event):void {
    FacebookDesktop.logout(onFacebookLogout);
    status = "Logging out...";
}

function onFacebookLogin(success:Object, fail:Object):void {
    if (success) {
        login_btn.enabled = false;
        logout_btn.enabled = true;
        status = "User is logged in.";
    } else {
        login_btn.enabled = true;
        logout_btn.enabled = false;
```

```
        status = "User failed to log in.";
    }
}

function onFacebookLogout(response:Boolean):void {
    login_btn.enabled = true;
    logout_btn.enabled = false;
    status = "User has logged out.";
}
```

How it works...

Aside from a few inconsistencies in the method signatures between the Desktop and the Web versions of the SDK, and the name of the classes, there's not much difference between the ActionScript code for a Flash Player or an AIR application.

The method signature for the initialization is a little different, but only because the Web version of the SDK includes some additional parameters—reflecting the fact that much of the Web SDK's authentication is a merely a conduit to the underlying JavaScript SDK. In contrast, the Desktop SDK—having no access to browser cookies or the JavaScript—has to manage its store of items like sessions and access tokens itself, which leads to the `manageSession` property of the SDK.

The `manageSession` property acts as you might expect—it replicates and mimics the functionality of the JavaScript SDK's session management cookies, and saves and loads the latest access token and token expiry date using the Flash Platform's Shared Object capabilities.

There's more...

Developing an application in AIR gives you more freedom over the login process than the Flash Player version can—the ability to launch a pop-up window from ActionScript, without requiring user interaction, is a useful capability.

How does the pop-up window work?

The pop-up window that the Desktop SDK launches is a native operating system window with a WebKit-powered HTML component inside. This pop-up window loads exactly the same content as the browser-based JavaScript SDK popups would load, and works in the same way, obtaining access tokens and session information from the URL redirect and POST variables of that component.

In addition, as all of the functionality behind launching new windows has been developed for the AIR runtime rather than the Flash Player, then should we wish to, we're not bound to launching those dialogs in response to user interaction, as we are with the web-based SDK.

See also

▶   *Automatic authentication with Facebook*

Logging out of Facebook

Logging the user out of Facebook is a simple task, but we'll include it anyway, as the ability to log our users out of Facebook is important, particularly when you consider situations where the wrong user might've been automatically logged in to our application, or that the user is accessing our application outside of the normal Facebook.com website, and would consequently may have no other immediate way of logging themselves out.

Logging out of Facebook doesn't require any user interaction, because it doesn't launch any additional pop-up windows. In this recipe, we're going to extend our previous authentication recipes to demonstrate how we'd use the ActionScript 3 SDK to log the current user out of Facebook.

Getting ready

For this recipe we're going to use the final code from the recipe on *Automatic authentication with Facebook* as our starting point and onto that we'll add an additional **Log out of Facebook** button, with an ID of `logout_btn`. Our application interface should therefore look like this:

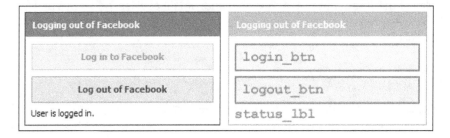

How to do it...

A simple function is all we need to log out of Facebook—we call the `Facebook.logout` method, which requires a single callback function as its parameter, and that's it.

```
Facebook.logout( callback function );
```

To add this code as a click handler function for the `logout_btn` component, and update the `status_lbl` component accordingly as we do so, we could introduce the following ActionScript to our application:

```
function logoutClickHandler(e:Event):void {
    Facebook.logout(onFacebookLogout);
    status_lbl.text = "Logging out...";
}

function onFacebookLogout(response:Boolean):void {
    login_btn.enabled = true;
    login_btn.enabled = true;
    logout_btn.enabled = false;
    status_lbl.text = "User has logged out.";
}
```

The function that we pass as the callback for the logout method will be called when the logout process is complete—that is to say, when the Facebook API confirms that the user has been logged out. The return function should expect a single parameter, and when the logout is complete the callback function will execute.

How it works...

There's not much to it—calling the `Facebook.logout` method in ActionScript will send a request back to the Graph API, which will then invalidate the current access token for that user. At the same time, the rest of the Facebook ActionScript 3 SDK also reacts to this logout, updating its internal variables, such as the `FacebookSession` object, accordingly.

There's more...

Any other applications or browser pages that are using the same access token will also find it stops working for future requests. Whether or not those applications get an immediate notification about the invalidated access token depends on the underlying JavaScript SDK—if the application is on the same page they'll likely get an update of the status as the user logs out; if they're in a different tab or window, probably not.

See also

▶ *Reacting to Facebook session changes that occur outside our Flash movie*

Retrieving information about the current session and active Facebook user

A key part to the logic of many of the validation checks for Facebook logins is retrieving information about the current user, or indeed finding out if there is an active user.

The underlying JavaScript SDK for Facebook has a function for getting the current user's session information in a synchronous way—meaning that the data that this function can return is instantaneous, and that makes it ideal for using in other functions as part of the validation process for our own code.

What does the session data actually contain? Well, it should contain the following elements:

- Access Token
- Application Secret Key
- Available Permissions
- Session Expiry Date
- Session Key
- Signature
- User ID

The User ID is really the only value you need to use from the session object, with many of the other elements only being there because they're used internally by the SDK. Thankfully, the User ID is all we need to start requesting more information from the Graph API.

Getting ready

Use one of the login and authentication examples from earlier in this chapter as the basis for this recipe. To retrieve information about the current session, we'll need to actually have an active session!

How to do it...

Once we've successfully authenticated with the Facebook API, we can use the `Facebook.getSession` method to return a `FacebookSession` object, such as:

```
function onFacebookLogin(success:Object, fail:Object):void {
    if (success) {
        login_btn.enabled = false;
        status_lbl.text = "User is logged in.";
        var session:FacebookSession = Facebook.getSession();
        trace(JSON.encode(session));
```

```
    } else {
        login_btn.enabled = true;
        status_lbl.text = "User failed to log in.";
    }
}
```

And this code would output a result similar to this, in the Flash Builder debug console:

How it works...

As part of the authentication process with the Facebook ActionScript 3 SDK, our application retrieves active session information from the Facebook API, if it is available.

The `Facebook.getSession` method doesn't actually make a request to the Graph API; it retrieves values are already stored locally in the JavaScript SDK. Technically speaking, you can always call this method and it will return a `FacebookSession` object. If no user is logged in, or the current user doesn't grant our application permission to access their data, then the properties of that `FacebookSession` object will be null.

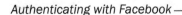

The `FacebookSession` object is really just a value object class for parsing and storing the session values that could be used by the SDK. Tracing out the object traditionally (using `trace(Facebook.getSession());`) will result in only the current user ID being shown, because the class has a defined `toString` method.

To see all of the values, you need some code similar to this:

There's more...

We shouldn't actually have to use the `FacebookSession` object too often—it's mainly used internally by other elements of the ActionScript 3 SDK, but there are only a few values, such as the User ID, that are of any real use to us outside of the internal workings of the SDK.

An easy way to check if a session is active is to call the `Facebook.getSession` method, and check the `uid` property of the session. If it's null then there's no active session, or the current user hasn't allowed our application access to their data. If it's anything other than null, there's an active user who's authorized our application.

Problems with the available permissions or the user object?

The available permissions and current user information are one part of the SDK that seem a little incomplete. Perhaps by the time you're reading this the next version of the Facebook ActionScript 3 SDK will be available and will fix this little issue, but it seems that the logical next steps for authentication—loading the current user information and permissions—are missing from the SDK. And oddly enough, the Desktop version of the SDK, when it is validating the access token, automatically loads the current user information; yet the web version of the SDK doesn't, and neither version loads the available permissions.

Not a massive issue, however—we can replicate this functionality easily ourselves. It's just a shame it's not automatic. To see how to load details about the current user, you can refer to the recipe *Loading the current users information* in *Chapter 4, Reading and Writing Data with the Graph API*.

But what about the permissions object? Well, according to the Facebook Developer Documentation, the `availablePermissions` object is only returned to our application when you actually request new permissions—all other times it will be returned as a null object.

Unfortunately, this is one of the issues with the server-side bias of the Facebook APIs, and doesn't really help very much for our client-side Flash Platform applications. When we request permissions we'll get some results under the `availablePermissions` parameter, but the response only contains any new permissions our application has been given, and not a complete list of permissions. So for the moment, ignore this limitation, and check out the other options in the *Chapter 3, Working with Facebook Permissions*.

- ▸ The following recipe in *Chapter 3, Checking for existing Extended Permissions*
- ▸ The following recipe in *Chapter 4, Loading simple Facebook user data*

Reacting to external session changes and JavaScript events

When using the web version of the Facebook ActionScript 3 SDK we can't assume that our application is the only point of entry for the user to interact with Facebook.

In fact our Flash application might just be a portion of a larger Facebook App, and our users could also be using other Facebook-enabled technologies elsewhere, in turn giving them the ability to, for example, log out of Facebook at any point, without acting through our application interface.

Whenever this situation occurs, Facebook should send a notification out through the JavaScript SDK, which interacts with our Flash movie, and that in turn will push the same notification through to our ActionScript 3 code, where we can then react accordingly.

Reacting accordingly should mean disabling those elements of our application that rely on Facebook functionality, or at least resetting the login elements so that they're always displaying the appropriate interface to our users.

The Facebook ActionScript SDK has some functions built in that make it possible to easily link events from the Facebook JavaScript SDK to functions in our ActionScript code. The functions are simple and functional, and they are:

```
Facebook.addJSEventListener(event, method);
Facebook.hasJSEventListener(event, method);
Facebook.removeJSEventListener(event, method);
```

In this example, we're going to react to login and logout events, updating the interface of our application to reflect the Facebook login status accordingly.

Getting ready

The nature of the events that get passed from the Facebook JavaScript SDK to Flash makes it difficult to test our code in a normal environment. Logging out of Facebook, while viewing our application on Facebook.com, is problematic because that same action redirects the user to the Facebook welcome page and away from our application.

With this in mind, and to test that our code is working, we're going to first add some additional code to our Flex application's HTML template page, which will call the `Facebook.logout` and `Facebook.login` functions in the JavaScript SDK.

In our HTML template, add the following code—which will create two hyperlinks on the page, which will allow us to log in and out of Facebook, without redirecting us away from the current page, so that we can watch as the JavaScript SDK events are passed into our Flash movie.

```
<a href="javascript:FB.login();">Log in to Facebook</a>
<a href="javascript:FB.logout();">Log out of Facebook</a>
```

In addition to these HTML changes, we'll also be using the ActionScript code and components from our earlier recipe, *Automatic Authentication with Facebook*, as the starting point for this recipe.

How to do it...

1. Following the initialization of the Facebook SDK in ActionScript, we need to add the following lines of code, which will associate functions in our ActionScript with Events coming in from the JavaScript SDK:

```
function applicationCompleteHandler(e:Event):void {
    var apiKey:String = "API_KEY";
    Facebook.init(apiKey, onFacebookInit);

    Facebook.addJSEventListener("auth.login", jsLoginHandler);
    Facebook.addJSEventListener("auth.logout", jsLogoutHandler);

    status_lbl.text = "Initializing Facebook SDK...";
}
```

The first parameter for these functions is the name of the event to react to—`"auth.logout"` or `"auth.login"`—and the second parameter is a reference to the ActionScript function to be executed. These functions must accept a single object as a parameter, which is a copy of the original JavaScript result object. The actual result object for a login event could look like this:

```
{
    "status": "connected",
    "session": {
        "uid": "526534401",
        "session_key": "2.AQCmpvI6ImCxmYvv.3600.1305759600.
            1-526534401",
        "secret": "AQAH4hZPRJOs-xFH",
        "access_token": "172944549389721|2.
            AQCmpvI6ImCxmYvv.3600.1305759600.1-
```

```
526534401|2CSu3FCM7XbhonQzEaCeZ0xeHgs",
        "sig": "5cf27b13af76b50418d662e5a30bee6f",
        "expires": 1305759600,
        "base_domain": "psyked.co.uk"
    }
}
```

2. The next step should be to create the callback functions for these events, which should look like this:

```
function jsLoginHandler(result:Object):void {
    if (result.status == "connected") {
        onFacebookLogin(Facebook.getSession());
    }
}

function jsLogoutHandler(result:Object):void {
    onFacebookLogout(result);
}
```

When we work with these authentication events, the response object contains two properties, `status` and `session`, although when we receive a logout event, both of those properties will be empty.

In our handler function for the login event, we check the `status` property of the result object—which can either be `"connected"`, `"notConnected"`, `"unknown"`—and if that value is acceptable, we invoke our already existing `onFacebookLogin` function, passing in the active Facebook session.

As for the logout event, the properties of the event aren't actually important—we only need to know that the user has logged out, nothing more—and so we can simply invoke our existing `onFacebookLogout` function to update our application's interface.

With the ActionScript and HTML code from this recipe added to our starting application, which is in turn based on the interface of our earlier recipe, *Logging out of Facebook*, we should be able to test our Flash Player application, using the HTML hyperlinks to log in and out of Facebook—with our Flash Player application instantly updating in response to the login status changes.

How it works...

Under the hood, the ActionScript 3 `ExternalInterface` class is able to provide an interface between the Flash movie and the external page's JavaScript. The Facebook ActionScript 3 SDK already uses this `ExternalInterface` class for the basics of connecting and logging in, so what these JavaScript event listeners are doing is allowing us to easily extend the Facebook SDK with our own functions.

You can register any number of functions against a single event, not just a single one. It's partially for this reason that there's also the `hasJSEventListener` and `removeJSEventListener` functions to accompany the `addJSEventListener` functions. The order they get executed in response to these events is the same order the event listeners were added.

The main difference between the JavaScript response handler (`jsLoginHandler`) and the pure ActionScript response handler (`onFacebookLogin`) is in the number of parameters returned to these functions. This differing number of parameters the functions expect, and what they expect, makes the two functions incompatible—which is why we've established a separate `jsLoginHandler` function, to act as an interim step that translates the single JavaScript response object into the dual-object format of the ActionScript 3 SDK response handlers.

There's more...

Aside from the obvious link to the JavaScript environment, how does listening to an event like `auth.logout` differ from using ActionScript's own `Facebook.logout` function?

Well, listening to the JavaScript event means you're always listening for a change in the Facebook session, until the point that you manually remove the listener. Calling the `Facebook.logout` function sets up a temporary listener for events, which is removed once the login is successful. So the result function we set up for a login only ever gets called once, but when listening for the event manually it can be called over and over again.

Other events from Facebook

There are more events than just logging out of Facebook. Here's a few more of the event types, as detailed by Facebook in their documentation:

- `auth.login`—fired when the user logs in
- `auth.logout`—fired when the user logs out
- `auth.prompt`—fired when user is prompted to log in or opt in to Platform after clicking a Like button
- `auth.sessionChange`—fired when the session changes
- `auth.statusChange`—fired when the status changes

More documentation and a full list of Events can be found in the Facebook documentation, which is available online at:
`http://developers.facebook.com/docs/reference/javascript/FB.Event.subscribe`

Is your user connected, not connected, or unknown?

One more useful element that we explore with JavaScript integration is checking the user's status, and seeing how they relate to our application. We've already encountered the status property as part of the `auth.login` event, but there is another dedicated event, `auth.statusChange`, that's far more useful to listen to if we want to see changes to the status.

According to the documentation from Facebook, the `auth.statusChange` event contains data with a status object that contains a value that is one of `connected`, `notConnected`, or `unknown`.

- "connected" users are those who are online and have allowed our application access to their data
- "notConnected" users are those who are online, but haven't allowed our application access to their data
- "unknown" users are those who are simply offline—those not logged in to Facebook at all

Why bother with the status? Well, the ability to distinguish between users who've allowed our application and those that haven't has got to be useful for something.

To add an event listener for changes to the Facebook status, we could add the following (highlighted) code:

```
function applicationCompleteHandler(e:Event):void
{
    var apiKey:String = "API_KEY";
    Facebook.init(apiKey, onFacebookInit);

    Facebook.addJSEventListener( "auth.statusChange",
    statusChangeHandler );
    Facebook.addJSEventListener("auth.login", jsLoginHandler);
    Facebook.addJSEventListener("auth.logout", jsLogoutHandler);

    status_lbl.text = "Initializing Facebook SDK...";
}
```

We could use the following response handler to display different status messages, dependent on the status of the current Facebook user (if they exist at all!):

```
function statusChangeHandler(result:Object):void {
    if (result && result.status) {
        switch (result.status) {
            case "connected":
                status_lbl.text = "User is logged in and authorised
our application.";
                break;
            case "notConnected":
                status_lbl.text = "User is logged in but has not
authorised our application.";
                break;
            case "unknown":
                status_lbl.text = "No Facebook user is logged in.";
                break;
        }
    }
}
```

See also

▶ *Authentication with the Web SDK, for Flash Player applications*

3
Working with Facebook Permissions

In this chapter, we will cover:

- ▶ Requesting Permissions at login
- ▶ Checking for existing Extended Permissions.
- ▶ Requesting extended permissions after the initial login
- ▶ Pre-emptively requesting additional Extended Permissions

Introduction

Regardless of permissions, any application has guaranteed access to three pieces of publicly-available data about a Facebook user—their `name`, their `picture`, and their Facebook `user ID`. To retrieve any information beyond that, the user in question has to either have made elements of their profile publicly-available, or our application has to have been authorized by that user, with the corresponding **Extended Permissions** allowing access to that information.

Private and publicly-available data on Facebook

To see for yourself what it meant by publicly-available information, have a look at the explanation of privacy and publicly-available data on the Facebook.com website: `http://www.facebook.com/privacy/explanation.php`

The next step up from publicly-available data is **Basic Profile Information**, which is the baseline level of data access given to any application that a user has authorized. This is granted automatically as part of the initial authorization process, and we don't actually have to specifically request any permissions to obtain this level of information—it comes as standard.

As we've seen in the previous chapter, when a user authorizes our application to access their data for the first time, they are presented with a dialog, requesting that they grant our application access to this **Basic Profile Information**, which looks like this:

Having this Basic Profile Information access extends the range of data our application can access to include more detailed profile information, such as the user's gender and a list of their friends.

More complete access to Facebook data, and the ability for our application to create, edit, or delete on the user's behalf, are governed by what's known as **Extended Permissions**. If we want our application to perform other actions on Facebook, such as reading or publishing to a News Feed, or simply retrieve further information about family connections, our application will require the appropriate Extended Permissions.

Requesting these Extended Permissions has the effect of changing the authorization dialogs slightly, so that they might look like this instead:

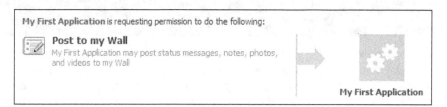

A full listing of the Extended Permissions available to an application is available online at the Facebook Developer Documentation page:

```
http://developers.facebook.com/docs/authentication/
permissions
```

Each user on Facebook has a separate listing of these Extended Permissions for each application they have allowed access to their information. It's not a global set of permissions that is granted to your application as a whole, but rather a per-user and per-application set of permissions, with the values being a hard and fast true or false.

Data access in Facebook has a very granular level of control—unlike other social networks (like Twitter, for example), it's not just a case of requesting read or write access, it's a case of requesting read or write access to *specific* aspects of our user's Facebook network. Of course, there's nothing to stop us from requesting permissions for every aspect of the network; it's just considered good practice to be a little more specific and focused with your permissions requests. Consider the following quote, again from the introduction to Extended Permissions, on the Facebook developer documentation:

> *"Applications that request more permissions tend to have a lower click-through rate on the permissions dialog. Therefore, you should only ask for the permissions you need from the user at a given time, as you can always ask for more later."*

Without the appropriate Extended Permissions granted to your application, your requests will fail—returning either an error message or blank data, depending on the type of request. One of the most common causes of the problems we're likely to come across during the course of our application development for Facebook stem from a lack of Extended Permissions.

Requesting permissions involves much the same process as when we authorized our application for the first time—everything is done through the OAuth 2.0 style methodology of launching pop-up windows containing content from the Facebook.com website, only instead of requesting authorization; we're requesting authorization, plus a specific set of permissions.

Extended Permissions can be requested at any point time from ActionScript—we could request them just before our application attempts to perform an action for example, or we could request those permissions upfront—when the user authenticates our application during their first-ever login.

There are many approaches we can take to managing Extended Permissions in our application, each with its own merits and drawbacks. The recipes in this chapter will demonstrate several of the strategies for requesting and validating the status of these Extended Permissions.

Requesting permissions at login

The Facebook Graph API, which applications use to obtain access tokens for use in requests, uses the same method for obtaining new Extended Permissions as it does for logging in—both of these actions work with the same underlying methods in the ActionScript and JavaScript SDKs, and both launch authentication pop-up windows with content from the Facebook.com website.

Transforming a login dialog request to a login-plus-permissions dialog is as simple as listing the codenames of the required Extended Permissions in an additional parameter on the login method call, and that will trigger a change in the style of the login window accordingly.

When an application requests permissions the user can only accept or deny the permissions request wholesale—they can't be selective about it.

The ideal workflow for any Facebook API request is to make sure that it succeeds first time, as the most common point of failure (besides an outright programming error on our part) is a lack of permissions.

In this recipe, we're going to create a sample application that requests additional permissions for our application at startup. This should ensure that for all successive API requests won't need to perform any additional checks for permission validity, and in planning our application, will allow us to assume that all API requests coming from authenticated users will automatically have the required Extended Permissions granted to them.

Getting ready

As our starting point we're going to use the setup from the earlier recipe, *Authentication with the Web SDK, for Flash Player applications*, from the previous chapter on authentication. Follow the instructions listed in the *There's more...* section of the recipe to create an example which automatically initializes the Facebook ActionScript 3 SDK, and our initial user interface should look like this:

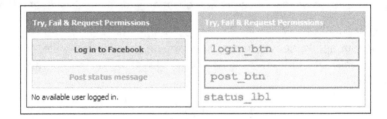

There's no specific need to be changing the user interface for this recipe, so it can stay as it currently is!

How to do it...

The Facebook Graph API ultimately expects the Extended Permission requirements for our application to be passed to it as a comma-delimited string of permission code names. How we pass those permissions in ActionScript depends on whether we're using the Desktop or Web versions of the SDK. The Web version expects your permissions as a comma-delimited String, passed under the `perms` property of the login options object, whereas the Desktop version expects an Array (of String objects).

The code necessary to pass an Array of permissions to the Desktop SDK looks like this:

```
FacebookDesktop.login( callback function, permissions );
```

Whereas the code to pass the same information into the Web SDK could looks like this:

```
var options:Object = new Object();
options.perms = permissions.toString();
Facebook.login( callback function, options );
```

1. The best way for us to put this together, in a manageable format, is to declare the required permissions as an Array of String instances. First we declare a new instance of the Array, and then we use the native `Array.push` method of ActionScript to populate the Array with the names of the Extended Permissions:

```
var permissions:Array = new Array();
  permissions.push("user_about_me" );
  permissions.push("publish_stream" );
  permissions.push("friends_status" );
```

Converting this Array of permissions to a single String for the Web version of the SDK is actually as simple as using the `toString` method built-in to the Array class, which returns the Array as a single comma-delimited String—just what we need.

2. Integrated into our existing `loginClickHandler` function from the original recipe, our code to request additional permissions at login should look like this:

```
function loginClickHandler(e:Event):void {
    var requiredPermissions = new Array();
    requiredPermissions.push("user_about_me");
    requiredPermissions.push("publish_stream");
    requiredPermissions.push("friends_status");

    var options:Object = new Object();
    options.perms = requiredPermissions.toString();
    Facebook.login(onFacebookLogin, options);
}
```

And clicking the **Log in to Facebook** button should yield the following pop-up window for a new visitor to our application:

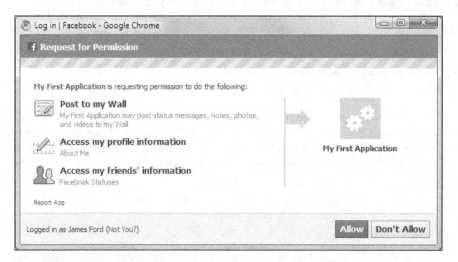

3. As with the basic authentication windows, our application waits for a response from the Graph API. As the method used and the response object is essentially the same as with basic authentication, we can use the same response handler function:

```
function onFacebookLogin(success:Object, fail:Object):void {
    if (success) {
        login_btn.enabled = false;
        status_lbl.text = "User is logged in.";
    } else {
        login_btn.enabled = true;
        status_lbl.text = "User failed to log in.";
    }
}
```

If the response is successful, the user has authorized and accepted all of the Extended Permissions—if not, they haven't.

How it works...

Assuming that our user doesn't take it upon themselves to visit the application settings section of their Facebook.com account's settings and revoke permissions after initially granting them, we can assume that a successful login means that all of the requested permissions have been granted to our application, and this should be true for both users that are logged-in automatically during the initialization phase, and those that log in manually by clicking the **Log in to Facebook** button.

This logic isn't infallible however, particularly if we are requesting different permissions at different points in our application, or are upgrading an existing application and need to add new permission requirements.

Progressing naturally from our previous example to this one, for example, it's possible for a user to be authenticated automatically, without the permissions that our application needs, but we have no way of preventing that login process.

Permissions that the user has already granted are automatically omitted from the request by Facebook itself, which is good because it makes things easier for us and reduces clutter for the user.

Our existing code doesn't include any permissions checking, and nor does the login response object return any reliable information on these permissions, so it's possible for a user to bypass our use of the `Facebook.login` method when we really actually need to use it to request any missing Extended Permissions.

There's more...

The downside of requesting all of the permissions at the start of our application is that it might discourage our users, causing some of them to not allow our application any access at all, especially given that the permissions granting process is an all-or-nothing affair. As stated in the Facebook Documentation:

> "There is a strong inverse correlation between the number of permissions your app requests and the number of users that will allow those permissions. The greater the number of permissions you ask for, the lower the number of users that will grant them; so we recommend that you only request the permissions you absolutely need for your app."

Sometimes staggering the requests for Extended Permissions in our application is a better option than doing the same upfront, particularly if functionality of our application can be split into manageable chunks. By adopting this approach, as we'll see in the next recipes, we can expect that users are more likely to grant our application the permissions it requests, as it is asking for less of them at a time, in a more familiar, granular fashion.

Using the ExtendedPermission class, instead of using hardcoded permission names

Within the community-driven version of the Facebook ActionScript 3 SDK there's a class which lists all of the names of the permissions on Facebook, and this is called the `ExtendedPermissions` class. This class is useful because it makes it much easier to add permissions to the requests without hardcoding the permission codenames, makes our code more manageable, and in turn reduces the chances of us misspelling those permission names.

For example, we could take the following ActionScript 3 code snippet:

```
var permissions:Array = new Array();
    permissions.push( "user_about_me" );
    permissions.push( "publish_stream" );
    permissions.push( "friends_status" );
    Facebook.login( callback, { perms:permissions.toString() } );
```

And swapping the hardcoded values for ones based off the `ExtendedPermission` class, this code snippet would look like this:

```
var permissions:Array = new Array();
    permissions.push( ExtendedPermission.USER_ABOUT_ME );
    permissions.push( ExtendedPermission.PUBLISH_STREAM );
    permissions.push( ExtendedPermission.FRIENDS_STATUS );
    Facebook.login( callback, { perms:permissions.toString() } );
```

See also

▶ *Checking for existing Extended Permissions*

▶ *Requesting Extended Permissions after the initial log in*

Checking for existing Extended Permissions

As a result of the server-side bias in the Graph API, the only way that our application gets informed of the user's extended permissions is when it specifically requested those permissions in the original request; that is, during the initial login—and not otherwise.

For example, if the user becomes authenticated automatically after initializing the Facebook SDK then our application won't be passed details of the user's permissions as, from the API's perspective, it hasn't attempted to authenticate—it's just retrieved an existing, valid access token.

Knowing which permissions our application has just isn't an easy task for a Flash Platform application, primarily because it's a client-side technology and only exists while the user is actually using it. If the user moves to a different computer, then everything the Flash Player might've stored about them is lost—not quite the same deal as with a server-side application.

In this recipe, we're going to use an **FQL query** to retrieve information about a set of Extended Permissions, and determine which of those permissions have been granted to our application by the current user, which we can then use to determine whether or not it's necessary to open a dialog to request missing permissions.

Getting ready

The starting point for this recipe should be one with basic authentication, such as that of the recipe *Authentication with the Web SDK, for Flash Player applications* from the previous *Chapter 2, Authenticating with Facebook*, giving our application two Button components, `login_btn` and `logout_btn`, and a Label component, `status_lbl`. To demonstrate visually the Extended Permissions we're checking for in this recipe, we'll add a few Checkbox components to the interface, with IDs corresponding to the permissions we'll be working with—`publish_chk` and `email_chk`, for example.

Our application's interface for this example should look like this:

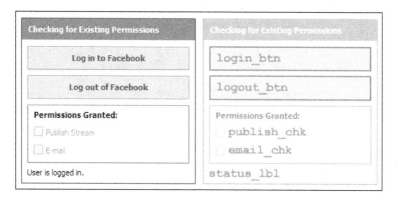

How to do it...

We need to be authenticated with Facebook before we start requesting data. The login/authentication process is already implemented by our starting code, and we don't need any further permissions or user interaction to start making these FQL requests, so we can jump right in.

1. Our first step is to create a new function that we can use to trigger our FQL request.

   The format of the ActionScript 3 method that we will need to use to execute an FQL query looks like this:

   ```
   Facebook.fqlQuery( "fql query", callback function, values );
   ```

   The first parameter that this method takes is the request as an FQL query template, the second is the callback function, and the third is an Array of values that are substituted for placeholders in the FQL query template.

2. As for the request itself, the information we need should come from the **permissions** table, where each permission is represented as a column within that table.

The FQL syntax to check for a single permission should be similar to this:

```
SELECT publish_stream FROM permissions WHERE uid = me()
```

When we construct our FQL request, we have to know what details we're asking for—we can't add wildcards, so we have to be specific. The previous query checks to see if the user has granted our application the `publish_stream` permission.

Multiple permissions can be checked by simply adding them as a comma-separated list of permissions names, for example,

```
SELECT publish_stream,email FROM permissions WHERE uid = me()
```

We can add as many permission names as we need to this request—we just have to be sure to format the FQL query correctly (names separated by commas, and no spaces in-between permission names, for example).

To create this FQL query in ActionScript, we'd use an FQL template like this:

```
SELECT {0} FROM permissions WHERE uid = me()
```

while at the same time passing an Array containing the String `"publish_stream,email"` as the third parameter of our `Facebook.fqlQuery` method.

 For more information on constructing FQL requests, you can refer to the recipes in *Chapter 5, Loading Data with FQL*.

3. With the FQL template, values, and ActionScript function determined, the complete ActionScript function to request the permissions should look like this:

```
function requestPermissionsInfo():void {
    var permissions:Array = new Array();
    permissions.push("publish_stream");
    permissions.push("email");

    if (permissions.length) {
        Facebook.fqlQuery("SELECT {0} FROM permissions WHERE uid =
me() ", onFQLResponse, [permissions.toString()]);
        status_lbl.text = "Retrieving Extended Permissions
information...";
    }
}
```

4. We would execute this function as soon as the user has logged in, by adding the (highlighted) code to the existing `onFacebookInit` and `onFacebookLogin` functions:

```
function onFacebookInit(success:Object, fail:Object):void {
    if (success) {
        logout_btn.enabled = true;
        status_lbl.text = "User is logged in.";
        requestPermissionsInfo();
    } else {
        login_btn.enabled = true;
        status_lbl.text = "No available user logged in.";
    }
}

function onFacebookLogin(success:Object, fail:Object):void {
    if (success) {
        logout_btn.enabled = true;
        status_lbl.text = "User is logged in.";
        requestPermissionsInfo();
    } else {
        login_btn.enabled = true;
        status_lbl.text = "User failed to log in.";
    }
}
```

5. Next, we need to look at handling the response from this query, by creating a new function, called `onFQLResponse`.

As with any other request on the Facebook APIs the callback function needs to accept two objects as parameters—the first for a successful response from the API, and the second to handle any network or communication errors.

The raw JSON-encoded response we get from the API might look something like this:

```
[{
    "publish_stream" : 1
},
{
    "email" : 0
}]
```

And in this case, the result signifies that the current user has granted our application the `publish_stream` permission, but not the `email` permission.

Looking at such a response, we can see that the basic result is an Array, populated with Objects, with those permissions represented as a parameter on separate Objects. To get at this data in ActionScript, we would cast the result as an Array (because by default JSON parses it as an Object rather than an Array), and then iterate through the parameters on each of these Objects, extracting their values.

There are two things we want to find out from this query—whether there are any permissions our application is missing, and what they are. To discover this, we can use the following code for our onFQLResponse function, which collates this information into two variables—isMissingPermission and missingPermissions:

```
function onFQLResponse(success:Object, fail:Object):void {
    var isMissingPermission:Boolean = false;
    var missingPermissions:Array = new Array();
    var results:Array = success as Array;
    if (success && results) {
        status_lbl.text = "Recieved Extended Permissions
        information.";
        for (var i:int = 0; i < results.length; i++) {
            var queryResult:Object = results[i];
            for (var param:String in queryResult) {
                if (Boolean(queryResult[param]) == false) {
                    isMissingPermission = true;
                    missingPermissions.push(param);
                }
            }
        }
    } else {
        status_lbl.text = "An Error occured.";
    }
}
```

This parsing function outputs the code names of any missing permissions into a separate Array, missingPermissions, which we can then use in another function to update our application's interface.

6. To update our user interface to reflect the results of our query, specifically to update the selected property of our interface's two Checkbox components, we can use the following function:

```
function updateInterface(missingPermissions:Array) {
    publish_stream_chk.selected = true;
    email_chk.selected = true;
    for (var i:int = 0; i < missingPermissions.length; i++) {
        switch (missingPermissions[i]) {
```

```
            case ExtendedPermission.PUBLISH_STREAM:
                publish_stream_chk.selected = false;
                break;
            case ExtendedPermission.EMAIL:
                email_chk.selected = false;
                break;

        }
    }
}
```

This `updateInterface` function is specialized to work with our current interface, and toggles the (non-interactive) Checkbox components to reflect the status of the permissions—initially toggling the component on, and then if the permission associated with the checkbox is included in the `missingPermissions` Array, it toggles it back off. Perhaps not the most efficient workflow, but it works.

7. We'd activate this new function by adding the (highlighted) line to the existing `onFQLResponse` function:

```
function onFQLResponse(success:Object, fail:Object):void {
    var isMissingPermission:Boolean = false;
    var missingPermissions:Array = new Array();
    var results:Array = success as Array;
    if (success && results) {
        status_lbl.text = "Recieved Extended Permissions
        information.";
        for (var i:int = 0; i < results.length; i++) {
            var queryResult:Object = results[i];
            for (var param:String in queryResult) {
                if (Boolean(queryResult[param]) == false) {
                    isMissingPermission = true;
                    missingPermissions.push(param);
                }
            }
            updateInterface(missingPermissions);
        }
    } else {
        status_lbl.text = "An Error occured.";
    }
}
```

If we run our application now, we should see a display similar to this:

(We added the `publish_stream` permission in our previous recipe, which is why it's shown as granted, of course.)

How it works...

For the majority of the information stored in Facebook, there's both Graph API and FQL representations of that data available to our application. However, the information about the user's Extended Permissions is only available through an FQL request.

We cover the technical side FQL queries in more detail in *Chapter 5, Loading Data with FQL*, but for now we just need to know that **FQL** is basically a method for making SQL-style queries on the Facebook API. As you may already understand from the syntax of our request, all of the Extended Permissions are stored in the `permissions` table in FQL, which contains a separate column for each of those permissions, and each of those columns contains either `0` (false) or `1` (true).

There's more...

Once we have the results of our FQL query, and have parsed them into meaningful information, we can have our application prompt the user to grant those permissions, or disable functionality in our application appropriately.

One of the more useful uses for this query is to use it to pre-emptively check for the Extended Permissions that our application has been granted, as we will see in the recipe later in this chapter, *Pre-emptively requesting additional Extended Permissions*.

Using the ExtendedPermission class constants to generate our FQL request

Our FQL request doesn't have to be hand-crafted—in fact, it's better if it isn't, as we're then less likely to make a typo. If we put all of your permission names into an Array, and then convert that Array into a String with the `toString` method, we can dynamically create a perfectly good FQL request statement that's also easier to manage:

```
function requestPermissionsInfo():void {
    var permissions:Array = new Array();
        permissions.push(ExtendedPermission.PUBLISH_STREAM);
        permissions.push(ExtendedPermission.EMAIL);

    if (permissions.length) {
        Facebook.fqlQuery("SELECT {0} FROM permissions WHERE uid =
me() ", onFQLResponse, [permissions.toString()]);
        status_lbl.text = "Retrieving Extended Permissions
information...";
    }
}
```

What about FacebookSession.availablePermissions?

You might have noticed that the `FacebookSession` class in the Facebook ActionScript 3 SDK contains the parameter `availablePermissions`, and think that it would be a very simple way to retrieve information about said permissions. However, you'd be wrong.

The `availablePermissions` property is only populated when permissions are requested by the `login` method, and even then it only returns a subset of the permissions originally requested—the new ones that are granted, making it pretty darn useless most of the time.

See also

▶ The recipe *Retrieving better data with FQL* in *Chapter 5*

Requesting additional Extended Permissions, following a failed API request

We've looked at requesting Extended Permissions from the user at the initial login stage, and seen how that works, but it's not infallible. Now we're going to look at actually requesting those permissions midway through our application.

There are two approaches we can take with regards to the management of permissions and requesting of additional ones. The first approach, which we'll explore in this recipe, is to try an API request, and if it fails, request the additional permissions we need for that request, before retrying the original API request. (The second approach we'll cover in the recipe *Pre-emptively requesting additional Extended Permissions*.)

In this recipe we're going to avoid requesting permissions during the initial login process, and instead request them midway through the application.

Getting ready

For this example, the starting point of our application should be that of our earlier recipe, *Authentication with the Web SDK, for Flash Player applications*, giving us a simple user interface and ActionScript code to log in and authenticate automatically, although neither of these processes request new permissions for the user—they simply authenticate them with no additional permission requirements.

> Testing this recipe in particular will involve a deal of granting and revoking permissions from your test accounts. A user's permissions can be easily modified by accessing the following URL on Facebook.com:
>
> ```
> http://www.facebook.com/settings/
> ?tab=privacy&section=app
> ```

To our initial user interface, we should add a Button component, with an **ID** of post_btn, which we will use to trigger the API request. Along with the existing login_btn components and status_lbl components, the initial user interface should look like this:

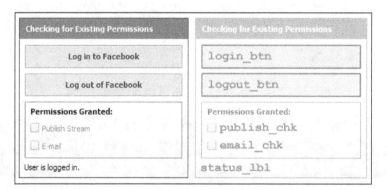

How to do it...

Our existing code should already enable and disable the **Log in to Facebook** button, inversely reflecting the login status of the Facebook ActionScript 3 SDK—if authorized, the button is disabled, and vice-versa.

1. Our **Post status message** button, `post_btn`, should reflect the authorization status of the Facebook ActionScript 3 SDK—if authorized, the button should be enabled. We can achieve this with the following (highlighted) code additions:

```
function onFacebookInit(success:Object, fail:Object):void {
    if (success) {
        login_btn.enabled = false;
        post_btn.enabled = true;
        status_lbl.text = "User is logged in.";
    } else {
        login_btn.enabled = true;
        post_btn.enabled = false;
        status_lbl.text = "No available user logged in.";
    }
}


function onFacebookLogin(success:Object, fail:Object):void {
    if (success) {
        login_btn.enabled = false;
        post_btn.enabled = true;
        status_lbl.text = "User is logged in.";
    } else {
        login_btn.enabled = true;
        post_btn.enabled = false;
        status_lbl.text = "User failed to log in.";
    }
}
```

For this recipe we are going to perform a simple API request that is restricted by default to a newly-authorized application—in this case, creating a status update for the user.

2. The ActionScript function needed to post a status update on the user's behalf could look like this:

```
function tryRequest():void {
    var data:Object = new Object();
    data.message = "Hello world!";
    Facebook.postData("/me/feed", onPostStatusCallback, data);
}
```

Successfully executing this status update request requires that the `publish_stream` permission is granted to our application (be sure to revoke it from your current test user if you've already granted them this permission previously).

3. In our application interface, we would link this function to our Button component with the following (highlighted) addition to the Button's MXML:

```
<s:Button buttonMode="true"
          click="tryRequest()"
          height="32" id="post_btn"
          label="Post status message" width="100%" />
```

4. In our response handler function, `onPostStatusCallback`, we will need to check for the existence of an error. A simple solution to this is to check the success parameter of the callback function, like this:

```
function onPostStatusCallback(success:Object,
                             fail:Object):void {
    if (success) {
        status_lbl.text = "Status update posted to Facebook.";
    } else {
        status_lbl.text = "Failed to post status update.";
    }
}
```

5. If there is an error, we assume it to be caused by a lack of permissions, and we can resolve this by interrupting the application flow to prompt the user to grant those permissions.

Direct user interaction via a mouse click is required to avoid upsetting any of the user's pop-up blockers, so the approach we're going to take in this example is to launch a new Alert component, which will look a little like this:

We can create and launch this Flash-based Alert window with the following code additions (highlighted) in the `onPostStatusCallback` function, and the new function, `showPermissionsRequestDialog`:

```
function onPostStatusCallback(success:Object,
                              fail:Object):void {
    if (success) {
        status_lbl.text = "Status update posted to Facebook.";
    } else {
        showPermissionsRequestDialog();
        status_lbl.text = "Failed to post status update.";
    }
}


function showPermissionsRequestDialog():void {
    Alert.okLabel = "Open Facebook Permissions Dialog";
    Alert.buttonWidth = 190;
    var dialog:Alert = Alert.show("This Application requires
      additional \npermissions from Facebook to continue.",
      "Additional Permissions required.", Alert.OK | Alert.CANCEL,
      null, alertCloseHandler, null, Alert.OK);
}
```

6. Once this Flash-based dialog window has been dismissed, it will call the `alertCloseHandler` function we've specified, which should look like this:

```
function alertCloseHandler(e:CloseEvent):void {
    if (e.detail == Alert.OK) {
        requestThePermissions();
    } else {
        // do nothing.
    }
}
```

7. The function that actually triggers the 'Request for Permissions' pop-up dialog should look like this:

```
function requestThePermissions():void {
    var permissions:Array = new Array();
        permissions.push("publish_stream");

    Facebook.login(permissionsRequestCallback,
                   {perms:permissions.toString()});
}
```

And the dialog that opens will look like this:

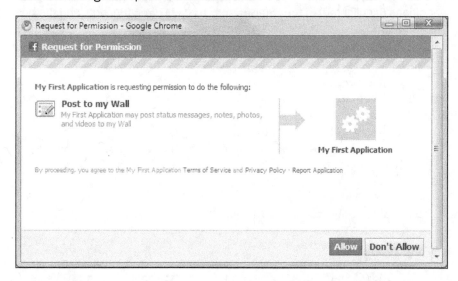

8. Once this window is dismissed, whether successful or unsuccessful in the granting of those Extended Permissions, the response will be passed to the `permissionsRequestCallback` function.

The type of Object returned in a successful response is a Facebook session. As we've just requested permissions that the current user was missing, a successful response will return details in the `availablePermissions` parameter, and it's this we need to check to see if the request was actually successful or not.

We can use the following function to check the response object, and if the result was successful, automatically retry our request:

```
function permissionsRequestCallback(success:Object,
                                    fail:Object):void {
    var session:FacebookSession = (success as FacebookSession);
    if (success && session) {
        if (session.availablePermissions && session.
        availablePermissions.indexOf("publish_stream") != -1){
                tryRequest();
                status_lbl.text =
                "Permissions granted, retrying...";
            } else {
                status_lbl.text = "Permissions not granted.
            Cannot continue.";
            }
        } else {
            status_lbl.text = "There was an error requesting the
            permissions.";
        }
}
```

And that's it for this recipe!

How it works...

In short, the process for dealing with requests that fail because of a lack of permissions, such as the one we've (slightly artificially) forced in this recipe is essentially this:

1. Graph API request fails, with returned error code of 200—OAuthException, a lack of required Extended Permissions.

2. Display a warning message to the user, which they can interact with to launch the Facebook *Request for Permission* dialog.

3. As you can see, the response isn't very helpful at working out which permissions are missing—we just have to know the required permissions in advance and plan accordingly.

4. If the result object passed back to our application contains a Facebook session instance, with our missing Extended Permissions listed under the `availablePermissions` property, automatically retry the original request.

There are better—or at least, more complex—methods we can develop in ActionScript to cache and retry the failed API requests. (This recipe is a demonstration of the process, rather than so much of a reusable example of best practice.)

In a failed API request, one which fails due to a lack of Extended Permissions, the response object would look like this:

```
{
    "error": {
        "type": "OAuthException",
        "message": "(#200) The user hasn't authorized the application to
perform this action"
    }
}
```

Knowing which missing permission is to blame for the failed API request falls to us, the developer, and has to be something which we build into our application.

There's more...

Regardless of how our Flash Platform application manages permissions elsewhere—whether it specifies Extended Permissions at the initial login, and even if it follows the approach of pre-emptively checking for permissions when our application starts up, it's always possible that our user could have revoked those permissions through the Facebook.com website in the meantime. So it's a good idea to always be checking the response for permission errors.

So, how can we distinguish between different API errors?

Checking if a failed API request is caused by (a lack of) Extended Permissions

It's not always permissions that are the problem—you might encounter issues with request limits on the API, your requests might be malformed, or Facebook itself could be suffering technical problems.

It would be disingenuous, and confusing for the user, to say the least, if we were to blame permissions for every error we come across when using the API. One error response we might get, for example, is the *Feed action request limit reached* for performing too many requests in a short space of time, which looks like this:

```
{
    "error":
    {
        "type": "OAuthException",
        "message": "(#341) Feed action request limit reached"
    }
}
```

This is obviously different from the response we'd get if it were a permissions problem. To programmatically check for the reasons behind errors, we're best to search for the error code itself, with code such as in this example:

```
function onPostCallback( success:Object, fail:Object ):void
{
    if ( success )
    {
        // successful call, so we have the correct permissions
    } else
    {
        // failed call
        if( fail.message.indexOf("#2") != -1 )
        {
            // failed because of permissions
        } else
        {
            // failed for something else
        }
    }
}
```

According to the documentation on Facebook API errors, an error with an ID of between 200 and 299 is due to a permissions error of some sort. In the preceding code sample we're searching through the error's 'message' property, which is where the error code is displayed, and checking the first digit of the error code, to see if it's in the two-hundred range. (Again, there are better ways to detect this, but the code here should suffice.)

A full list of the error codes and messages that can be returned by the Facebook API currently isn't available from the Facebook documentation, but it is available elsewhere online, such as at the following URL, which is a copy of the previous list of error codes from Facebook, before they inadvertently removed it from their documentation:

```
http://www.takwing.idv.hk/tech/fb_dev/faq/general/gen_
10.html
```

See also

▶ *Checking for existing Extended Permissions*

Pre-emptively requesting additional Extended Permissions

Another approach to managing Extended Permissions, that does not require requesting all of the Extended Permissions upfront, is to combine it with the FQL request from our *Checking for existing Extended Permissions* recipe—check for any missing permissions, request them, and then go on to attempt the API request.

In this recipe, we'll create an interface which we can use to authenticate with Facebook requiring no additional Extended Permissions. Our application will still authenticate with Facebook when it starts up, giving it basic access to the user's information, but it's not until we need to start making API requests that we need to check for those permissions.

Getting ready

For this example, the starting point of our application should be that of our earlier recipe, *Authentication with the Web SDK, for Flash Player applications*, giving us a simple user interface and ActionScript code to log in and authenticate automatically, although neither of these processes request new permissions for the user—they simply authenticate them with no additional permission requirements.

Testing this recipe in particular will involve a deal of granting and revoking permissions from your test accounts. A user's permissions can be easily modified by accessing the following URL on Facebook.com:

```
http://www.facebook.com/settings/
?tab=privacy&section=app
```

To our initial user interface, we should add two new Button components, `request_btn` and `post_btn`, which we will use to separately request permissions and post a status update. Along with the existing `login_btn` components and `status_lbl` components, the initial user interface should look like this:

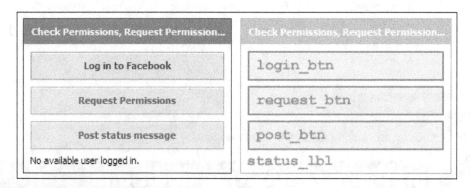

How to do it...

Once our application has authenticated with the Graph API, we should update the user interface to initially disable the **Request Permissions** and **Post status message** buttons, and automatically dispatch an FQL query to retrieve a list of the Extended Permissions granted to our application.

1. First, make the following (highlighted) changes to the existing functions, `onFacebookInit` and `onFacebookLogin`, which will start by disabling the two additional Button components we've added to the stage, and begin the FQL request the moment that the user becomes authenticated with the Graph API:

```
function onFacebookInit(success:Object, fail:Object):void {
    request_btn.enabled = false;
    post_btn.enabled = false;
    if (success) {
        login_btn.enabled = false;
        status_lbl.text = "User is logged in.";
        requestPermissionsInfo();
    } else {
        login_btn.enabled = true;
        status_lbl.text = "No available user logged in.";
    }
}

function onFacebookLogin(success:Object, fail:Object):void {
    request_btn.enabled = false;
    post_btn.enabled = false;
    if (success) {
```

```
        login_btn.enabled = false;
        status_lbl.text = "User is logged in.";
        requestPermissionsInfo();
    } else {
        login_btn.enabled = true;
        status_lbl.text = "User failed to log in.";
    }
}
```

For this recipe we are ultimately going to perform a simple API request that is restricted by default to a newly-authorized application—in this case, creating a status update for the user.

2. The function we'd need to request these Extended Permissions should look like this:

```
function requestThePermissions():void {
    var permissions:Array = new Array();
    permissions.push("publish_stream");
    Facebook.login(permissionsRequestCallback, {perms:
permissions.toString()});
}
```

3. And we would associate this function with our **Request Permissions** Button component with the following (highlighted) addition to the button's MXML:

```
<s:Button buttonMode="true"
          click="requestThePermissions()"
          enabled="false" height="32" id="request_btn"
          label="Request Permissions" width="100%" />
```

4. The ActionScript function needed to post a status update on the user's behalf could look like this:

```
function tryRequest():void {
    var data:Object = new Object();
    data.message = "Hello world!";
    Facebook.postData("/me/feed", onPostStatusCallback, data);
}
```

Successfully executing this status update request requires that the publish_stream permission is granted to our application (be sure to revoke it from your current test user if you've already granted them this permission previously).

5. In our application interface we would link this function to our Button component with the following (highlighted) addition to the buttons' MXML:

```
<s:Button buttonMode="true"
          click="postClickHandler(event)"
          enabled="false" height="32" id="post_btn"
          label="Post status message" width="100%" />
```

6. Next we need to copy the `requestPermissionsInfo` function and its response handler, `onFQLResponse`, from the *Checking for existing Permissions* recipe, changing only the permissions we request to remove request for the "email" permission.

```
function requestPermissionsInfo():void {
    var permissions:Array = new Array();
    permissions.push("publish_stream");
    if (permissions.length) {
        Facebook.fqlQuery("SELECT {0} FROM permissions WHERE uid =
me() ", onFQLResponse, [permissions.toString()]);
        status_lbl.text = "Retrieving Extended Permissions
information...";
    }
}


function onFQLResponse(success:Object, fail:Object):void {
    var isMissingPermission:Boolean = false;
    var missingPermissions:Array = new Array();
    var results:Array = success as Array;
    if (success && results) {
        status_lbl.text = "Recieved Extended Permissions
information.";
        for (var i:int = 0; i < results.length; i++) {
            var queryResult:Object = results[i];
            for (var param:String in queryResult) {
                if (Boolean(queryResult[param]) == false) {
                    isMissingPermission = true;
                    missingPermissions.push(param);
                }
            }
            updateInterface(missingPermissions);
        }
    } else {
        status_lbl.text = "An Error occured.";
    }
}
```

7. Once response for the FQL query has been received, our `onFQLResponse` function is set up to call the `updateInterface` function, passing an Array of the missing Extended Permissions, which we can use to update the interface accordingly.

If there are no permissions missing from our application, we can enable the `post_btn` component and our user can post a status message to Facebook, but if there are, we should keep the `post_btn` component disabled, in favor of the `request_btn` component.

We can use the following function to update our application's interface accordingly:

```
function updateInterface(missingPermissions:Array):void {
    if (missingPermissions.length == 0) {
        request_btn.enabled = false;
        post_btn.enabled = true;
        status_lbl.text = "Has all required permissions.";
    } else {
        request_btn.enabled = true;
        post_btn.enabled = false;
        status_lbl.text = "Does not have all required permissions.";
    }
}
```

All of this gives us an application that does not require any Extended Permissions from Facebook before it authenticates, and then updates the user interface to reflect what the user can and can't do.

How it works...

The approach towards managing Extended Permissions that we've taken in this recipe is essentially:

1. Authenticate with the Facebook Graph API.

2. Use an FQL request to retrieve the status of relevant Extended Permissions.

   ❑ If the Extended Permissions are available:

      i. Disable the 'Request Permissions' button.

      ii. Enable the 'Post to Status update' button.

   ❑ If the Extended Permissions are *not* available:

      i. Enable the 'Request Permissions' button.

      ii. Disable the 'Post to Status update' button.

The main technical aspect of this recipe—making and parsing the results of the FQL request itself is covered in the earlier recipe *Checking for Extended Permissions*. This recipe demonstrates more of a pattern for integrating this information into any application's workflow.

There's more...

There's no hard and fast rule about when you should be requesting extended permissions from your users—it depends largely on the what you're trying to do and how much you can develop your application so that it gracefully degrades without those permissions.

The danger with a progressive approach is that if you have too many pop-up windows you'll annoy your users. On the other hand, asking for too many permissions initially, when you've not even let your users experience your application, is likely to discourage them altogether—especially when you're asking for those permissions in a single dialog, where they can't be individually accepted or rejected.

See also

▶ *Checking for existing Extended Permissions*

▶ *Requesting additional Extended Permissions, following a failed API request*

4
Reading and Writing Data with the Graph API

In this chapter, we will cover:

- ▶ Building a 'Test Console' for the Graph API
- ▶ Loading a Graph API object from Facebook
- ▶ Loading specific data fields for a Graph API object
- ▶ Loading Graph API connections
- ▶ Loading multiple Graph API objects in a single request
- ▶ Limiting request lengths and paging results
- ▶ Filtering requests to a specific time period
- ▶ Loading a Facebook profile image
- ▶ Using the search capabilities of the Graph API
- ▶ Creating, editing, and deleting Graph API objects

Introduction

The vast majority of data stored on Facebook is available to developers through what is known as the **Graph API**, which is a system that closely resembles the REST protocols. This Graph API makes data available as Objects, through specific URLs, and it is using those URLs that we send and retrieve information.

The introduction to the Graph API, from Facebook's own Developer Documentation (`http://developers.facebook.com/docs/api`) describes the Graph API like so:

> *"[...]The Graph API presents a simple, consistent view of the Facebook social graph, uniformly representing objects in the graph (e.g., people, photos, events, and pages) and the connections between them (e.g., friend relationships, shared content, and photo tags).*
>
> *Every object in the social graph has a unique ID. You can access the properties of an object by requesting* `https://graph.facebook.com/ID`. *For example, the official page for the Facebook Platform has id* `19292868552`, *so you can fetch the object at* `https://graph.facebook.com/19292868552`."

With the Graph API we can also create, edit, and delete data from Facebook, in addition to simply being able to read that information—unlike FQL, which although more flexible, is limited to purely reading data.

In this chapter, we're going to look at how we can retrieve and manage data from Facebook using the Graph API, and how we can convert the returned data into more usable, strict-typed ActionScript objects.

Building a 'Test console' for the Graph API

For the recipes in this and the next chapter, there is less need for us to be developing a specific user interface for each recipe. Instead, we'd be better off developing a single, flexible interface which we can use to test a variety of different requests.

In this recipe, we're going to develop a simple user interface in the Flash Player (or AIR runtime, if you wish) that allows us to quickly see the results of a Graph API request URL and modify that URL without the need to continually re-build our project.

Once completed, our 'Test Console' should contain a sizable `TextArea` component, where we will output formatted JSON objects; a `TextInput` component, for specifying the Graph API object (or Graph API connection) URLs; a `CheckBox` component, for including additional Metadata (primarily to view Graph API connections); and a `Button` component, for triggering the request itself.

When complete, our 'Test Console' should look like this:

Graph API Object Test Console

```
http://graph.facebook.com/   [me                    ]   [ Get details ]   ☐ Include Metadata

{
    "timezone": 1,
    "id": "526534401",
    "username": "psyked",
    "first_name": "James",
    "verified": true,
    "significant_other": {"id": "            ", "name": "            "},
    "last_name": "Ford",
    "link": "https://www.facebook.com/psyked",
    "gender": "male",
    "name": "James Ford",
    "relationship_status": "In a relationship",
    "updated_time": "2011-05-31T10:17:40+0000",
    "birthday": "            ",
    "locale": "en_GB"
}
```

Getting ready

The base class for our test console application should be that of the `ApplicationBase` class, from the recipe *Creating the ApplicationBase class* in *Chapter 11, Bridging the Flash and Application Gap*, which gives us a template that is set up to automatically authenticate with, and manage Extended Permissions for, the Graph API.

Our user interface should include a **Button** component, with an ID of `graph_api_request_btn`; a **TextInput** component, `uid_inpt`; a **TextArea** component, `results_txt`; and a **CheckBox** component, `metadata_chk`.

You could add more UI elements, such as the text: `http://graph.facebook.com/` as in the preceding screenshot, but that's up to you.

How to do it...

This test console will allow us to make requests to the Graph API, which essentially involves just constructing the URL for that request, dispatching it, and waiting for a response. The response that we receive from the Graph API is a JSON-encoded object, and we'll output that, with a little bit of formatting, to our TextArea component.

With our components added to the stage, we can start adding the functionality:

1. Add a click handler function, `requestClickHandler`, to the `graph_api_request_btn` in MXML:

    ```
    <s:Button buttonMode="true"
              click="requestClickHandler(event)"
              height="25" id="graph_api_request_btn"
              label="Get details" />
    ```

2. The click handler function will take the current text value of the `uid_inpt` component and use it to perform a basic API request, setting the function `requestCallback` as the response handler, with the following function:

    ```
    import com.facebook.graph.Facebook;

    function requestClickHandler(e:Event):void {
        Facebook.api(uid_inpt.text, requestCallback);
    }
    ```

3. And in the `requestCallback` function, we will output a JSON-encoded version of the responses, with the following code:

    ```
    import com.adobe.serialization.json.JSON;

    function requestCallback(success:Object, fail:Object):void {
        if (success) {
            results_txt.text = JSON.encode(success);
        } else {
            results_txt.text = JSON.encode(fail);
        }
    }
    ```

    At this point, we should be able to run our application, enter a value (such as me) into the `uid_inpt` component, click the `graph_api_request_btn` component, and receive a result similar to this:

Graph API Object Test Console

http://graph.facebook.com/ `me`   [Get details]   ☐ **Include Metadata**

```
{"timezone":1,"id":"526534401","updated_time":"2011-05-31T10:17:40+0000","username":"psyked","first_name":"James","
verified":true,"significant_other":{"id":"          ","name":"          "},"last_name":"Ford","link":"https://
www.facebook.com/psyked","gender":"male","name":"James Ford","relationship_status":"In a
relationship","birthday":"          ","locale":"en_GB"}
```

4. Finally, there is the `metadata_chk` component that we added to the application. We can use this component to toggle on and off the loading of metadata in our requests.

This metadata contains the details of all of a Graph API object's connections, which as we will see in our later recipes, is very handy to know for testing purposes, if not in our real-world applications. To include metadata in our request, we need to add a third parameter to the `Facebook.api` method of the `requestClickHandler` function, a new Object with a property of `metadata`, containing an integer with a value of `0` or `1`, as demonstrated in the following code:

```
function requestClickHandler(e:Event):void {
    var options:Object = new Object();
    options.metadata = int(metadata_chk.selected);
    Facebook.api(uid_inpt.text, requestCallback, options);
}
```

That's it for this recipe, although you may well want to improve upon this with the further suggestions in this recipe's *There's more...* section. To test the application at this point, I'd suggest adding the value `me` to the `uid_inpt` component, and see for yourself what results you get!

How it works...

This recipe gives us a basic application that we can use to quickly experiment with the Graph API. By keeping much of our application essentially dumb, with no validation of inputted URLs and no parsing of the results into strict-typed ActionScript classes, we have ensured that our application is able to work with both individual Graph API objects and Graph API connections, all from the same code base.

The specifics of how the URLs for Graph API objects and Graph API connections are constructed and how they work is discussed in more detail in the next few recipes of this chapter.

There's more...

To improve this basic application further, and make the output more human-readable and user-friendly, we can look at the following enhancements:

Using an animation to indicate load progress

With our application being built on top of the `ApplicationBase` class, we have access to two functions—`showLoader` and `hideLoader`—which are inherited from that class, and which display a Facebook-style loading animation while our application is awaiting a response from the Graph API.

Add the highlighted lines of code in ActionScript to integrate these functions into our application's workflow:

```
function requestClickHandler(e:Event):void {
    showLoader();
    var options:Object = new Object();
    options.metadata = int(metadata_chk.selected);
    Facebook.api(uid_inpt.text, requestCallback, options);
}

function requestCallback(success:Object, fail:Object):void {
    hideLoader();
    if (success) {
        results_txt.text = JSON.encode(success);
    } else {
        results_txt.text = JSON.encode(fail);
    }
}
```

Getting a human-readable JSON string from the API

The current response information isn't the nicest thing to look at—in fact, it's downright horrendous to understand by just looking at it. What we need is some nicely formatted response data, using a technique referred to as **pretty-printing**.

Luckily, there is a version of the ActionScript 3 JSON libraries that handles pretty-printed outputs. It is based off the same **as3corelib** JSON encoder that we're already using as part of the Facebook ActionScript 3 SDK, but has been expanded to introduce some options for outputting human-readable versions of encoded JSON data.

A version of the ActionScript 3 JSON class with support for pretty-printed output has been developed by Larry Maccherone of http://maccherone. com/ and is available for download from the following locations:

Introduction and blog post: http://maccherone.com/larry/ projects/a-pretty-json-encoder-for-actionscript-3-as3/

Subversion source control: http://svn.maccherone.com/json/ trunk/src/

To use this JSON encoder class with pretty-printing support, rather than the Adobe-standard JSON class, we would add this library/source code to our project, and change the class import statement to read:

```
import com.maccherone.json.JSON;
```

The code formatting is an additional optional parameter of this JSON class, which is disabled by default. To enable the pretty-printing we pass a second parameter to the `JSON.encode` method, with a value of `true` to enable the pretty-printing, like so:

```
function requestCallback(success:Object, fail:Object):void {
    if (success) {
        results_txt.text = JSON.encode(success, true);
    } else {
        results_txt.text = JSON.encode(fail, true);
    }
}
```

With this pretty-printing code in place, our application should look like the image at the top of this recipe.

See also

▶ *Chapter 11, Creating the ApplicationBase class*

Loading a Graph API object from Facebook

All information in the Facebook Graph API is stored as either an object, a property of an object, or as a connection between two or more objects. In this recipe, we're going be looking specifically at loading a single object from the Graph API.

This 'object' can represent practically any single element of Facebook—be it a **User**, an **Event**, or a **Status message**—with the properties of that object being determined by the object's type and our application's Extended Permissions.

Each Graph API object has its own ID, which is an identification number that is unique across the entire Facebook ecosystem, and each object can be referenced and retrieved from the Graph API based on an URL schema which revolves around the use of that ID.

There are two main steps to retrieving, and working with, an object from the Graph API:

1. The first step is to know the unique ID of the object to be loaded.
2. The next step is to anticipate the type of object that will be returned by the Graph API, and handle it accordingly—for instance, parsing it into a strict-typed class instance.

In this recipe we're going to load some publicly-accessible sample objects from the Graph API, and then parse the raw, loosely-typed dynamic Object instances into strongly-typed, predefined, ActionScript class instances.

Getting ready

As the starting point for this example, we're going to use the test console interface that we created in our previous recipe, which already handles authentication and permissions management. We need make no further additions to the interface of this application, as our changes will all revolve around the ActionScript code.

How to do it...

To request data from the Graph API, we need to use the `Facebook.api` (or for the Desktop SDK, the `FacebookDesktop.api`) method. The signature for this method is:

Facebook.api("URL", response handler[, options, "method"]);

As for the parameters of this method:

▶ The first parameter is the partial URL to load, which for an individual object is simply the Facebook object's ID.

▶ The second parameter is the **callback function**, which will be executed when a result (be it successful or not) is received from the API request.

▶ The optional third and fourth parameters, **options** and **method**, aren't needed when we are loading objects from the Graph API, so we can omit them from our request.

To load information about the 'Facebook Platform' page object, which has an ID of **"19292868552"**, we can simply enter this object's ID into our interface and execute the request, which should yield a result similar to this:

Graph API Object Test Console

http://graph.facebook.com/ [19292868552]   [Get details]   ☐ Include Metadata

```
{
    "link": "https://www.facebook.com/platform",
    "username": "platform",
    "id": "19292868552",
    "name": "Facebook Platform",
    "category": "Product/service",
    "company_overview": "Facebook Platform enables anyone to build social apps on Facebook and the web.",
    "picture": "https://fbcdn-profile-a.akamaihd.net/hprofile-ak-snc4/211208_19292868552_8264376_s.jpg",
    "likes": 2054886,
    "website": "http://developers.facebook.com",
    "founded": "May 2007",
    "mission": "To make the web more open and social."
}
```

How it works...

A typical request to the Graph API, such as the one in this recipe, would load data from the URL: `https://graph.facebook.com/19292868552`, which when loaded yields a JSON-formatted String of data. This JSON data is then parsed into a dynamic Object instance by the JSON serialization classes of the `AS3CoreLib` library, which comes bundled as part of the Facebook ActionScript 3 SDK.

What the ActionScript 3 SDK is actually doing here is taking the values that we supply into the `Facebook.api` method, formatting them into an URL to be loaded, and then using the built-in `URLLoader` class of the Flash Platform to load that data.

There's more...

Unfortunately, there's no validation happening on the new object instances that we create using the `fromJSON` method (most likely because it's technical implausible to do so) which means that, regardless of the contents of the object that we pass in to this function, this method will return a valid new instance of that class.

Converting raw results into ActionScript class instances

The returned data from the Graph API arrives as a JSON-encoded object, which is then converted into an ActionScript Object instance by the Facebook ActionScript 3 SDK. We could use this Object instance as-is, but it would be easier for us, and better for our long-term development process, if we converted those returned objects into strict-typed objects.

Fortunately, the community-supported version of the Facebook ActionScript 3 SDK that we're using already includes a set of built-in value object classes that represent each of the possible object types of the Graph API. And each of these value object classes implement the `IFacebookGraphObject` interface, meaning that they feature a static `fromJSON` method, to be used when parsing the responses from the Graph API.

The 'Facebook Platform' object that we've loaded is a Graph API object of the type **Page**. The equivalent value-object class in ActionScript 3 is `FacebookPage`, and to convert the result object from our API call to an instance of this class, we would use the following ActionScript code:

```
var page:FacebookPage = FacebookPage.fromJSON(success);
```

What this code does is create a new instance of the `FacebookPage` class and copy all of the parameters from the source object (that we passed in to the `fromJSON` method) to the new `FacebookPage` instance. Using this strict-typed object in ActionScript has many advantages for us as developers, not least from the Flash Builder's code hinting and precompiler validation features.

Therefore, knowing a Graph API object's type and its corresponding class in ActionScript is something that falls to us as developers, rather than being something that gets worked out automatically by the Facebook ActionScript 3 SDK.

The URL pattern that we use in an API request for a Facebook Page is the same as that for a **User**, **Event**, or **Photo**. For example, the 'Facebook Developer Garage Austin' Event, another sample object from the Developer Documentation, has an **ID** of 331218348435.

To request this object, we use the following ActionScript:

```
Facebook.api("331218348435", requestCallback);
```

And to parse the result into the appropriate ActionScript class we'd use the follow code:

```
var result:FacebookEvent = FacebookEvent.fromJSON(success);
```

Every object in the Facebook Graph API has an equivalent ActionScript 3 class, and they should be easy enough to work out—FacebookEvent, FacebookApplication, FacebookGroup—they all follow a logical naming convention.

Detecting errors in Graph API requests

There are two types of error that we might encounter when working with the Graph API—actual communication errors, and problems with the data passed between our application and the Graph API.

All response handler functions that work with the Facebook ActionScript 3 SDK must take two parameters—an Object for a successful response, and one for a failed response. The failed response object is only triggered if there is an actual communications error—a failed connection, or something similar.

If the communication with the Graph API is successful, but the request sent was invalid, the response handler function still receives an Object under the success parameter, but instead of the results we're interested in, the response object contains information under the parameters error_code and error_message. Validation of the results from our API requests should be performed on all of our requests.

Usernames and Vanity URLs

Graph API objects, such as **Applications**, **Pages**, or **Users** may also have a Facebook **username,** which is interchangeable with the object's ID, but their presence (and indeed, their existence) is not guaranteed for each Graph API object in the same way that the ID is.

For example, as we can see in the previous screenshot, the Facebook Platform has an ID of 19292868552 and also has a **username** of platform. They both return the same information, but it means that we could use the following request instead for this recipe, and still receive the same response from the API:

```
Facebook.api("platform", requestCallback);
```

From a development point-of-view, it makes little difference whether we're requesting data from a vanity URL or an ID-based URL, as using either URL will return the same object.

Using the 'me' shortcut to reference the current user

In addition to the usernames and IDs, the Facebook Graph API provides us with a shortcut for retrieving information about the current user, in the form of an URL synonym or shortcut, cunningly called **me**.

Whenever we're loading information from a Graph API URL, instead of needing to supply the current user's ID as part of the request, we can substitute that ID for this *me* shortcut—so instead of loading an URL that contains the current user's ID, we can instead load:
`http://graph.facebook.com/me` and receive the same information.

With this in mind, loading information about the current user is as simple as using this line of ActionScript:

```
Facebook.api( "me", requestCallback );
```

This shortcut applies to any URL request—it doesn't just work when it's used in isolation. As we'll see in later recipes, we can also use this shortcut as part of Graph API connections, and in our later chapter on FQL, we'll see that there's also an equivalent shortcut for FQL requests.

The magic here is all performed by Facebook and their servers; it's nothing to do with the ActionScript or JavaScript SDKs. Using the me keyword in an URL returns information about the current user. So as long as the request would work with a user ID, it will work with this keyword.

/[OBJECT_ID] vs. [OBJECT_ID] in requests

Notice a difference between the URLs listed in the Facebook Developer Documentation and those that we're using in this recipe? It doesn't matter whether you choose to make your request with the URL me or /me; both requests are treated the same and are combined (by the Facebook ActionScript 3 SDK) with the hardcoded Graph API base URL (`https://graph.facebook.com/`) to produce valid request URLs.

Whether you choose to include a leading forward-slash character is up to you!

See also

▶ The recipe *Loading Graph API connections* in this chapter
▶ *Chapter 5, Loading Data with FQL*

Loading specific data fields for a Graph API object

When we request an object from the Graph API, without explicitly specifying the data fields we're interested in, we receive a default set of properties for that object, properties which are determined by Facebook.

Alternatively, we can improve the efficiency of our requests by explicitly listing the data fields we're interested in, and the API will only return those properties.

For example, were we seeking information about user's birthdays, rather than loading all of the user's information—including their name, gender, and locale—with each request, we could specify that we only want to load that user's birthday information, via the `birthday` data field.

Specifying data fields in this manner obviously doesn't give us access to information that a user hasn't supplied, and it doesn't bypass any privacy restrictions that the user has set up for their data, but it does ensure that responses from the Graph API will return that information if it is available.

In this recipe, we'll again be requesting information about the Facebook Platform Page, only this time around, we'll be specifying the data fields to be returned by the API. In doing so, we cut out unnecessary properties from the response, and (if we were to pay particular attention to the download times) we experience a faster load time for the response. We'll also modify our application's interface, so that we can see the two different responses, side-by-side.

Getting ready

To compare the results of the original API request and one that specifies data fields, we can make a simple modification to our application's interface—duplicating the `results_txt` component with an ID of `limited_results_txt` and positioning the two components side-by-side, like this:

How to do it...

To explicitly request properties for a Graph API object, we need to make use of the third parameter of the `Facebook.api` method, which is where we input the options for the API requests.

The input type for the third parameter of this method is an Object, and to request specific properties we give it a property with the name `fields`, which should contain a comma-delimited String of the required data fields to request.

1. To create the information that will go into the `fields` property of the request, we should first create an Array, populated with the data field values, which can be supplied using the following code:

```
var dataFields:Array = new Array();
dataFields.push(FacebookPageField.CATEGORY);
dataFields.push(FacebookPageField.NAME);
```

2. To convert this Array into a single comma-delimited String, we then use the `toString` method of the Array class on our `dataFields` Array, and associate the output with the options objects' `fields` parameter, like this:

```
options.fields = dataFields.toString();
```

3. In this recipe, we're going to make two different requests in parallel, and we have two different components to which we're going to output the results of those requests. The way we're going to achieve this is with the following modifications to the `requestClickHandler` function, which should look like this (with modifications highlighted):

```
function requestClickHandler(e:Event):void {
    showLoader();

    Facebook.api(uid_inpt.text, requestCallback);

    var options:Object = new Object();

    var dataFields:Array = new Array();
    dataFields.push(FacebookPageField.CATEGORY);
    dataFields.push(FacebookPageField.NAME);
    options.fields = dataFields.toString();

    Facebook.api(uid_inpt.text, requestCallbackTwo, options);
}
```

4. To output the results of these requests into separate components, we're simply making a copy of the original `requestCallback` handler function, so that the two of them look like this:

```
function requestCallback(success:Object, fail:Object):void {
    hideLoader();
    if (success) {
        results_txt.text = JSON.encode(success, true);
    } else {
        results_txt.text = JSON.encode(fail, true);
    }
}

function requestCallbackTwo(success:Object, fail:Object):void {
    hideLoader();
    if (success) {
        results_restricted_txt.text = JSON.encode(success, true);
    } else {
        results_restricted_txt.text = JSON.encode(fail, true);
    }
}
```

With these functions in place, we should be able to run our application and use it to request a Facebook Page and compare the results of a request with restricted and default sets of parameters, as in this following screenshot:

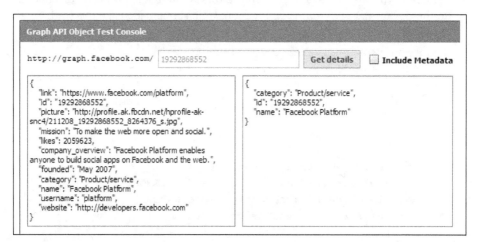

How it works...

When we request an object from the Graph API without explicitly specifying the data fields, as we did in our previous recipe *Loading a Graph API object*, the data fields that get returned usually consist of every field that we have access too. Once we start explicitly requesting the data fields, the responses will be limited to those fields plus the Facebook ID of the object they're associated with, or if none of the fields we requested are available, the response will just contain a set of objects with only the Facebook IDs!

> The names of all the possible data field values are detailed in the Facebook Developer Documentation, which is available online at:
>
> `http://developers.facebook.com/docs/reference/api/`
>
> Alternatively, as part of the Facebook ActionScript 3 SDK, each of the Graph API value object classes has an accompanying field class—`FacebookPageField` for the `FacebookPage` class, `FacebookPostField` for the `FacebookPost` class, and so on.
>
> Each of these classes contains a set of constants that map out the official structure of the Graph API object types, which, combined with Flash Builder's code completion capabilities, makes developing our code faster because we have to spend less time cross-referencing the documentation and our own code!

There's more...

The Facebook platform isn't likely to suffer many ill effects from your application unnecessarily requesting information it doesn't need when you're loading a single object, but when you start scaling up your requests to multiple objects you may well start to see the benefits of keeping your data requests a little more trim.

The undocumented fringes of the Graph API

Oddly enough, not all of the potential information and data fields available from a Graph API request follow the official documentation, or perhaps that documentation is simply incomplete.

For Facebook Pages in particular there is an official list of properties for the object type, and then there's a few non-standard oddities that exist, but only on certain pages, and they aren't officially documented.

Whether these mystery undocumented fields are the result of legacy code or represent future features is yet to be established, but there's a listing of them available online in the unofficial Facebook Developer documentation, should you be interested:

```
http://fbdevwiki.com/wiki/Graph:Page
```

See also

▶ The recipe *Loading a Graph API object* in this chapter

Loading Graph API connections

Connections are what Facebook is all about—the interlinking and associations between different objects. In the previous recipes, we have looked at loading individual objects and their properties, but a connection is an entirely different beast.

A connection is an Array of Graph API objects, and is used to represent News Feeds, Photo Albums, Event Attendees, Links, Comments, and much more. Each type of Graph API object has its own different set of connections, ranging from a **Comment** object, with its single / `likes` connection to a **User** object, with multiple connections, detailing just about every piece of data Facebook stores about its users (as listed in the following table).

There are two main routes for discovering a Graph API object's connections:

1. Comprehensive details of the connections available for a particular type of Graph API object are available as part of the Developer Documentation, from the URL: `http://developers.facebook.com/docs/reference/api/`.

2. We can request the Metadata parameter of an individual Graph API object, which will return a list of its available connections, as per this quote from the Developer Documentation:

    The Graph API supports introspection of objects, which enables you to see all of the connections an object has without knowing its type ahead of time.

For example, the connections available for a Facebook User object—that are relevant to a Flash Platform application—are as follows:

User Connection URL	Description
/USER_ID/home	The user's news feed
/USER_ID/feed	The user's wall
/USER_ID/tagged	The photos, videos, and posts in which this user has been tagged
/USER_ID/posts	The user's own posts

User Connection URL	Description
/USER_ID/picture	The user's profile picture
/USER_ID/friends	The user's friends
/USER_ID/activities	The activities listed on the user's profile
/USER_ID/interests	The interests listed on the user's profile
/USER_ID/music	The music listed on the user's profile
/USER_ID/books	The books listed on the user's profile
/USER_ID/movies	The movies listed on the user's profile
/USER_ID/television	The television listed on the user's profile
/USER_ID/likes	All the pages this user has liked
/USER_ID/photos	The user's photos and/or the photos user is tagged in
/USER_ID/albums	The photo albums this user has created
/USER_ID/videos	The videos this user has been tagged in
/USER_ID/groups	The groups this user is a member of
/USER_ID/statuses	The user's status updates
/USER_ID/links	The user's posted links
/USER_ID/notes	The user's notes
/USER_ID/events	The events this user is attending
/USER_ID/inbox	The threads in this user's inbox
/USER_ID/outbox	The messages in this user's outbox
/USER_ID/updates	The updates in this user's inbox
/USER_ID/checkins	The places that the current user has checked into
/USER_ID/friendlists	The user's friend lists

In this recipe, we're going to load one of these connections; specifically, the current user's list of friends. The same basic process applies to other connections, such as **News feeds** or **Photos** and **Albums**, but those connections are covered in detail in our later chapters, and so we won't repeat ourselves here.

Getting ready

As with our other recipes, our starting point for this recipe is the Test Console that we developed as part of our earlier recipe, *Building a Test Console for the Graph API*. Graph API connections don't have the option to supply Metadata, so we can remove the `metadata_chk` component from the interface, as it's useless for this recipe, and update the click handler function for the `graph_api_request_btn` Button component accordingly, so that it looks like this:

```
function requestClickHandler(e:Event):void {
    showLoader();
    Facebook.api(uid_inpt.text, requestCallback);
}
```

How to do it...

Just as with *individual* Graph API objects, connections are specified through an URL scheme (as shown in the preceding table). Therefore, to request a list of friends, we use the friends connection, `/USER_ID/friends`, (although obviously we're going to replace the `USER_ID` value).

1. To request the friends list of the current user we can use the /me/friends URL in our existing `uid_inpt` component, run the request and our results should look like this:

```
Loading Graph API Connections

http://graph.facebook.com/  me/friends                         Get details

[
  {"id": "100002985847264",: "name": "Chandra Ting"},
  {"id": "100001739503845",: "name": "Lenore Devenport"},
  {"id": "100001048493485",: "name": "Nelson Mccleery"},
  {"id": "100003485893947",: "name": "Noemi Hurston"},
  {"id": "100001938594033",: "name": "Javier Timbers"},
  {"id": "100003267476345",: "name": "Max Toller"}
]
```

Entering this URL in our application is equivalent to running the following ActionScript:

```
Facebook.api("me/friends", requestCallback);
```

The response we receive from this request will be an array of Graph API User objects, instead of a single object. It has been encoded and decoded from a JSON String, and so still arrives in our response handler function as an Object class instance, but the way we parse the results and convert them into strict-typed instances is little more complex.

2. To parse the results of a Graph API connection, what we need to do is attempt to cast the response object as an Array, and if that conversion is successful, we can then iterate through the contents of that Array, converting the individual Objects within that Array into strict-typed ActionScript class instances. To parse the results in this manner, our response handler function, `requestCallback`, should look like this:

```
function requestCallback( success:Object, fail:Object ):void {
    var results:Array = success as Array;
    if ( success && results ) {
        for ( var i:int = 0; i < results.length; i++ ) {
            var friend:FacebookUser = FacebookUser.
fromJSON(results[i]);
        }
    }
}
```

We can easily detect if there was an error with our request—perhaps by mistyping our connection URL—by inspecting the `success` parameter and `results` variable in the preceding code. If either parameter is **null**, there was a problem with the request.

If the connection that we're requesting is actually restricted due to a lack of Extended Permissions, we'll receive a valid response from the Graph API, but the content of that response will be empty—in other words, we'll receive an array, but an empty one.

How it works...

A successful response from the Graph API returns an Array of Objects, which have been decoded from a JSON string. We can treat the response as an Array and iterate through it because it actually *is* an Array; it's just the transition from JavaScript to ActionScript and String to Objects and function parameters that result in the overall response object being cast as an Object instance.

If the `success` parameter is **null** then the Facebook ActionScript 3 SDK will populate the `fail` parameter, which represents a technical communications error with the Graph API, just as it does for other Graph API requests.

We know that the expected results format for a connection request is an Array, so if we're unable to cast the `success` parameter as an Array, using the code: `success as Array` (which will either return an Array or null value), then we know that the request was unsuccessful without having to look for error codes or messages.

If we request an unrecognized connection, for example, the response may look like this (following) which will return a null value if we try to cast it as an Array:

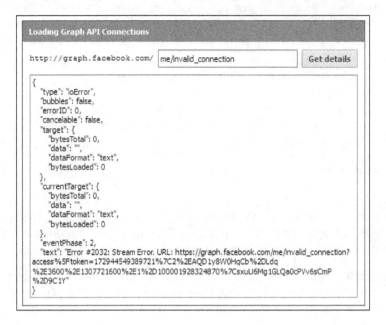

As we explore the contents of the results Array, we come across the same issues as when we request individual objects from the Graph API, which is that the Facebook ActionScript 3 SDK, on its own, cannot determine whether an object returned is of the type that we are expecting. We can make it attempt to parse the results into a strict-typed instance, but with no built-in validation of the result, the burden of correctly matching the results to their correct ActionScript class ultimately rests on us as developers.

You may have noticed that the results of a Graph API connection, particularly the /USER_ ID/friends connection, returns a different set of results to that of the direct /USER_ID connection. That behavior essentially boils down to a different set of default data fields for the connection; the resulting object types remain the same, and we can still explicitly request the missing data fields—but the defaults are different.

There's more...

As we'll see in our later recipes, connections are not just for retrieving information—when we start uploading images for example, we'll see that we upload them to an /USER_ID/albums connection to put the image in that album.

Handling responses with mixed results content types

Most connections—such as the me/friends, me/photos or me/checkins connections—consist of elements of a single type. For those connections, interpreting the results should be a simple task. Others however, like the me/tagged, me/home or me/feed connections, can contain a mix of different object types.

Take the me/home connection as an example—when a user wants to post something, they can do it in several formats:

The objects returned by a typical home feed will be a mixture of **Status update**, **Photo**, **Link**, and **Video** objects. Some of the properties for objects overlap, but they're all different object types, and we'll want to convert these into FacebookStatusMessage, FacebookPhoto, FacebookLink, and FacebookVideo objects, respectively.

Fortunately, the Graph API response for these kinds of connection have anticipated our needs in this area, and provide to us an additional **type** parameter, which we can introspect and use in our handler to run the correct conversions.

For example, the raw response from the Graph API for the me/home connection might look like this:

```
[
    {
        "type": "status",
        "id": "108734602494994_167760323267610",
        "created_time": "2010-12-31T17:35:12+0000"
    },
    {
        "type": "video",
        "id": "503204088_177059452326877",
        "created_time": "2010-12-31T14:22:03+0000"
    },
    {
        "type": "link",
        "id": "647357194_10150114315727195",
        "created_time": "2010-12-31T09:24:48+0000"
    },
    {
        "type": "photo",
```

```
            "id": "110274552356073_152287188154809",
            "created_time": "2010-12-30T18:10:58+0000"
        }
    ]
```

As we'll see in more detail in the *News Feed and Status updates* recipes in *Chapter 6*, we can use this `type` parameter in our parsing function, with a function similar to this—parsing the response contents into different ActionScript classes based on the type listed by the Graph API.

```
function requestCallback( success:Object, fail:Object ):void {
    var result:Array = success as Array;
    if ( success && result ) {
        for ( var i:int = 0; i < result.length; i++ ) {
            switch (result[ i ].type) {
                case "status":
                    var statusMessage:FacebookStatusMessage =
FacebookStatusMessage.fromJSON( feed[ i ] );
                    break;
                case "link":
                    var link:FacebookLink = FacebookLink.fromJSON(
feed[ i ]);
                    break;
                case "photo":
                    var photo:FacebookPhoto = FacebookPhoto.fromJSON(
feed[ i ]);
                    break;
                case "video":
                    var video:FacebookVideo = FacebookVideo.fromJSON(
feed[ i ]);
                    break;
            }
        }
    }
}
```

See also

- ▶ *Loading a Graph API object*
- ▶ *Loading specific data fields for a Graph API object*
- ▶ *Limiting Graph API request lengths*
- ▶ *Requesting data for a specific time period*
- ▶ *Chapter 6, Loading a user's status updates*

Loading multiple Graph API objects, in a single request

Multiple objects can be loaded in a single Graph API request. As explained in the Developer Documentation:

> *You can also request multiple objects in a single query using the "ids"
> query parameter. For example, the URL* `https://graph.facebook.`
> `com?ids=arjun,vernal` *returns both profiles in the same response.*

This differs from the URL-oriented approach used for the other Graph API methods, but luckily, implementing it doesn't require much of a change to our ActionScript code, so long as we have the IDs or usernames of the objects we want to load.

In this recipe, we're going to load the data for a series of Facebook Pages, information that we would otherwise have to load with separate requests.

How to do it...

In this recipe, we're going to load the Facebook Page objects of a few well-known companies—Facebook, Coca-Cola, and Pepsi. If we were to load their data separately, we'd need to make the following three requests, with code similar to this:

```
Facebook.api( "facebook", onFBInfoLoaded );
Facebook.api( "cocacola", onCocaColaInfoLoaded );
Facebook.api( "pepsi", onPepsiInfoLoaded );
```

As we saw from the documentation, the IDs of the objects to be loaded need to be passed into the Graph API as part of the query string of the request URL, rather than the main URL itself. To translate this into values suitable for the ActionScript SDK, we need to remove the contents from the first (URL) parameter and instead add them as part of the optional third parameter, under the property `ids`.

The property itself should be formatted as a comma-delimited string of the object IDs (or usernames), and is best created by populating an Array with multiple String values, and then converting that Array into a single String, using the native `toString` method of the Array class.

The ActionScript code we should use to request these three objects in a single request should look like this:

```
var idsToLoad:Array = new Array();
idsToLoad.push( "facebook" );
idsToLoad.push( "cocacola" );
idsToLoad.push( "pepsi" );
```

```
    var options:Object = new Object();
    options.ids = idsToLoad.toString();

    Facebook.api( "", requestCallback, options );
```

When it comes to interpreting the response, the format of the response is a little different to both the normal Graph API requests and Graph API connection responses.

A single Graph API object is returned as that raw object, and a connection is returned as an Array of objects. However, when it comes to making multiple object requests, the data returned from the Graph API again comes as a single object, but it is instead a custom object, with properties corresponding to the values passed in the original request.

Using this code, the response received from the Graph API should look like this (with the responses limited to only include the `name` and `category` fields, for the sake of brevity).

```
{
    "cocacola": {
        "category": "Food/beverages",
        "id": "40796308305",
        "name": "Coca-Cola"
    },
    "facebook": {
        "category": "Product/service",
        "id": "20531316728",
        "name": "Facebook"
    },
    "pepsi": {
        "category": "Food/beverages",
        "id": "56381779049",
        "name": "Pepsi"
    }
}
```

We can still iterate through this result object, but we need to use a different parsing function than that which we've used for previous examples. Instead of treating the result as an Array, and iterating through its length as we do with a connection, we instead treat the response as an object, similar to a Dictionary, and loop through its properties.

The following code will achieve this, iterating through the properties of the response object and parsing them into their strict-typed ActionScript class equivalents:

```
function requestCallback( success:Object, fail:Object ):void {
    if ( success ) {
        for ( var key:String in success ) {
```

```
        var page:FacebookPage = FacebookPage.
fromJSON(success[key]);
            }
        }
    }
```

How it works...

The REST-style approach of mapping objects to URLs in our data requests works until the point we start wanting to request multiple pieces of data simultaneously, at which point it breaks down and simply isn't suitable. As there isn't an URL scheme that can handle this, we have to abandon the URL approach and start using query string parameters instead.

To add a query string parameter we add its values to the options object of the `Facebook.api` method, under the parameter `ids`, and the ActionScript SDK combines those values with the ones it adds itself (like the access token) to produce the final URL request, which it then loads.

We can still load multiple objects as part of a connection, of course, but the contents of those connections are managed by Facebook and are out of our control. In contrast, when we are manually combining objects into a single request ourselves, we could ask for completely unrelated items in a single request.

The three ways of loading information from Facebook—single object, multiple objects, and an object connection—are distinct because they all return their information in a different format.

A request of this style returns a single object, with parameters equal to the IDs of the objects requested. This is different from a connection or a single object request, and thus requires a different parsing function.

There's more...

Why would we request a batch of Graph API objects in a single API request? It's all about performance, really. Facebook's own rule of thumb is to:

Combine as many requests as possible.

Succinct. But it is a good rule.

Whenever we make a data request, there's a certain amount of overhead that comes from forming a request, dispatching it, waiting for the response, and so on. With the Facebook Platform, the internal systems are very quick to respond and it's actually the connection between the user and the Graph API that takes the largest chunk of time, rather than actually waiting for, or downloading the response.

In my own (totally unscientific) testing, the data from this recipe when loaded separately can take 700 to 1000 ms to receive, whereas the same data loaded in a single request can take 350 to 400 ms, which demonstrates how effective optimizing these requests can be.

For more information on how combining queries helps performance, and for other performance tips, check out the Facebook Developer Guidelines for Application Performance, available online at:

`http://developers.facebook.com/docs/guides/performance`

See also

▶ *Loading a Graph API object from Facebook* recipe
▶ *Loading Graph API connections* recipe

Limiting request lengths and paging results

We can limit the number of responses that we receive from a Graph object connection by simply using the **limit** option in our requests. By taking advantage of the **limit** and **offset** capabilities of the Graph API we can add paging to our data—requesting a large set of data in several smaller chunks.

In this recipe, we're going to implement paging for a connection request—reducing what would otherwise be a list of hundreds of images down to only ten at a time, with components onscreen that allow us to customize the number of results for each 'page' and navigate forward and backward through those pages.

Getting ready

The initial starting point for this recipe should be that of our earlier recipe, *Building a Test Console for the Graph API*. To this basic interface, we should add several components to test the pagination capabilities of our requests. These should be a **NumericStepper** component, `increments_stp`; two **Button** components, `prev_btn` and `next_btn`; and a **Label** component, `indicator_lbl`.

The layout of our user interface should look like this:

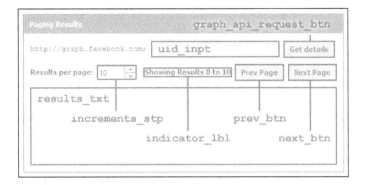

How to do it...

The `limit` and `offset` parameters must be added as parameter of the options for an API request, which will then see them added to the Facebook query string correctly.

To limit a photos connection to only 10 items, we could use the following code:

```
var options:Object = new Object();
options.limit = 10;
Facebook.api("me/photos", requestCallback, options);
```

Implementing paging on those the photos would mean adding an additional offset parameter to the options object, like the following, which would load results 11 through to 20 from the `me/photos` connection:

```
var options:Object = new Object();
options.limit = 10;
options.offset = 10;
Facebook.api("me/photos", requestCallback, options);
```

To test this functionality in our own interface, we should:

1. Add a new variable in our application's scope, `currentPage`, an integer which keeps track of the current page of results that we're requesting from the API, which should look like this:

```
var currentPage:uint = 0;
```

2. In the actual request function, `requestClickHandler`, we want to extract the current values from our `NumericStepper` component (which defines the number of results in each page) and combine them with the `currentPage` variable, by changing this function so that it looks like this:

```
function requestClickHandler(e:Event = null):void {
    showLoader();
    var options:Object = new Object();
    options.limit = increments_stp.value;
    options.offset = increments_stp.value * currentPage;
    Facebook.api(uid_inpt.text, requestCallback, options);
}
```

3. By default our current page number is zero, and we have no way of changing that. So now we need to be able to change the current page, by creating and attaching our click handler functions for the `next_btn` and `prev_btn` components:

```
function nextClickHandler(e:Event):void {
    currentPage++;
    requestClickHandler();
}


function prevClickHandler(e:Event):void {
    if (currentPage > 0) {
        currentPage--;
        prev_btn.enabled = true;
    } else {
        prev_btn.enabled = false;
    }
    requestClickHandler();
}
```

And we can associate these functions with our components in MXML by adding the following (highlighted) parameters:

```
<s:Button buttonMode="true"
          click="prevClickHandler(event)"
          height="25" id="prev_btn"
          label="Prev Page" />


<s:Button buttonMode="true"
          click="nextClickHandler(event)"
          height="25" id="next_btn"
          label="Next Page" />
```

4. Finally, in our `requestCallback` function we should update the contents of the `indicator_lbl` component that we added to our application, so that it would read **"Showing Results 1 to 10"** or **"Showing Results 11 to 20"**:

```
function requestCallback(success:Object, fail:Object):void {
    hideLoader();
    var results:Array = success as Array;
    if (success && results) {
        results_txt.text = JSON.encode(success, true);
        indicator_lbl.text = "Showing Results " +
        (increments_stp.value * currentPage) + " to " +
        (increments_stp.value * (currentPage + 1));
    } else {
        results_txt.text = JSON.encode(fail, true);
    }
}
```

Now we have an interface that implements Graph API connection results paging—if your application has the `"user_photos"` permission, try loading the `me/photos` connection, or a publicly-accessible equivalent, like `platform/photos`.

How it works...

The limit works as you'd expect—a limit of 10 will give a maximum of 10 results. Similarly, an offset of 10 will return results from 11 onwards, while an offset of five would return results from five onwards, and setting either of these values to zero is essentially the same as not specifying them at all.

The application we've developed in this recipe can effect pagination on any Graph API connection. Of course, our requests need to be large enough to make pagination worthwhile—many connections have an automatic limit to a few tens of results or the last 30 day's worth of content. Unfortunately, there's no easy way for us to count the total number of possible results from our request—we're essentially working blind, paging results until the point that we stop receiving results from the connection.

There's more...

The advantage of implementing paging is that it means we can exercise more control over the data we load and keep it more optimized, while at the same time still being able to load the remaining results on demand. Better optimization of your API requests should help your application's performance by reducing the amount of memory it requires, and should also serve to speed up your Graph API request response times.

For more information on how limiting the length of queries and implementing paging will improve the Graph API's response times, check out the Facebook Developer Guidelines for Application Performance, available online at:

http://developers.facebook.com/docs/guides/performance

See also

▶ *Loading Graph API connections* recipe

Filtering requests to a specific time period

Time-based filtering is also a feature offered to us by the Graph API. Its usefulness is much the same as that of limiting the number of requests, only that instead of simply limiting the number of responses, it allows us to perform our filtering based on the time that the objects were created or updated.

The Facebook platform is much more geared towards time-oriented information, with features like the News and Home Feed connections, so this type of filtering makes a lot of sense for applications that would display this information.

Time-based results can be filtered to those results that are either before or up to a specific time. By combining both the until and since properties, we can achieve filtering for a date range.

How to do it...

For this example, we're going to load the status updates for the Facebook platform, using the URL value of facebook/statuses. To limit the results we would load to those from the last week, we would use the since option, with a value of "-1 week".

```
var options:Object = new Object();
options.since = "-1 week";
Facebook.api( "facebook/statuses", callback, options);
```

To invert this search, and retrieve all of the results up to one week prior, we would change the since option for the until option:

```
var options:Object = new Object();
options.until = "-1 week";
Facebook.api( "facebook/statuses", callback, options);
```

Should we wish to retrieve the results between two points in time, we would combine both the `until` and `since` properties, such as:

```
var options:Object = new Object();
options.until = "-1 week";
options.since = "-2 week";
Facebook.api( "facebook/statuses", callback, options);
```

How it works...

We can specify whether we want to fetch results from either before or after our timestamp by adding or changing the `until` and `since` properties.

All Graph API objects have a created or updated time, and those can be used out-of-the-box to filter our API responses. In addition, the Graph API accepts either Unix timestamps (such as "December 31, 1998 23:59:60") or English-language **datetime** strings supported by PHP, such as "+1 week" or "10 September 2000".

 For more information on the supported date formats, see the PHP **strtotime** method documentation:

`http://php.net/manual/en/function.strtotime.php`

There's more...

Some Graph API objects have both a created date and an updated date—when it comes to filtering requests based on the time, the API makes use of the latest time rather than the oldest time.

See also

▶ *Loading Graph API connections* recipe

Loading a Facebook profile image

Many of the objects in Facebook—such as Users, Places, Events, Groups, Applications, Photos, and Videos—can have profile pictures associated with them. In the technical sense, these pictures are described as Facebook connections, but at the same time they're also different than other Facebook connections.

There are two ways to obtain the URL of a profile picture for an object—it can either come as a property of an object, obtained by specifying the correct fields when you load an object, or you can use a method in the ActionScript SDK to load different sized thumbnail versions of the profile image.

We need no additional permissions for loading profile images—as long as the current user can load the basic object, they can load the profile image for that object, as it is covered by a different set of permissions from those that govern access to the photo or video connections.

In this recipe, we're going to use the methods that come as part of the ActionScript SDK to load different size versions of the profile image. In the follow-up we'll also look at the values that we can obtain from the Graph API object, and show how they correspond to the versions returned in this recipe.

How to do it...

The method we will be using is `Facebook.getImageUrl`, which is a helper function that comes as part of the Facebook ActionScript 3 SDK. It returns the URL of the image immediately, as a String, which we can then use in a standard image load request.

Facebook.getImageUrl("url" [, "size"]);

The `getImageUrl` method can take two parameters—the Facebook ID of the object, which is always required, and the size of the image, which is optional. There are currently three options for the image size, determined by Facebook.

The image sizes available through Facebook are **square**, **small**, and **large**.

 ▶ A square image is 50 x 50 pixels in size
 ▶ A small image has a maximum width of 50 pixels and a maximum height of 150 pixels
 ▶ A large image is 200 pixels wide and up to 600 pixels tall

If we choose to not specify a size for the image, then the Graph API defaults to returning the square size image thumbnail.

To obtain the image for the current user, we can use this code:

```
Facebook.getImageUrl( "me" );
```

To get the URL of a large image for the current user, we would use the following code:

```
Facebook.getImageUrl("me", "large");
```

What this method does is just convert values into URLs—me becomes `http://graph.facebook.com/me/picture`—but to actually load the image we'd need to tie this in with the `URLLoader` class or `Image` component.

Once our Facebook class is initialized, and the user logged in, we could run this code:

```
profile_image.source = Facebook.getImageUrl("me", "large" );
```

Assuming we have an `Image` component in our application, with an ID of `profile_image`—created with MXML such as this:

```
<s:Image id="profile_image" width="200" />
```

Which will set the source of the `Image` component, and the component will then automatically start loading a new image from that URL.

How it works...

The method we're using here is simply a utility function—all it's actually doing is reformatting the values we enter into the method and combining them with some constants from the SDK.

The output from these functions will look something like this:

```
http://graph.facebook.com/526534401/picture?type=large
```

We could easily generate these values ourselves, but if we don't have to do things that way, we might as well not do so.

When we make a request to those URLs what we will actually get is not an image at that URL, but a server-side 302 redirect to the actual URL where that image is located, which comes from a far more cryptic Content Delivery Network URL, which might look something like this:

```
http://profile.ak.fbcdn.net/hprofile-ak-snc4/hs455.snc4/49855_
526534401_2568_n.jpg
```

Luckily, we don't need to do anything more to load the correct URL—the browser or the underlying AIR runtime will handle all of the redirects to serve up the correct data.

There's more...

In this recipe we've used the shortcut for retrieving information about the current user, but if we wanted to get an image for the 'Facebook Developer Garage Austin' event that we used in our previous recipes, we simply need to use its Facebook ID in the call:

```
Facebook.getImageUrl( "331218348435", "large" );
```

The method would, of course, return to us the following URL:

`http://graph.facebook.com/331218348435/picture?type=large`

Getting image URLs from Graph API objects

As well as this `getImageUrl` method, it's also possible to retrieve a picture's URL for a Graph API object. If an object's `picture` property isn't already available in the object returned by the Graph API, it's possible to request it specifically, as a data field. See the recipe *Loading specific data fields for a Graph API object* for more information.

When *picture* is specified as one of the fields to load, the returned object should have a field that contains the URL of the profile image. This image URL doesn't follow the same pattern as the method we've used in this recipe returns, but rather it is the URL that those URLs ultimately redirect to. From that point of view it's more direct, but it also means we're not able to specify the size of image we're after, and the URL will point to the smaller squared-off image.

```
{
    "id": "526534401",
    "picture": "http://profile.ak.fbcdn.net/hprofile-ak-snc4/
      hs455.snc4/49855_526534401_2568_q.jpg"
}
```

GetImageURL and the 'me' shortcut

Using the 'me' shortcut in the `Facebook.getImageURL` function doesn't work out-of-the-box. Using the object's ID works fine, because those values are always accessible, whether or not there is a valid, active Facebook session.

For the 'me' shortcut to work the URL needs a valid access token. The Facebook SDK normally handles the addition of the access token to outbound URLs, but in this instance it doesn't have anything to do with the load process. To get around this problem, we can add the access token to the URL ourselves:

```
var urlToLoad:String;
var rawURL:String = Facebook.getImageUrl( "me", "large" );
var sess:FacebookSession = Facebook.getSession();

if ( rawURL.indexOf( "?" ) != -1 ) {
    urlToLoad = rawURL + "&access_token=" + sess.accessToken;
} else {
    urlToLoad = rawURL + "?access_token=" + sess.accessToken;
}
```

See also

▶ *Loading Graph API objects* recipe

▶ Chapter 5, *Loading Data with FQL*

Using the search capabilities of the Graph API

In addition to the 'natural discovery' method of locating content in the Facebook Platform, the major discovery route for content is through the search functionality of the platform. The search capabilities available to us as developers through the Graph API are almost, if not exactly, the same as the search capabilities available to the user through the Facebook.com website.

As detailed in the online Facebook Developer Documentation, the available object types for searching are:

▶ Publicly-available posts, such as those by a Facebook User, Application, Page, or Organization in their Profile Feed

▶ People (Facebook Users)

▶ Pages (Businesses, Organizations, and so on)

▶ Facebook Events

▶ Facebook Groups

▶ Facebook Places, which can be retrieved by location as well as name

▶ Facebook User Check-ins

▶ News Feeds for a specific Facebook User

As you might expect, the search capabilities are flexible, allowing us to make searches by name and by type, and in the case of Facebook Places, by location or proximity to a location.

Getting ready

The starting point for this recipe should be the end result of our earlier recipe, *Building a Test Console for the Graph API*. The search functionality we will explore in this recipe can take two parameters; a free-text search query, for which the existing uid_inpt component will suffice: and a search type, for which we will need to introduce a new component to our application's stage.

Create a `DropDownList` component, named `type_ddl`, and populate it with the options for the results type, using the following MXML:

```
<s:DropDownList height="26" id="type_ddl">
    <s:dataProvider>
        <mx:ArrayCollection>
            <fx:Object data="" label="All" />
            <fx:Object data="post" label="Post" />
            <fx:Object data="user" label="User" />
            <fx:Object data="page" label="Page" />
            <fx:Object data="event" label="Event" />
            <fx:Object data="group" label="Group" />
            <fx:Object data="place" label="Place" />
            <fx:Object data="checkin" label="Checkin" />
        </mx:ArrayCollection>
    </s:dataProvider>
</s:DropDownList>
```

With this component added to the stage, our user interface should look like this:

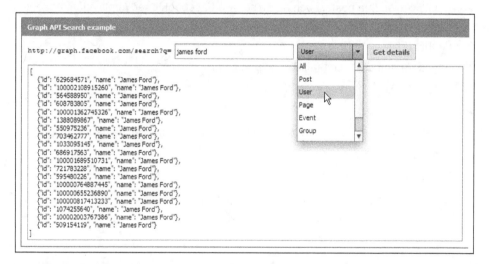

How to do it...

The format of a search query is slightly different to that of loading a single Graph API object or connection, in that it uses a fixed URL and passes the search queries in the options object of the request.

The starting point for our code in this recipe looks like this:

```
var options:Object = new Object();
options.metadata = int(metadata_chk.selected);
Facebook.api(uid_inpt.text, requestCallback, options);
```

1. Instead of supplying a Graph API object ID as the URL parameter of the `Facebook.api` request, we should hardcode the URL to read `"search"` and supply our search query as the **'q'** parameter of the request's options Object, with ActionScript such as this:

```
var options:Object = new Object();
options.metadata = int(metadata_chk.selected);
options.q = uid_inpt.text;
Facebook.api("search", requestCallback, options);
```

2. The next step is to limit the results of this search request by specifying the type of results we're looking for—Post, User, or Event, for example—and to do that, we need to add an extra `type` parameter to our API request options, coming from the selected item in the `type_ddl` component:

```
var options:Object = new Object();
options.metadata = int(metadata_chk.selected);
options.q = uid_inpt.text;
if (type_ddl.selectedItem) {
    options.type = type_ddl.selectedItem.data;
}
Facebook.api("search", requestCallback, options);
```

With this code in our `requestClickHandler` function we can make our search query, limiting the search results type if there's one selected in the `type_ddl` **DropDownList** component, and otherwise leaving it blank. The results of this search query come in the format of an Array, containing each Graph API result object.

As these results come in the same format as a Graph API connection, we can use a similar function to parse them—casting the results as an Array and then iterating through them.

How it works...

We perform searches in the Graph API by making a request through the normal Graph API methods, but using the value `search` as the URL and passing the text-based query itself as parameters of the request, producing a final request URL such as:

```
https://graph.facebook.com/search?q=QUERY&type=OBJECT_TYPE
```

This search URL makes it possible to search the entire publicly-accessible Facebook 'social graph', giving it a wider scope for results than any of the other connections offer.

Helpfully, the results from our search request will always return a `type` parameter for the object in question—`video`, `status`, `link`, `photo` for Posts, or `user`, `event`, `group`, `page`, `place`, or `checkin`, and we can parse the results with a switch statement, as we did in our earlier recipe, *Loading Graph API connections*.

There's more...

In addition to simple text-base searches, we are also able to use the search functionality of the Graph API to locate the location-based Facebook Places.

See also

▶ *Loading Graph API connections* recipe

Creating, editing, and deleting Graph API objects

The Graph API is what we should use when we want to create, edit, or delete information on Facebook. Following the REST style approach, we create objects on Facebook by making `POST` requests to Graph API connections.

In addition to creating new objects, we can edit or delete existing objects, although not all of the objects in the Graph API are editable once they've initially been created. User information can be edited for example, but comments or status messages cannot be edited, only deleted.

In our later chapters, we'll cover the specifics of creating different Graph API object types, such as Photos. In this recipe, we'll examine the general approach needed to make requests that create, edit, or delete Graph API objects.

Getting ready

For this recipe, we have no specific user interface, but we can use the `ApplicationBase` class created in *Chapter 11* for authentication and permissions management. To create and manage Graph API objects on the user's behalf, our application will require the `pubish_stream` Extended Permission.

How to do it...

To change the default API request (which is a `GET` request) into a `POST` request, we should be invoking the fourth optional parameter of the `Facebook.api` method, supplying a value of `"post"`, which will cause the Facebook ActionScript3 SDK to adjust the internals of the SDK to change the actual method of the URL request it performs.

```
Facebook.api("URL", response handler[, options, "method"]);
```

The fourth parameter of this function is optional, and if omitted defaults to the value `"get"`. When creating our `POST` request, we use the options object to supply the parameters for our request.

1. Creating a new Graph API object:

   New objects can be created in the Graph API by issuing a request to an existing object's connection.

   Referring to the Facebook Developer Documentation, we can see that one connection that we can use to create an object on Facebook is:

Method	Description	Arguments
/PROFILE_ID/feed	Publish a new **post** on the given profile's feed/wall	message, picture, link, name, caption, description, source

   We can use the publicly accessible profile of **"My First Application"** (`172944549389721`) with this connection, and create a new **Post** object by supplying one of the arguments as a parameter of the options object, with code such as this:

```
var options:Object = new Object();
options.message = "I am creating a new message from Flash.";
Facebook.api("172944549389721/feed", requestCallback, options,
"post");
```

   A request like this will return a single object, with an `id` parameter, which is that object's unique ID on Facebook, in this instance, returning the object:

```
{"id": "172944549389721_233830563301119"}
```

2. Editing an existing Graph API object:

   Not all Graph API objects can be edited, but for those that can, we can make `POST` requests to the individual object's URL.

   The process is much the same as for creating a new object—`POST` data to the object's connection URL, with the new parameters and values. As long as there are no errors—which are most commonly caused by attempting to edit non-editable parameters.

3. Deleting a Graph API object:

   As we are unable to make requests from the Flash Player using the `DELETE` header, we need to make a `POST` request to an individual object's Graph API URL and supply the parameter `method` with a value of `delete` in the options, using code such as this:

   ```
   var options:Object = new Object();
   options.method = "delete";
   Facebook.api("172944549389721_233830563301119", requestCallback,
   options, "post");
   ```

How it works...

Creating a new object is referred to in the Facebook ecosystem as **Publishing**. All publishing that happens exclusively through our own application requires an **Extended Permission** to do so, which would be either `pubish_stream` or `publish_checkins`. With the ability to publish to Facebook on the user's behalf also comes the ability to edit or delete data from Facebook on the user's behalf.

For an application to follow a true REST approach to managing objects, it should rely on `GET`, `POST`, and `DELETE` requests to specific URLs. In an AIR application, this is no problem, but the Flash Player runtime is limited by the capabilities of its containing web browser, and can only make `GET` or `POST` requests—hampering its ability to provide a true REST client. JavaScript-based applications suffer from the same limitation, which is why the Facebook Developer Documentation states:

> *To support clients that do not support all HTTP methods (like JavaScript clients), you can alternatively issue a POST request to an object URL with the additional argument* `method=delete` *to override the HTTP method. For example, you can delete a comment by issuing a POST request to* `https://graph.facebook.com/COMMENT_ID?method=delete`.

All of the information that we transmit to the Graph API is sent together in the ActionScript 3 `Facebook.api` method's options Object. Complex objects such as Arrays often have to be flattened into comma-delimited equivalent String data for these requests, but most of the time simple text-based parameters are all that we need to supply.

There's more...

Other recipes in this cookbook give specific examples of creating, editing, or deleting objects in the Graph API—uploading Photos, for example.

See also

▶ *Chapter 6, Creating a status update with ActionScript*

▶ *Chapter 6, Posting a Link with ActionScript*

▶ *Chapter 6, Deleting a status update with ActionScript*

▶ *Chapter 7, Adding a comment to a Graph API object*

▶ *Chapter 7, Removing a comment from a Graph API object*

▶ *Chapter 7, Adding a Like to a Facebook Post*

▶ *Chapter 7, Removing a Like for a Graph API object or URL*

▶ *Chapter 8, Creating an Album with the Graph API*

▶ *Chapter 8, Uploading Photos to Facebook*

▶ *Chapter 9, Changing current user's RSVP status*

▶ *Chapter 10, Checking in to an existing Facebook Place with Flash and the Graph API*

5
Loading Data with FQL

In this chapter, we will cover:

- ▶ Loading data with FQL
- ▶ Using subqueries in FQL
- ▶ Using logical operators in FQL requests
- ▶ Loading large data sets with FQL multiquery
- ▶ Cross-comparing data sets to find overlapping results
- ▶ Sorting FQL results
- ▶ Limiting and paging FQL results
- ▶ Searching for text strings in FQL

Introduction

Facebook Query Language (**FQL**), provides us with a much more optimized and flexible mechanism for retrieving both specific and lengthy sets of data. In this chapter we're going to explore FQL, and use it to retrieve data from Facebook that we couldn't so easily obtain using the standard Graph API, as well as loading some more optimized versions of data that's already accessible to us through Graph API objects and connections.

FQL is database-style approach to loading data from the Facebook API. The syntax is very similar to that of SQL, which makes it inherently both more complex and more adaptable, and allows for much more precise data requests, with comparatively smaller like-for-like responses than the standard Graph API.

All of the objects available through the Graph API are represented in FQL tables, and all of the Graph API connections can be replicated with FQL queries. Objects and connections in the Graph API are simply a representation of the most common information requested from the API, whereas FQL is almost-raw access to all of the data from Facebook.

> A full list of the database tables and data fields available through a FQL request is available online, in the Facebook Developer Documentation at:
>
> `http://developers.facebook.com/docs/reference/fql/`

FQL can only be used for reading data from Facebook, but not for adding, editing, or deleting objects. To add, edit, or delete objects from Facebook we must use the standard Graph API or even the older REST API (although that is currently being depreciated, and won't be around forever).

We load data from Facebook by constructing and sending FQL queries to the API, with these queries being sent either as single requests, or bundled into a batch of multiple requests to be executed simultaneously. The FQL queries themselves can be standalone or self-referencing, with further nested queries (or subqueries) and logical operators helping to narrow down the range of results.

Loading data with FQL

In this recipe, we're going to load information about a Facebook object from an FQL table. Specifically, we're going to replicate the data requests from the previous chapter's recipe, *Loading a Graph API object*, which pulled information from the Graph API about the Fan page for the 'Facebook Platform', a Graph API object with an ID of `19292868552`.

Getting ready

In this recipe, and all of the recipes in this chapter, we'll require the same basic setup and Facebook authentication code discussed in the previous chapters. Specifically, our application will need a basic interface to display the results of our queries, and for our own sake, a display of the FQL query itself.

Create an application interface, which includes two main components—a **TextArea** component with an ID of `results_display` and a **RichText** component with an ID of `query_display`:

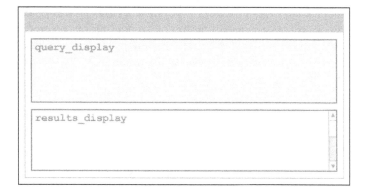

Our application should be built on top of the `ApplicationBase` class, which is detailed in the recipe *Creating the ApplicationBase class* in *Chapter 11, Bridging the Flash and Application Gap*, and which gives us authentication and permission-requesting capabilities.

Unlike the 'Test console' that we developed in the previous chapter, we won't be specifying our FQL queries via the interface, but adding the queries to our application by modifying the application's ActionScript code. To execute our FQL request immediately after authenticating with Facebook, we can override the internal `facebookReady` method of the `ApplicationBase` class, with the following ActionScript template:

```
override public function facebookReady():void {
    // your code here
}
```

The ActionScript code that we develop in these recipes should all be triggered from inside this `facebookReady` method, for them to happen automatically. When we make our requests, we can use the `results_display` component to display the output of our request, and the `query_display` component to display the inputted FQL request, using code such as this:

```
query_display.text = query;
```

An FQL query requires no more permissions than any other Graph API request, and just like the rest of the Graph API, our application can only make queries against users that it has access to or data that it has the correct set of extended permissions for. In this recipe, we're going to be loading public data for public objects, so no worries there.

How to do it...

In the Facebook ActionScript 3 SDK, FQL queries can be executed with the `Facebook.fqlQuery` method, the code for which looks like this:

```
Facebook.fqlQuery("query", callback function, values);
```

Into the first parameter of this function we supply our FQL query, in **String** format. The second parameter is the `callback function`, and the third is an **Object**, the properties of which can be combined with values supplied in the first parameter, to produce an FQL request that is slightly more protected against syntax errors (both accidental and malicious).

To make an FQL request, we first need to construct our FQL query:

That query has a few consistent elements. Those basic elements themselves are very similar to those of SQL—`SELECT`, `FROM`, and `WHERE` to construct our query and we can also extend those queries with the `IN`, `ORDER BY`, `AND`, `OR`, `NOT`, and `LIMIT` keywords.

We'll cover those extended keywords in the next few recipes, so no need to worry about them yet—for now, all we need is the minimal elements:

```
SELECT x
FROM x
WHERE x
```

The Graph API object we want to load is a Facebook Page object, with an ID of `19292868552`. Facebook Pages are stored in the table `page`, and the data field that the Facebook ID is stored in is called `page_id`.

```
SELECT x
FROM page
WHERE page_id = 19292868552
```

To load the data fields, we put those field names under the `SELECT` clause, specifying multiple fields as a comma-separated String. To select the same data as we'd get in the standard Graph API, we can use this query:

```
SELECT page_id,name,pic,page_url,type,website,founded,
company_overview,mission
 FROM page
 WHERE page_id = 19292868552
```

There's a slight difference in the field names between a Graph API object and an FQL object, but the data remains the same.

To execute this FQL query in ActionScript, we supply it as a single line String in the query parameter of the `Facebook.fqlQuery` method, with the following ActionScript code:

```
var query:String = "SELECT page_id,name,pic,page_url,type,
website,founded,company_overview,mission FROM page WHERE page_id =
19292868552";
Facebook.fqlQuery(query, responseHandler);
```

This supplies our query as-is—but in addition to this approach of supplying the entire request in a single String, we can also take a template-based approach to our FQL queries, using placeholders in conjunction with the method's values parameter to dynamically construct our requests.

Placeholders are denoted in our query with the { and } brackets, enclosing named parameters. These parameter names should then correspond to the values of properties on the values Object. A template version of our query String would look like this:

```
SELECT page_id,name,pic,page_url,type,
website,founded,company_overview,mission
    FROM page
    WHERE page_id = {uid}
```

In ActionScript, the code needed to make this request should look like this:

```
override public function facebookReady():void {
    var query:String = "SELECT page_id,name,pic,page_url,type,
    website,founded,company_overview,mission FROM page WHERE
    page_id = {uid}";
    var values:Object = new Object();
    values.uid = "19292868552";

    Facebook.fqlQuery(query, responseHandler, values);
}
```

Results from a FQL query come back JSON-encoded, just like standard Graph API requests, and are returned as an Array, just as they are from a connection request.

As for the response handler function, we can use almost the same function as we'd use when parsing a response from the standard Graph API request, which can look like this:

```
function responseHandler(success:Object, fail:Object):void {
    var results:Array = success as Array;
    if (success && results) {
        for (var i:int = 0; i < results.length; i++) {
            var page:FacebookPage = FacebookPage.fromJSON(results[i]);
            results_display.text += page.toString();
        }
    }
}
```

Of course, with such a specific request as this, there will only be one result, but it's also possible to get multiple results from an FQL query, and they'll be returned in the same format as this one—objects in an Array.

The response object from the request in this recipe should look like this:

```
[{
    "page_id": 19292868552,
    "name":" Facebook Platform",
    "pic": "http://profile.ak.fbcdn.net/hprofile-ak-snc4/hs451.snc4/50414_
19292868552_7650_s.jpg",
    "page_url":"http://www.facebook.com/platform"
    "type": "PRODUCT/SERVICE",
    "website": "http://developers.facebook.com",
    "founded": "May 2007",
    "company_overview": "Facebook Platform enables anyone to build social
applications on Facebook and the web.",
    "mission": "To make the web more open and social."
}]
```

How it works...

Unlike the standard Graph API, where we only need an object's ID and a vague idea of the returned object type, constructing FQL requests requires a lot more cross-referencing with the documentation; FQL is a much easier syntax to get wrong, and the API is unforgiving, although that's not necessarily a bad thing!

Like any other request on the Graph API, the return type of our FQL request is in JSON format, which is automatically decoded by the SDK into ActionScript Object instances. Whether there's single or multiple results returned, a successful result always comes back as an Array, and so to parse those results we need to cast the response handler's `success` property as an Array and iterate through its contents to access them—exactly as we would for the response object of a Graph API connection, using the code:

var results:Array = success as Array;

There are a few key points to understand when working with FQL:

▶ Results can only come from a single table at a time

Each FQL query can only return data from a single table—no merged results from separate tables, which means that all of the returned data fields have to come from the same table as the one listed in the `FROM` clause.

For example, if we're looking for information in the `album` table, the most information that we can obtain about the user is their ID, because that is stored in the table under the `owner` field. We can't get any more information, such as the owner's name, from this same request because the scope of the query is limited to the `album` table.

▶ Results must be based on indexable columns

A key point with FQL queries—besides getting the syntax correct—is making use of an indexable field in the WHERE clause of the request.

That means that at least one of the fields we're comparing against for our query has to be marked as indexable. An indexable field is usually one of the fields that has a unique ID, such as the Facebook object ID, and doesn't include fields like the description. We can use non-indexed fields to narrow the scope of our search afterwards, but there always has to be an indexed field involved somewhere.

An indexable field is denoted in the online Developer Documentation with an asterix (*) in the **Indexable** column, for example:

Indexable	Name	Type	Description
*	page_id	int	The ID of the Page being queried.
*	name	string	The name of the Page being queried.
	pic_small	string	The URL to the small-sized picture for the Page being queried. The image can have a maximum width of 50px and a maximum height of 150px. This URL may be blank.
	pic_big	string	The URL to the large-sized profile picture for the Page being queried. The image can have a maximum width of 200px and a maximum height of 600px. This URL may be blank.
	pic_square	string	The URL to the square profile picture for the Page being queried. The image can have a maximum width and height of 50px. This URL may be blank.
	pic	string	The URL to the medium-sized profile picture for the Page being queried. The image can have a maximum width of 100px and a maximum height of 300px. This URL may be blank.

> The full version of the Developer Documentation for the FQL Page object is available online at:
>
> https://developers.facebook.com/docs/reference/fql/page/

Why do we need an indexed field involved? Well, it's all about optimization. On a small database of our own you might be able to do non-indexed searches, but Facebook isn't small, and besides, it's not good practice. You couldn't do a plain text search on a database with half a billion users, but if you first narrowed that search to the hundreds (with a subquery looking for friends) then such a search becomes plausible.

Unfortunately, indexable fields are necessary for FQL queries, and which fields are indexed is entirely down to Facebook, which ends up making some things horribly complex or impossible to do with FQL.

There's more...

We can only load data from a single table at a time, and the selectors have to be strung together with keywords (like AND or OR), but loading multiple data fields is a case of stringing those field names together in a comma-delimited concatenation.

Of course, you don't have to stick to the bounds of the Facebook SDK—it provides an implementation and structure for your classes, but using it isn't something you have to do. The ActionScript SDK mirrors the Facebook API structure, nothing more.

Formatting (pretty-printing) our FQL requests

We can't format the actual FQL request that we send to Facebook, but when we're displaying the FQL request for our own benefit, we can make the results a little bit prettier, using the following function:

```
function formatFQL(input:String, values:Object = null):String {
    var output:String = "";
    var indent:String = "";
    var queries:Array = input.split("SELECT");
    for (var i:int = 1; i < queries.length; i++) {
        indent += "    ";
        output += "SELECT" + queries[i].split("FROM").join("\n"
        + indent + "FROM").split("WHERE").join("\n" + indent +
        "WHERE").split("IN").join("\n" + indent +
        "IN").split("ORDER").join("\n" + indent + "ORDER");
        indent += "    ";
        output += "\n" + indent;
    }
    for (var n:String in values) {
        output = output.replace(new RegExp('\\{' + n + '\\}', 'g'),
values[n]);
    }
    return output;
}
```

We can use this function in the following way:

```
query_display.text = formatFQL(query);
```

And the result of this function should be the transformation of a basic FQL request from this:

```
SELECT page_id, name, pic, page_url, type, website, founded, company_overview,
mission FROM page WHERE page_id = 19292868552
```

To this:

```
SELECT page_id, name, pic, page_url, type, website, founded, company_overview, mission
    FROM page
    WHERE page_id = 19292868552
```

Using the FQL name classes to construct requests

Not all of the field names in FQL objects correspond exactly with the parameter names of the Graph API objects, so there's a few classes supplied with the Facebook ActionScript 3 SDK that provides those table and field names as constants.

As of the ActionScript SDK version 1.5, these classes are:

▶ **FQLTable**, which supplies the name of the FQL tables

▶ **FQLUserField**, which contains the names of all of the user fields in FQL (as they're slightly different than the standard Graph API ones, which are stored in the `FacebookUser` class)

▶ **FQLFriendField**, which supplies the names of the friend table

Most of the remaining classes map directly to their Facebook{Type} class, that we'd use for standard Graph API objects.

When it comes to parsing the results from FQL, there is also a variant of the `FacebookUser` class, called **FQLUser**. Both classes are simply strict-typed versions of the returned object from the API, and don't actually offer any functionality, but the `FQLUser` field has slightly different named properties, which match the differences in the field names from an FQL request. When working with FQL, it's better to use this class instead of the `FacebookUser` class, as you can be sure that all of the returned properties are converted correctly into the new strict-typed instance.

Using me() to reference the current user

Much like we can use the shortcut /me in the URL of a Graph API request, we can quickly reference the current user in FQL by using a similar shortcut for our FQL requests.

The me () shortcut is a replacement for obtaining and inputting the current user's Facebook ID into our queries. Whenever we would attempt to locate a user based on their ID, we can replace that ID with me (). This is not something we couldn't do manually, extracting data from the active Facebook session, but it does make things a little easier, and makes our final code all the more readable.

Take this simple request, loading the name of a specified user:

```
SELECT name
    FROM user
    WHERE uid = 526534401
```

This request, if executed, would return the data "James Ford". We could reference the current user by extracting their user ID from the current Facebook session using the following ActionScript code:

```
var query:String = "SELECT name FROM user WHERE uid = {uid}";
var values:Object = new Object();
values.uid = Facebook.getSession().uid;
Facebook.fqlQuery(query, responseHandler, values);
```

If we were using the `me()` shortcut however, our request would be more human-readable, and the ActionScript code much shorter:

```
SELECT name
    FROM user
    WHERE uid = me()
```

Which looks like this, in ActionScript:

```
var query:String = "SELECT name FROM user WHERE uid = me()";
Facebook.fqlQuery(query, responseHandler);
```

This shortcut code all works on the server-side, and is interpreted by the Graph API when it processes your request. The `me()` shortcut references the unique ID for a Facebook user, so it can only be used for comparisons against the **uid** data field—it won't work for the user table's other indexable data fields, such as the **username**.

See also

▶ In *Chapter 4, Reading and Writing Data with the Graph API* the recipe *Loading specific data fields for Graph API objects*

▶ *Chapter 4*, the recipe *Loading a Graph API object from Facebook*—using the 'me' shortcut to reference the current user

▶ *Using subqueries in FQL* recipe in this chapter

▶ *Using logical operators in FQL queries* recipe in this chapter

Using subqueries in FQL

Almost anything you would want to do through the Facebook Graph API is possible with FQL and the Facebook ActionScript 3 SDK. But wrapping your head around the structure of a query, and how you can actually use one to retrieve the data you want, requires a bit of effort and a shift in mindset—particularly if you've not done any SQL before!

Subqueries are an integral part of FQL; they allow us to perform multiple queries within an overall query, and the results of those nested queries feed in to the larger overall query, affecting its results. The big bonus to using subqueries is that everything is done on the server side, which speeds things up tremendously compared to the alternative of not using subqueries, having to go back-and-forth between the client and server to generate the final query.

One of the most common types of subquery would be that which returns a list of the user's friends. In this recipe, we're going to use a subquery to return user details of the current user's friends.

How to do it...

To use FQL to retrieve a group of users, we have to make our overall request on the `user` table, which means that we will need to use one of the three indexable columns, `uid`, `name`, or `username`, in the WHERE clause of the request.

What we want to retrieve in this recipe is the `uid` and `name` of a user. A simple request to do this for the current user would look like this:

```
SELECT uid,name
    FROM user
    WHERE uid = me()
```

And the value that it returns might look like this:

```
[{uid: "526534401", name: "James Ford"}]
```

We can widen the range of results to include the user's friends by introducing a subquery. This subquery must return data which matches the content of the indexable field listed in the WHERE clause of its container query.

Our subquery will be looking at the `friend` table; a table which only contains two columns—`uid1` and `uid2`—columns which contain the IDs of users, either of which can be matched against the `uid` column of the `user` table in the containing query.

```
SELECT uid2
    FROM friend
    WHERE uid1 = me()
```

Were we to execute this FQL query on its own, the response would be similar to this:

```
[
    {"uid2":"6731427901"},
    {"uid2":"5280830943"},
    {"uid2":"1475529147"},
    {"uid2":"1361183838"},
    {"uid2":"1361183838"}
]
```

Subqueries are wrapped in brackets, and are deemed to return an Array of results, so our comparison should use the `IN` clause rather than an `=` (equals) comparison to match against the results from the subquery.

When we combine both of these queries together, our FQL syntax should look like this:

```
SELECT uid,name
    FROM user
    WHERE uid
    IN (
        SELECT uid2
        FROM friend
        WHERE uid1 = me()
        )
```

And the result of this request should look like this:

```
[
    {"uid":"6731427901", "name":"Friend name #1"},
    {"uid":"5280830943", "name":"Friend name #2"},
    {"uid":"1475529147", "name":"Friend name #3"},
    {"uid":"1361183838", "name":"Friend name #4"},
    {"uid":"1361183838", "name":"Friend name #5"}
]
```

Flatten that request out into a single-line String, and we can execute it with the following ActionScript code:

```
var query:String = "SELECT uid,name FROM user WHERE uid IN (SELECT
uid2 FROM friend WHERE uid1 = me())";
Facebook.fqlQuery(query, responseHandler);
```

If we take the results of this query and decode the response, we'll see that it consists of an Array, populated by objects, whose parameters correspond to the data fields that we specified—uid and name. We can parse this response in the same way that we parse Graph API connections; and the corresponding ActionScript value object class for user details retrieved via FQL is called FQLUser, so our response handler function for this recipe should look like this:

```
function responseHandler( success:Object, fail:Object ):void {
    var feed:Array = success as Array;
    if ( success && feed ) {
        for ( var i:int = 0; i < feed.length; i++ ) {
            var user:FQLUser = FQLUser.fromJSON( feed[ i ] );
            trace( user.name );
        }
    }
}
```

How it works...

Subqueries can be used to expand or reduce the number of results from a single FQL request. They can't remove the single-table restriction on individual requests, but they do allow us to combine two (or more) similar queries on the server side, removing some of the overheads associated with making multiple requests and manually comparing or processing the results.

There is no real limit to the number of subqueries that can go into a query, nor how deep they can be nested, but our main request is the only one that will determine what data is returned, and the table the data is returned from—the subquery can only be used to widen or narrow the scope of results.

There's more...

Not all filtering actions have to take place with the aid of subqueries—there are many things that can also be achieved with logical operators alone. Here's a couple more examples which make use of subqueries to return some useful data:

Loading the current user's family

Retrieving a list of the current user's family is fairly easy—the query is much the same approach as for retrieving a list of friends. Tables and data fields are of course, slightly different, but the logic is the same:

```
SELECT uid,name
    FROM user
    WHERE uid
    IN (
```

```
        SELECT uid
        FROM family
        WHERE profile_id = me()
    )
```

There's more to the family information than that though. Unlike friend lists, where users are simply linked, family members also have details of the relationship between those users. The possible relationship types are `parent`, `mother`, `father`, `sibling`, `sister`, `brother`, `child`, `son`, and `daughter`.

To retrieve the information about a family relationship, we can use this query:

```
SELECT uid,relationship
    FROM family
    WHERE profile_id = me()
```

And the results of such a request should look similar to this:

```
[
    {"uid":"6731427901", "relationship":"sister"},
    {"uid":"1361183838", "name":"mother"}
]
```

In addition to the linking of other Facebook users with a family relationship, users can add family information about others that aren't on Facebook. This information also gets stored in the `family` table, even if the other user doesn't exist or doesn't accept the request, and we can access that information through a query to the `family` table.

As with Facebook users that we don't have permission to access, all we know about these non-Facebook users is their name and relationship to the current user. To retrieve this information, we can use the following query:

```
SELECT name,relationship
    FROM family
    WHERE profile_id = me()
```

Of course when the family member isn't on Facebook (or alternatively, hasn't accepted the family request from the current user) we don't know their **uid** and can't retrieve a profile picture for them, so we would need to supply a profile picture of our own.

No results?

Don't panic if this FQL query doesn't give any results—like much of the data available in Facebook, it relies entirely on the user having entered this information and making it available to third-party applications—which not every user cares to do.

Loading a list of users that have been tagged in photos, alongside the current user

Loading a list of users tagged alongside the current user is another perfect example of a nested FQL query—first, we would need to get a list of all of the photos where a user is tagged, and then we would need to add another query, for the other tagged users in each individual photo. Our final result wouldn't be the photo, and it wouldn't be the tags, it would be the users themselves—and all from a single query.

To receive results from this query, our application will require the `"user_photo_video_tags"` and `"user_photos"` extended permissions.

To make this query, the first information we need to retrieve is the ID of the photos that the current user is tagged in. This information is stored in the `photo_tag` table, and that table has the data fields `pid` for the photo ID, and `subject` for the tagged users themselves. Therefore, to locate the photos the current user is tagged in, we'd use this query:

```
SELECT pid
    FROM photo_tag
    WHERE subject = me()
```

By itself, this query should return a result which looks something like this:

```
[
    {"pid": "2225255558586398800"},
    {"pid": "2225255558586398807"},
    {"pid": "2225255558586398814"}
]
```

The `subject` data field is a single, indexable field for the `photo_tag` table, so it only returns a single result. To retrieve the rest of the user IDs for each photo, we need to make a further request on this same table, using the first as a subquery:

```
SELECT subject
    FROM photo_tag
    WHERE pid
```

```
IN (
    SELECT pid
    FROM photo_tag
    WHERE subject = me()
)
```

The results of this FQL request should look a little like this:

```
[
    {"subject": "515537192"},
    {"subject": "527598125"},
    {"subject": "716402233"}
]
```

And to convert the results from this query from plain **user IDs** to FQL user objects, we can use this as a further subquery, comparing the resulting IDs against the user table:

```
SELECT uid,name,pic_big
    FROM user
    WHERE uid
    IN (
        SELECT subject
        FROM photo_tag
        WHERE pid
        IN (
            SELECT pid
            FROM photo_tag
            WHERE subject = me()
        )
    )
```

And the final result of this FQL query should look like this:

```
[
    {
        "name": "Random User #1",
        "pic_big": "https://fbcdn-profile-a.akamaihd.net/hprofile-ak-
snc4/49151_515537192_2934_n.jpg",
        "uid": 515537192
    },
```

```
    {
        "name": " Random User #2",
        "pic_big": "https://fbcdn-profile-a.akamaihd.net/hprofile-ak-snc4/70761_527598125_4126757_n.jpg",
        "uid": 527598125
    },
    {
        "name": " Random User #3",
        "pic_big": "https://fbcdn-profile-a.akamaihd.net/hprofile-ak-snc4/186485_518107684_1735026_n.jpg",
        "uid": 716402233
    }
]
```

Advanced data types in FQL

Some of the fields available in FQL return more than just an integer, string or array—they can actually return complex objects as well. These objects are sent in a JSON-encoded format, which is then expanded into ActionScript objects, just like the rest of the SDK, and so using them is no different to any other parameter, although our requests have to make use of dot-notation to reference those complex object properties.

For example, the `checkin` table has the field `coords`, which is an object with three parameters—`longitude`, `latitude`, and `accuracy`. Some other examples of complex objects can be found in the `group | venue` field, or the `user | family` fields.

See also

▶ *Using logical operators in FQL requests*
▶ *Cross-comparing data sets to find overlapping results*

Using logical operators in FQL requests

With an FQL request you have the ability to use the core Boolean logical operators—**AND, OR** and **!=** (not equal to). Combine these with subqueries and you've got a lot of power available to help you filter out results from your queries.

In this recipe we're going to use subqueries and logical operators to retrieve a list of Facebook user objects. We'll be using a nested subquery to get a list of other Facebook users that the current user is tagged in photos with. We're then going to use the OR operator to expand our search results, and include all of the current user's friends, so our overall query will return both friends and tagged users.

Once we have that list, we're going to flip the results and use the AND operator to exclude results, and only return a list of users that are both friends and tagged in photos alongside the current user.

Getting ready

For this recipe, we'll need the "user_photo_video_tags" and "user_photos" Extended Permissions granted to our application.

Assuming that our application is built on top of the ApplicationBase class, created in the recipe *Creating an ApplicationBase class* in *Chapter 11, Bridging the Flash and Application Gap*, we can add the following ActionScript to our application to ensure that we have those Extended Permissions:

```
override protected function get requiredPermissions():Array {
    if (!_requiredPermissions) {
        var perms:Array = new Array();
        perms.push(ExtendedPermission.USER_PHOTOS);
        perms.push(ExtendedPermission.USER_PHOTO_VIDEO_TAGS);
        _requiredPermissions = perms;
    }
    return _requiredPermissions;
}
```

In this recipe, we're going to combine two queries; one which will retrieve information about all of the other users that are tagged in photos alongside the current user, which looks like this:

```
SELECT uid,name
    FROM user
    WHERE uid
    IN (
        SELECT subject
        FROM photo_tag
        WHERE pid
        IN (
            SELECT pid
            FROM photo_tag
            WHERE subject = me()
        )
    )
```

And another query, which will retrieve information about the current user's friends:

```
SELECT uid,name
    FROM user
    WHERE uid
    IN (
        SELECT uid2
        FROM friend
        WHERE uid1 = me()
    )
```

Both of these examples pull the same data fields (`uid`, `name`) from the same FQL table (`user`) but are currently written as separate requests.

How to do it...

In this recipe, there are two types of operator that we will be looking at. The first is the OR operator, which allows us to make an FQL request which would contain results from both of these queries, combined into a single response:

1. Using OR operator to combine sets of results.

   Using the OR operator means that the content of the results from the FQL query conforms to one or more of the conditions set out by the FQL result. It widens the net, as it were, and makes it easier for a result object to qualify as a valid response.

```
SELECT uid,name
    FROM user
    WHERE uid
    IN (
        SELECT uid2
        FROM friend
        WHERE uid1 = me()
    )
    OR uid
    IN (
        SELECT subject
        FROM photo_tag
        WHERE pid
        IN (
            SELECT pid
```

```
                              FROM photo_tag
                              WHERE subject = me()
                    )
          )
```

Translated into ActionScript, this query would look something like this:

```
var query:String = "SELECT uid,name FROM user WHERE uid IN (SELECT
uid2 FROM friend WHERE uid1 = me()) OR uid IN (SELECT subject FROM
photo_tag WHERE pid IN (SELECT pid FROM photo_tag WHERE subject =
me()))";
Facebook.fqlQuery( query, responseHandlerFunction );
```

The same approach that we'd use to define the WHERE statement (see the recipe *Loading data with FQL* for more information) also applies to the OR statement, and any of the other logical operators that we'll look at in this recipe.

2. Using the AND operator to filter responses.

   Using the AND operator reduces the number of results from a request, because it means that the results themselves have to conform to all of the conditions in the query, not just any of them.

   To make our previous example less liberal, we could change that original request to load only the users who are both tagged in the same photos as the current user and are friends of the current user, simply by swapping a keyword:

```
SELECT uid,name
     FROM user
     WHERE uid
     IN (
          SELECT uid2
          FROM friend
          WHERE uid1 = me()
     )
     AND uid
     IN (
          SELECT subject
          FROM photo_tag
          WHERE pid
          IN (
               SELECT pid
               FROM photo_tag
               WHERE subject = me()
          )
     )
```

How it works...

The AND and OR keywords make it possible to chain multiple queries together, as we've seen. AND reduces the range of results, whereas OR widens it. It's not quite as capable as SQL, but it's a good start. For more complex comparisons, we have to look instead at doing the comparisons on the client side, with ActionScript.

 More information about FQL, how it works and what it supports is available online: `http://developers.facebook.com/docs/reference/fql/`

There's more...

The AND and OR operators are likely to be the most commonly used operators, but there's also a couple more to explore.

Removing the current user from the results

With the queries in this recipe, you may notice that amongst the results is the current user. Logically speaking this is because we're requesting the information about all of the users tagged in photos, and the current user is indeed one of these.

This is the situation where we would use the **!=** (not equal to) operator. To exclude the current user, we would use the **AND !=** operator to make our query look like this:

```
SELECT uid,name
    FROM user
    WHERE uid
    IN (
        SELECT uid2
        FROM friend
        WHERE uid1 = me()
    )
    AND uid
    IN (
        SELECT subject
        FROM photo_tag
        WHERE pid
        IN (
            SELECT pid
```

```
        FROM photo_tag
        WHERE subject = me()
    )
)
AND uid != me()
```

Excluding results with 'NOT IN'?

Unfortunately, such useful logical operators as **NOT IN** are not supported in FQL requests. For those cases where we would think to use the **NOT** operator, this means we need to be a little more creative about our requests, or start duplicating variations on requests, and comparing the results.

See also

▶ *Using subqueries in FQL* recipe

▶ *Cross-comparing data sets to find overlapping results* recipe

Loading large data sets with FQL multiquery

In situations where we want to load a large chunk of data at once, or we want to pull a lot of data from different tables, we can use what's known on Facebook as an FQL multiquery.

A multiquery is exactly what you might think—multiple FQL queries. They don't have to be related to each other, unlike subqueries, and they can each pull data from different FQL tables.

One of the original appeals for the FQL multiquery capability was the ability to perform what is now referred to as subqueries in FQL. Before this functionality was made available, there was presumably no other way for developers to perform complex subqueries. At present, the main attraction for using multiqueries is that they negate some of the overheads of making and managing multiple FQL requests, as all of the requests are packaged into a single request and single response.

In this recipe we're going to create a multiquery request to load information simultaneously about two tables—retrieving simultaneously details of a set of users (the current user's friends), and those user's status updates.

Getting ready

To retrieve details of our friend's status updates, our application will need the `ExtendedPermission.FRIEND_STATUS` permission, otherwise we'll simply receive empty results.

Assuming that our application is built on top of the `ApplicationBase` class that we developed in the recipe *Creating an ApplicationBase class* in *Chapter 11*, we can add the following ActionScript to our application to ensure that it has those Extended Permissions:

```
override protected function get requiredPermissions():Array {
    if (!_requiredPermissions) {
        var perms:Array = new Array();
        perms.push(ExtendedPermission.FRIEND_STATUS);
        _requiredPermissions = perms;
    }
    return _requiredPermissions;
}
```

The FQL requests that we want to execute in this recipe look like this:

1. To request the current user's friends' status updates:

```
SELECT uid,message
    FROM status
    WHERE uid
    IN (
        SELECT uid2
            FROM friend
            WHERE uid1 = me()
    )
```

2. To request details about the user's friends:

```
SELECT uid,name
    FROM user
    WHERE uid
    IN (
        SELECT uid2
        FROM friend
        WHERE uid1 = me()
    )
```

How to do it...

The method we can use to dispatch a multiquery request looks like this:

```
Facebook.fqlMultiQuery(queries, response handler);
```

The first parameter of this request expects an instance of the `FQLMultiQuery` class. The second parameter, the response handler function, follows the same format as for other Graph API response handlers.

To create the property for the queries parameter, we first create a new instance of the `FQLMultiQuery` class, using the following code:

```
var instance:FQLMultiQuery = new FQLMultiQuery();
```

On this instance we then call the `FQLMultiQuery.add` method, passing in the FQL query and a name for that query. As with single requests, there's also a third parameter, where we can supply an options object, so that we can treat the query as a template and supply variables for the request separately.

The format of the method itself looks like this:

```
instance.add("query", "name", values);
```

To execute the two FQL requests as an FQL multiquery, we would use the following ActionScript code, which defines our two FQL queries as Strings—`statusQuery` and `friendDetailsQuery`—and adds them to a new instance of the `FQLMultiQuery` class under the names `status-updates` and `friend-details`:

```
var statusQuery:String = "SELECT uid,message FROM status WHERE uid IN
(SELECT uid2 FROM friend WHERE uid1 = me())";
var friendDetailsQuery:String = "SELECT uid,name FROM user WHERE uid
IN (SELECT uid2 FROM friend WHERE uid1 = me())";

var queries:FQLMultiQuery = new FQLMultiQuery();
queries.add(statusQuery, "status-updates");
queries.add(friendDetailsQuery, "friend-details");

Facebook.fqlMultiQuery(queries, responseHandler);
```

The response handler function for such a request should expect to receive an Object, with the parameters of that object corresponding to the names of the queries passed in the original request.

For example, a response from a request like this might look like this:

```
{
    "status-updates": [
        {"uid": 100001928326570, "message": "FOTB :D :D :)"},
        {"uid": 100001928326570, "message": "woo!"},
        {"uid": 100001748483346, "message": "Pizzzzzzaaaa :)"}
    ],
```

```
"friend-details": [
    {"uid": 100001928326570, "name": "Random user #1"},
    {"uid": 100001938437734, "name": "Random user #2"},
    {"uid": 100001748483346, "name": "Random user #3"}
]
}
```

The format of this response is very similar to the format of Graph API requests when we're requesting multiple objects (as in our earlier recipe from *Chapter 4, Loading multiple Graph API objects in a single request*).

To parse this response, we can use the following ActionScript function:

```
function responseHandler(success:Object, fail:Object):void {
    var i:int;
    if (success) {
        for (var key:String in success) {
            switch (key) {
                case "status-updates":
                    for (i = 0; i < success[key].length; i++) {
                        var status:FQLStatus = FQLStatus.fromJSON(success[k
ey][i]);

                        results_display.text += status.toString() + "\n";
                    }
                    break;
                case "friend-details":
                    for (i = 0; i < success[key].length; i++) {
                        var friend:FQLUser = FQLUser.fromJSON(success[key][
i]);

                        results_display.text += friend.toString() + "\n";
                    }
                    break;
            }
        }
    }
}
```

As you can see it's a pretty extensive amount of code in this function, but what we're doing is looping through properties of the results object—treating it as a Dictionary instance. A quick check against the name of the property allows us to change the parsing function, and from there it's business as usual, looping through the results and converting them into strict-typed ActionScript class instances.

How it works...

Under the hood, the FQL multiquery capability is only available as part of the Old REST API, at least for the moment. Luckily, the Facebook ActionScript 3 SDK makes it easy for us to implement FQL multiqueries, using its dedicated set of SDK methods.

The official Developer Documentation for the underlying `fql.multiquery` function that powers the multiquery capability can be found online at:

`http://developers.facebook.com/docs/reference/rest/fql.multiquery`

There's more...

Unsurprisingly, multiqueries take longer to respond than a smaller single query, and sometimes less than all of the queries combined. The total time taken for the response comes from a mix of execution time for the FQL query and the HTTP transfer time. Using separate requests might result in a faster response for a few of the requests, but the overall load time would be improved by removing duplicate HTTP transfer times.

When it comes to making HTTP requests, the web browser controls the number of simultaneous requests, which will also have an effect on how quickly data can be loaded.

What's faster?

Here's an example of the load times involved when loading FQL queries separately, compared to the same request as a multiquery request:

- ▶ Multiquery approach:
  - ❑ Waiting time (for response from Facebook): 1.04 s
  - ❑ Loading time (for the data from Facebook): 448 ms

  Total time: 1.49 seconds

- ▶ Separate queries approach:

  - ❑ Query 1 waiting time (for response from Facebook): 371 ms
  - ❑ Query 1 loading time (for the data from Facebook): 2 ms
  - ❑ Query 2 waiting time (for response from Facebook): 390 ms
  - ❑ Query 2 loading time (for the data from Facebook): 2 ms
  - ❑ Query 3 waiting time (for response from Facebook): 782 ms
  - ❑ Query 3 loading time (for the data from Facebook): 428 ms

  Total time: 1.22 seconds

The methods we're using in this example are due to be depreciated in future updates to the Graph API, but Facebook as a platform is committed to maintaining the multiquery capability within its platform. So even if they remove or depreciate this functionality, they'll replace it beforehand with a newer equivalent in the standard Graph API.

There's no public timeframe placed on the depreciation process itself, but hopefully these methods and solutions will remain in a working condition for the foreseeable future.

See also

▶ FQL multiquery documentation on Facebook: `http://developers.facebook.com/docs/reference/rest/fql.multiquery/`

▶ FQL `Batch.run` documentation on Facebook: `http://developers.facebook.com/docs/reference/rest/batch.run`

Cross-comparing data sets to find overlapping results

There are some things that a subquery alone can't manage, and there are some times when it suits us better to perform cross-referencing on the client side. Subqueries for example, are very good for excluding and narrowing down results, but they don't really help by providing any further information about the results or many clues to common similarities.

In this recipe we're going to make two FQL requests: one to retrieve information about the current user's friends, and another to retrieve information about users that are tagged in photos alongside the current user—the same FQL queries as we used in our earlier recipe *Using logical operators in FQL requests*.

In our previous recipe, we combined these two separate queries as subqueries, grouping together the results of both queries into a single set of results. In this recipe we want to be able to distinguish between the results of each query, and identify results that don't overlap in the two queries.

This couldn't be achieved with an FQL subquery, but we can cross-compare the results of these queries using ActionScript in order to find and group the overlapping results, in ways that aren't possible with FQL queries alone, and could for example, work out which of the current user's friends have not been tagged with the current user.

Getting ready

For this recipe, we'll need the `"user_photo_video_tags"` and `"user_photos"` Extended Permissions granted to our application.

In this recipe, we're going to combine two queries, one which will retrieve information about all of the other users that are tagged in photos alongside the current user, which looks like this:

```
SELECT uid,name
    FROM user
    WHERE uid
    IN (
        SELECT subject
        FROM photo_tag
        WHERE pid
        IN (
            SELECT pid
            FROM photo_tag
            WHERE subject = me()
        )
    )
```

And another query, which will retrieve information about the current user's friends:

```
SELECT uid,name
    FROM user
    WHERE uid
    IN (
        SELECT uid2
        FROM friend
        WHERE uid1 = me()
    )
```

Both of these examples pull the same data fields (`uid`, `name`) from the same FQL table (`user`) but are currently written as separate requests.

How to do it...

We need to make two FQL queries that are completely separate from each other, and the simplest way to execute that is with a multiquery, using the following ActionScript:

```
var taggedUsers:String = "SELECT uid,name FROM user WHERE uid IN
(SELECT subject FROM photo_tag WHERE pid IN (SELECT pid FROM photo_tag
WHERE subject = me()))";
var friends:String = "SELECT uid,name FROM user WHERE uid IN (SELECT
uid2 FROM friend WHERE uid1 = me())";

var queries:FQLMultiQuery = new FQLMultiQuery();
queries.add(taggedUsers, "tagged-users");
queries.add(friends, "friends");

Facebook.fqlMultiQuery(queries, responseHandler);
```

The results of both of these requests will be a list of FQL users, and we want to parse the results of both of these queries into separate ActionScript Array instances, named `taggedUsers` and `friendUsers`.

```
function responseHandler(success:Object, fail:Object):void {
    var i:int;
    if (success) {
        var taggedUsers:Array = new Array();
        var friendUsers:Array = new Array();
        for (var key:String in success) {
            switch (key) {
                case "tagged-users":
                    for (i = 0; i < success[key].length; i++) {
                        var userFriend:FQLUser = FQLUser.fromJSON(succ
ess[key][i]);

                        taggedUsers.push(userFriend);
                    }
                    break;
                case "friends":
                    for (i = 0; i < success[key].length; i++) {
                        var userFriend:FQLUser = FQLUser.fromJSON(succ
ess[key][i]);

                        friendUsers.push(userFriend);
                    }
                    break;
            }
        }
    }
}
```

Once we've parsed the results of both the queries, we can start comparing the data in those two Arrays, to find a list of those which don't overlap, and we can do that using the following ActionScript:

```
function responseHandler(success:Object, fail:Object):void {
    var i:int;
    if (success) {
        var taggedUsers:Array = new Array();
        var friendUsers:Array = new Array();
        for (var key:String in success) {
            switch (key) {
                case "tagged-users":
                    for (i = 0; i < success[key].length; i++) {
                        var userFriend:FQLUser = FQLUser.fromJSON(succ
ess[key][i]);

                        taggedUsers.push(userFriend);
                    }
                    break;
                case "friends":
                    for (i = 0; i < success[key].length; i++) {
                        var userFriend:FQLUser = FQLUser.fromJSON(succ
ess[key][i]);

                        friendUsers.push(userFriend);
                    }
                    break;
            }
        }
        var i:int;
        var j:int;
        var cleanTagged:Array = friendUsers.concat();
        for (i = 0; i < friendUsers.length; i++) {
            for (j = 0; j < cleanTagged.length; j++) {
                if (friendUsers[i].uid == cleanTagged[j].uid) {
                    cleanTagged = cleanTagged.slice(0,
j).concat(cleanTagged.slice(j + 1, cleanTagged.length));
                }
            }
        }
        var cleanFriends:Array = friendUsers.concat();
        for (i = 0; i < taggedUsers.length; i++) {
            for (j = 0; j < cleanFriends.length; j++) {
                if (taggedUsers[i].uid == cleanFriends[j].uid) {
                    cleanFriends = cleanFriends.slice(0,
j).concat(cleanFriends.slice(j + 1, cleanFriends.length));
```

```
            }
          }
        }
        var combinedUsers:Array = cleanTagged.concat(cleanFriends);
        results_display.text = "";
        for (i = 0; i < combinedUsers.length; i++) {
            results_display.text += combinedUsers[i] + "\n";
        }
      }
    }
```

What this (rather lengthy) response handler function should do is loop through the results of both of the queries and extract duplicates from each Array. Once the results are combined into a single Array (`combinedUsers`) the contents of that Array will represent all of the users which the current user has not been tagged with in a Photo on Facebook.

How it works...

What we've done in this recipe is essentially an FQL multiquery, but with a more complex response handler function to parse the results of that query into Array instances.

Once the results of both queries have been parsed, we can then loop through the separate Arrays of results that we made for each query. If the same object (exactly the same object) appears in both Arrays, it's an overlap and we discard it. Anything left at the end of the comparison is the data we're after.

There's more...

The main reason for this example is because such a comparison can't be done server side, but that doesn't mean it's the only time you'll want to do a client-side comparison.

As fast as FQL is, requesting data from the server all the time is going to be slower than doing things locally, provided you've all the data readily available locally. So requesting unfiltered data is sometimes the better way to go about things, particularly if you're going to be displaying it in multiple different fragments in a UI.

Why use server-side comparisons?

There are two main reasons why you might want to perform your cross-comparisons on the server-side, rather than in ActionScript:

1. The results are going to be faster—it's always going to be faster to filter Facebook data at-source, rather than sending full sets back to your client to filter. There's more data to transmit otherwise, more to send, and extra time to package, send, and unpackage on the client, before you even start processing it yourself.

2. The other is that these comparisons have a little more access to Facebook than your application has. The API appears to have unfettered access to its own data for the purposes of subquery comparisons. You still can't see or retrieve that data, but so long as the only eyes that see that data are Facebook, you can perform those comparisons.

See also

▶ *Using logical operators in FQL requests*

▶ *Loading large data sets with FQL multiquery*

Sorting FQL results

FQL results can be sorted before they're returned, by making use of the ORDER BY query, just like you would do in a SQL request. Results can be sorted alphanumerically ascending or descending, and both normal data fields and advanced data fields can be used in the sort process.

In this recipe we're going to create an FQL request for the current user's friends, which will also apply a sort to the data prior to returning it to our application.

Getting ready

Our starting FQL request should look like this:

```
SELECT uid,name
    FROM user
    WHERE uid
    IN (
        SELECT uid2
        FROM friend
        WHERE uid1 = me()
    )
```

How to do it...

To apply sorting to the results of our request, we need to add the ORDER BY statement to our requests, specifying one of the table's columns as the target, and whether the sort should be ascending (**ASC**) or descending (**DESC**).

To retrieve the list of the current user's friends, and then sort the results based on the name of the user, we would use the following FQL query:

```
SELECT uid,name
    FROM user
    WHERE uid
    IN (
        SELECT uid2
        FROM friend
        WHERE uid1 = me()
    )
    ORDER BY name ASC
```

To reverse the order of the results, we could simply change the ORDER BY statement to the following:

```
    ORDER BY name DESC
```

If we add an ORDER BY clause, but don't specify the results as either ascending or descending, the results will default to an ascending order.

How it works...

The sorting of results for this example is alphanumeric and case-sensitive, so the results for a String-based field such as the name would be ordered by numbers, then capital letters, and then lowercase letters.

If the field we were querying was actually an integer or date-based field, the results would come out as expected—proper numeric sorts or date comparisons, as the FQL parsers interpret and handle different kinds of data types without any additional information, much like SQL.

FQL requests can be sorted ascending or descending on any column of the main return table. The results of a subquery can also be sorted, although that's only going to have an actual difference on the final output if there's actually any limits or paging used in that subquery.

There's more...

If we don't specify the order in which we want to receive the results, everything is left up to Facebook itself. There's a semblance of order, in that the results tend to all be returned in repeatable patterns, but those patterns are more representative of the order that the results are stored in the database than any kind of default ordering.

Case-insensitive sorting

We could actually make this sort function case-insensitive by using the built-in `lower()` or `upper()` FQL statements, like this:

```
ORDER BY lower(name) ASC
```

Sorting results with advanced objects

The properties of returned objects can be used in the sorting in the same way as they can be used in other subqueries—through dot-notation of their properties. Facebook check-ins for example, has an advanced property for coordinates. Sorting results based on the accuracy of a check-in could look like this:

```
SELECT checkin_id,coords
    FROM checkin
    WHERE author_uid
    IN (
        SELECT uid2
        FROM friend
        WHERE uid1 = me()
    )
    ORDER BY coords.accuracy ASC
```

See also

> ▶ *Limiting and paging FQL results* recipe

Limiting and paging FQL results

Just like we can limit the number of results from a Graph Connection, we can also place a limit on the number of results from FQL requests, a practice recommended by Facebook in the Developer Documentation.

In this recipe we're going to request a small list of the user's friends, using the `LIMIT` capabilities of the FQL language to return only 10 results.

Getting ready

The requests in this recipe build on those explored for the earlier recipe *Using subqueries in FQL*. We don't require any additional Extended Permissions from Facebook, just an authenticated user.

How to do it...

Paging and limiting results from an FQL query uses much the same syntax as in SQL—the
`LIMIT` key word. It's easier to show than it is to explain so, to load the first 10 friends of the
current user, we'd use the following FQL query:

```
SELECT uid,name
    FROM user
    WHERE uid
    IN (
        SELECT uid2
        FROM friend
        WHERE uid1 = me()
    )
    LIMIT 10
```

That would grab the friend results 1 through 10, but if we wanted to load the next results, we'd
need to use paging. To implement paging, and grab the results 11 through to 20, we'd use the
limit keyword in conjunction with two parameters, like this:

```
SELECT uid,name
    FROM user
    WHERE uid
    IN (
        SELECT uid2
        FROM friend
        WHERE uid1 = me()
    )
    LIMIT 10, 10
```

Beyond the number of queries, the result from the FQL query is little different than a normal
FQL query, so the code to request and parse the results would look like this:

```
var query:String = "SELECT uid,name FROM user WHERE uid IN ( SELECT
uid2 FROM friend WHERE uid1 = me() ) LIMIT 10";
Facebook.fqlQuery(query, responseHandler);
```

Our response handler function can remain the same or similar to the parsing functions from
our previous recipes, and can look like this:

```
function responseHandler( success:Object, fail:Object ):void {
    var feed:Array = success as Array;
    if ( success && feed ) {
```

```
        for ( var i:int = 0; i < feed.length; i++ ) {
            var user:FQLUser = FQLUser.fromJSON( feed[ i ] );
            trace( user.name );
        }
    }
}
```

How it works...

This limit key word can be used with either one or two parameters. The first parameter would be the offset for results, and the second is the limit on the number of results. If you only use a single parameter then the parameter you use counts as the limit (the offset defaults to zero). So using `LIMIT 10` returns results 1-10, `LIMIT 10,10` returns results 11-20, and `LIMIT 5,10` would return results 5-15.

There's more...

Unlike limiting request lengths in the JSON and Graph API connections, it is at least possible to specify an ordering system for FQL results, by combining the `LIMIT` keyword with the `ORDER BY` keyword that we explored in the previous chapter.

Should we add limits to FQL requests?

You're not *forced* to add a limit to your requests—if there is a problem with the number of requests, the Facebook API will place limits on the results anyway, and some of the FQL tables have fixed limits on the number of results.

The tables that have these fixed limits are those that often contain the highest number of results—check-ins for example, return up to 20 results by default, with a maximum of 500 results. Status updates are either the last 30 or 50 days worth of results.

 Comprehensive information about the limits you might encounter are detailed in the developer documentation, under each table:

http://developers.facebook.com/docs/reference/fql/

Thankfully, most tables don't have limitations on the number of results, unless we put them in place ourselves with the `LIMIT` keyword.

See also

▶ *Chapter 4, Limiting Graph API request lengths recipe*

Searching for text strings in FQL

FQL isn't as powerful as SQL, and doesn't have access to selectors such `LIKE`, but it does have built-in support for some basic functions, ones that make it possible to get similar results.

The basic functions available in FQL queries are `now()`, `strpos()`, `substr()`, and `strlen()`. Only the `strpos()` function would actually be used in a text search—it returns the position of one string, in another string. We can use this function to determine if the text we're looking for exists within the contents of a result's data field, and that's how we can power a simple FQL search.

In this recipe we're going to build an application which can search the status messages of the current user's friends, for occurrences of the text we supply.

Getting ready

In this recipe, we're going to be querying the current user and their friend's status updates, so we'll need to ensure that our application has the `"user_status"` and `"friends_status"` extended permissions.

To explore the text searching abilities of FQL, we can add two new components to our existing FQL examples interface—`search_inpt` and `search_btn`, with an interface that looks like this:

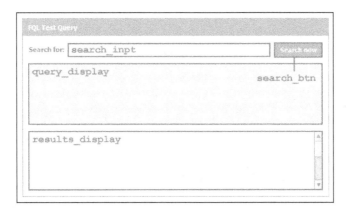

For this recipe, we will need an initial FQL query, which will return all (of the available) status updates for the current user's friends. This query looks like this:

```
SELECT uid,message
    FROM status
    WHERE uid
```

```
    IN (

        SELECT uid2

        FROM friend

        WHERE uid1 = me()

    )
```

How to do it...

Our search would be performed against the `message` data field, and we will use the `strpos()` function to exclude all messages that don't include the term specified in the `search_inpt` component.

This function takes two parameters—the first is the data field to interrogate, and the second is the string to search for. It returns the position of the string within the data field (if it exists), and it's that position we can test against to see if the string exists. If the index comes back as -1, it doesn't exist, 0 or higher and the string exists.

The `strpos` part of our FQL query should look like this:

> AND strpos(message, 'query') > '-1'

Of course, not everyone would use the same capitalization, so one further task we can perform is to make things case-insensitive, using the `lower()` function to compare values in a case-insensitive fashion:

```
SELECT uid,message

    FROM status

    WHERE uid

    IN (

        SELECT uid2

        FROM friend

        WHERE uid1 = me()

    )

    AND strpos( message, lower('query') ) > '-1'
```

To make this FQL request in response to a click of the `search_btn` component, we should use the following ActionScript code:

```
function searchClickHandler(e:Event):void {
    var query:String = "SELECT uid,message FROM status WHERE uid IN
    (SELECT uid2 FROM friend WHERE uid1 = me()) AND strpos( message,
    lower('{searchquery}') ) > '-1'";
```

```
    var values:Object = new Object();
    values.searchquery = search_inpt.text;

    Facebook.fqlQuery(query, responseHandler, values);

    query_display.text = formatFQL(query, values);
}
```

We can keep the same `responseHandler` and `formatFQL` functions as with our original FQL test application and with this code in place, the results of our final application might look like this:

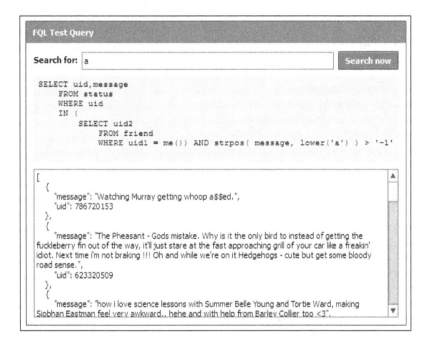

How it works...

If the supplied string exists within the specified data field, the position that the string appears in the data is returned, otherwise a value of -1 is returned—just like the native ActionScript 3 `String.indexOf` method. FQL understands basic math operations, so we can use a numeric comparison on the `strpos` subquery to exclude results that don't include the search string.

Text comparisons are case-sensitive, so to get better search results it helps to force them to the same case for the purposes of the comparison, which is what combining the results with the `lower()` or `higher()` functions will do.

There's more...

If you didn't get any results from that example, it's probably because there were no results to obtain. The scope of the text search in this recipe is limited to the users and their results that we've already got access rights for—the recipe here is simply filtering the results we could otherwise load from FQL without this textual search.

 For a broader-scope search which would return more results, it is perhaps easier to use the standard Graph API search function.

If we were to try and replicate the non-FQL search capabilities, we'd have to make a pretty complex and lengthy search using FQL multiqueries to search different tables, multiple OR statements, and textual matches against multiple data fields.

See also

▶ In *Chapter 4, Search results in the Graph API* recipe

6
Facebook News Feeds and Status Updates

In this chapter, we will cover:

- ▶ Loading a user's status updates
- ▶ Creating a status update with `ActionScript`
- ▶ Posting a link with `ActionScript`
- ▶ Deleting a status update with `ActionScript`
- ▶ Adding custom actions to Facebook posts

Introduction

In the chapters so far, we've looked at some of the different parts of the Facebook APIs, and how we can use the `ActionScript` 3 SDK in a general sense to perform actions on Facebook.

In this chapter, we're going to be looking at news feeds and profile feeds in particular. News and profile feeds are available for Facebook **Users**, **Pages**, **Applications**, and **Groups**, as part of their Graph API connections.

When we reading data from these feeds, we see that they can be populated by four different types of Graph API object: **Status message**, **Link**, **Photo**, or **Video**.

Only the first two of those are objects which can be posted directly to those feeds; photos and videos get uploaded elsewhere, to other Graph API connections, and the appearance of those photos and video items in the news feed is decided by Facebook.

Loading a user's status updates

In this first recipe, we're going to load **Status message** updates from Facebook, using the Graph API object connection. There are several Graph API connections which can return Status updates, links, photos, or videos.

For a Facebook user, these connections are:

- `/PROFILE_ID/home`
- `/PROFILE_ID/feed`
- `/PROFILE_ID/posts`
- `/PROFILE_ID/statuses`

For a Facebook page or Facebook application, the connections are:

- `/PAGE_ID/feed`
- `/PAGE_ID/posts`
- `/PAGE_ID/statuses`

And for a Facebook group, there is:

- `/GROUP_ID/feed`

All of these connections return an array of Graph API post objects, which can be transformed into their equivalent `ActionScript 3` value object class, `FacebookPost`.

 The developer documentation for the Graph API Post object is available from: `http://developers.facebook.com/docs/reference/api/post/`

Getting ready

As with our earlier recipes, we'll need a starting point application, one that handles the initialization of the Facebook SDK, the authentication and required permissions. The easy way to achieve that is to build our application on top of the `ApplicationBase` class that we build in the recipe from *Chapter 11, Building the ApplicationBase class*.

In this recipe, we can load any one of the six feeds listed previously. Access to feeds, and thus, the extended permissions our application will require depends on the accessibility of the feed itself. If we're inspecting a publicly-accessible Facebook **Group** or **Page**, then we'll require no permissions. If we intend on loading the current user's, or a friend of the current user's feeds, then our application will require the `"read_stream"` permission.

As for the component structure of our application, for this recipe we're not going to need a complex layout; add a `List` component which covers the entire stage to the application. The MXML tag for this component can be very simple, like this:

```
<s:List width="100%" height="100%" />
```

We don't need to give our `List` component a specific id—instead we can use Flexs' data binding capabilities to connect the component with its data provider.

How to do it...

As you can see in the introduction, the URL we'd need to load the profile feed for a Graph API object is of the format `/OBJECT_ID/feed`.

To obtain this feed for the current user, we would use the URL `me/feed`, or for the `Facebook Platform Page` object—which has an ID of `19292868552` and a username of `platform`—would be `19292868552/posts` or `platform/posts`.

In the Facebook `ActionScript` 3 SDK, this translates into the following `ActionScript` code:

```
Facebook.api("platform/feed", responseHandler);
```

To display the results from our request, we're going to use that `List` component that we've already added to our application. The contents of this `List` will come from a data-bound `ArrayCollection` instance, and we'll use a custom item renderer with this `List` to render each individual status update.

1. First, we need to declare an `ArrayCollection` instance—to be used as a data provider for the List component—and associate the `List` and `ArrayCollection` instances.

2. Create a new `ArrayCollection` instance in `ActionScript`, using the following code:

   ```
   [Bindable]
   private var newsFeed:ArrayCollection;
   ```

3. To assign this `ArrayCollection` instance as the `dataProvider` for our `List` component, we should change that component's MXML tag to look like this:

   ```
   <s:List dataProvider="{newsFeed}"
           width="100%" height="100%" />
   ```

4. Next, we want to load the selected profile feed and then parse the results.

5. The `ApplicationBase` class is set up to call the `facebookReady` method once the user has authenticated successfully, so the best place for us to automatically request the feed is by overriding that default function, using the following `ActionScript`:

```
override public function facebookReady():void {
    Facebook.api("platform/posts", responseHandler);
}
```

6. The results of this query should be an array of objects, of type `FacebookPost`, and to parse the results, we'd use the following response handler function, which outputs the results to our `ArrayCollection` instance:

```
function responseHandler(success:Object, fail:Object):void {
    newsFeed = new ArrayCollection();
    var results:Array = success as Array;
    if (success && results) {
        for (var i:int = 0; i < results.length; i++) {
            var postUpdate:FacebookPost = FacebookPost.
fromJSON(results[i]);
            newsFeed.addItem(postUpdate);
        }
    }
}
```

7. As the `ArrayCollection, newsfeed`, is data bound and linked with our `List` component, any changes to the collection will be immediately reflected in the `List` component, and new item renderers created and reused when necessary.

8. If we run our application now, the result might look like this:

[id: 19292868552_113649195392798, name: Inside Facebook HQ: future-proofing the social network]

[id: 19292868552_10150226205938553, name: Platform Updates: Operation Developer Love]

[id: 19292868552_10150225142278553, name: The Send Dialog, for Integrated Private Sharing]

[id: 19292868552_10150224420378553, name: Facebook Credits: New Payment Methods and Workflows Extend Global Reach]

[id: 19292868552_10150220433413553, name: Platform Updates: Operation Developer Love]

9. The next step for our application is to create an item renderer to use to display the results of our request.

10. With the aid of a background image, an image component, and some text-based components, we can make the status updates look like this instead:

11. To create this interface, add a new MXML-based item renderer under the package `itemrenderer`, with the name `StatusMessageItemRenderer`. Into our item renderer, we add several new key components: a `RichText` component, `message_lbl`, an `Image` component, `profile_img`, and the `Label` components, `user_name_lbl` and `time_lbl`.

12. In addition to these components, we can add some basic background graphics—a speech bubble, for example. The layout of these components in our item renderer should look like this:

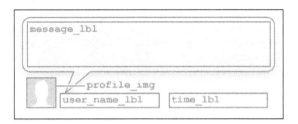

13. To populate these components with values, we should override the default `data` setter function. The first step for our function should be to parse the data into the appropriate `ActionScript` class—`FacebookPost`:

```
override public function set data(value:Object):void {
    super.data = value;
    var post:FacebookPost = value as FacebookPost;
    if (value && post) {
        //
    }
}
```

14. Once we've successfully converted the data object into a `FacebookPost` instance, we can populate our item renderer's components with the appropriate values—for example, the `message` parameter into the `message_lbl` component—and then post the owner's user name into the `user_name_lbl` component.

15. Populating all four components, our `data` setter function might look like this:

```
override public function set data(value:Object):void {
    super.data = value;
    var post:FacebookPost = value as FacebookPost;
    if (value && post) {
        message_lbl.text = post.message;
        user_name_lbl.text = post.from.name;
        profile_img.source = Facebook.getImageUrl(post.from.id,
        "square");
        var dateFormatter:DateFormatter = new DateFormatter();
        dateFormatter.formatString = "EEEE, MMM. D, YYYY at L:NN:
        QQQ A";
```

```
                    time_lbl.text = dateFormatter.format(post.updated_time);
            }
    }
```

16. Now that we have our item renderer set up, we need to use it in our application.

17. To apply this item renderer to our `List` component we specify the name of our renderer under its `itemRenderer` property, like this:

```
<s:List dataProvider="{newsFeed}"
        itemRenderer="itemrenderers.StatusMessageItemRenderer"
        width="100%" height="100%" />
```

18. With our custom renderer applied and the feed loading successfully, our application might look something like this:

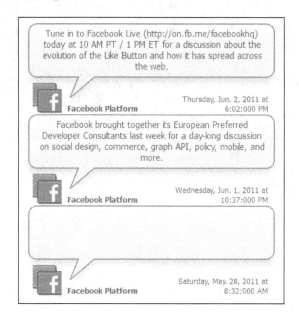

19. Of course, for status messages this works fine, but it also demonstrates the limitations of using a single type of item renderer when multiple object types can be returned in the connection.

20. In the next step, our recipe starts using different item renderers for each of the different update types.

    Each element returned by our feed request is a post object, but the posts themselves have different collections of properties and different types. Knowing this, we can use a selection of different item renderers to customize the display based on the type of the update. Create three additional components—`PhotoItemRenderer`, `VideoItemRenderer`, and `LinkItemRenderer`, which will accompany the existing `StatusMessageItemRenderer`.

Our first two types of item renderer, `PhotoItemRenderer` and `VideoItemRenderer`, should contain the additional component `preview_img`:

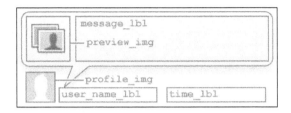

Both `video` and `photo` objects contain a preview image under the property `picture`. In those item renderer's `data` setter function, we'll need to add the additional line of `ActionScript` code:

```
preview_img.source = post.picture;
```

Links posted on Facebook can contain anything from a single `link` property to a more complete post featuring `message`, `name`, `caption`, `description`, `picture`, and `link` properties. Accordingly, the `LinkItemRenderer` component should include the components for each, with provisions for hiding those components, if there's no data under those parameters. The layout of the item renderer should look like this:

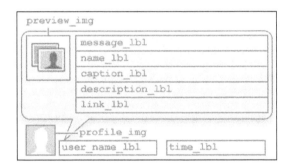

And the `data` setter function for this item renderer might look like this:

```
override public function set data(value:Object):void {
    super.data = value;
    var post:FacebookPost = value as FacebookPost;

    if (post) {
        profile_img.source = Facebook.getImageUrl(post.from.id,
"square");
        profile_img.visible = profile_img.includeInLayout = (post.
picture != null);
```

```
        var dateFormatter:DateFormatter = new DateFormatter();
        dateFormatter.formatString = "EEEE, MMM. D, YYYY at L:NN:
QQQ A";
        time_lbl.text = dateFormatter.format(post.updated_time);

        name_lbl.text = post.name;
        name_lbl.visible = name_lbl.includeInLayout = (post.name
!= null);

        message_lbl.text = post.message;
        message_lbl.visible = message_lbl.includeInLayout = (post.
message != null);

        caption_lbl.text = post.caption;
        caption_lbl.visible = caption_lbl.includeInLayout = (post.
caption != null);

        description_lbl.text = post.description;
        description_lbl.visible = description_lbl.includeInLayout
= (post.description != null);

        link_lbl.textFlow = post.link;
        link_lbl.visible = link_lbl.includeInLayout = (post.link
!= null);
    }
}
```

Now that we have a selection of different item renderers to use in our `List` component, we can set the `itemRendererFunction` property of the `List` component, which allows us to specify the type of the item renderer to used for individual items in that `List`.

21. The function which specifies the different item renderer for each post in the List component should look like this:

```
function feedRendererFunction( item:Object ):IFactory {
    var rtnType:Class;
    if ( item.type == "status" ) {
        rtnType = StatusMessageItemRenderer;
    } else if ( item.type == "photo" ) {
        rtnType = PhotoItemRenderer;
    } else if ( item.type == "video" ) {
        rtnType = VideoItemRenderer;
    } else if ( item.type == "link" ) {
        rtnType = LinkItemRenderer;
    } else {
        rtnType = Label;
    }
    return new ClassFactory( rtnType );
}
```

This function checks against the `type` property of each individual item in the `List` component's `dataProvider`, and returns a different `ClassFactory` instance based on that value, defaulting to the `Label` class if there's a problem parsing the item's type.

22. Now that we have our item renderer selector function created, we can associate it with the `List` component by making the following (highlighted) change to the `MXML`:

```
<s:List dataProvider="{newsFeed}"
        itemRendererFunction="feedRendererFunction"
        width="100%" height="100%" />
```

The `itemRendererFunction` property makes it possible to dynamically switch the item renderers in a way that's consistent with the Flex frameworks' reusable item renderer component model.

How it works...

With this code, we've loaded a Graph API connection, which returns only Facebook post objects. By parsing the results of the API request into an `ArrayCollection` instance, we are able to display the results in a Flex `List` component, using item renderers to better display the contents of the individual posts.

However, a post object represents any of the four update types: `status`, `link`, `photo` and `video`, but not each type of element stores the same properties. Setting an `itemRendererFunction` allows us to change the item renderer class to better suit the post type.

There's more...

So far, we've loaded data from Facebook and displayed it in a `List` with custom item renderers. Making those renderers more visually appealing and ultimately, a little more userfriendly, is something that we will have to achieve with `ActionScript` alone.

Taking the Facebook website as an example, there are two elements that are missing—functional hyperlinks, and user-friendly timestamps.

Displaying the "time since" on status updates

When we see updates on the Facebook website, those updates don't actually display the time as a timestamp, but instead display their updates/created time relative to the current time.

To transform the associated timestamp into a relative time, we can use a simple `ActionScript` method, such as the `timestamptoRelative` function shown here, which is a code snippet that can be found online, at: `http://snipplr.com/view/43419`.

```
function timestampToRelative( timestamp:String ):String {
    //-- Parse the timestamp as a Date object
    var pastDate:Date = new Date( timestamp );
    //-- Get the current data in the same format
    var currentDate:Date = new Date();
    //-- seconds inbetween the current date and the past date
    var secondDiff:Number = ( currentDate.getTime() - pastDate.
getTime()) / 1000;

    //-- Return the relative equivalent time
    switch ( true ) {
        case secondDiff < 60:
            return int( secondDiff ) + ' seconds ago';
            break;
        case secondDiff < 120:
            return 'About a minute ago';
            break;
        case secondDiff < 3600:
            return int( secondDiff / 60 ) + ' minutes ago';
            break;
        case secondDiff < 7200:
            return 'About an hour ago';
            break;
        case secondDiff < 86400:
            return 'About ' + int( secondDiff / 3600 ) + ' hours ago';
            break;
        case secondDiff < 172800:
            return 'Yesterday';
            break;
        default:
            return int( secondDiff / 86400 ) + ' days ago';
            break;
    }
}
```

This method takes a UTC-formatted timestamp string as its input value, parses it into a `Date` object, does a little calculation against the current time, and outputs a more context-friendly date representation. To get a UTC version of the `Post` object's creation time, we can call the `toUTCString` method, which is built into the `Date` class.

In order to display the "time since" we'll need to add a new `Label` component to the display, such as this:

```
<s:Label id="time_lbl" />
```

Once we've added this function to our code, we can extend our item renderer's setter function for the `data` property so that it makes use of the function:

```
override public function set data( value:Object ):void {
    super.data = value;
    var post:FacebookPost = value as FacebookPost;
    if (post) {
        profile_img.source = Facebook.getImageUrl( post.from.id,
"square" );
        time_lbl.text = timestampToRelative( post.updated_time.
toUTCString());
    }
}
```

This way whenever the data is changed in the item renderer, the relative time will be worked out and displayed in the `Label` component, `time_lbl`. It's not completely perfect—after all, the time will only be set once, when the `data` is set.

To improve this further we could use an instance of the `Timer` class, which would update the display every second or so, and keep the view up-to-date:

```
var updateTimer:Timer;

override public function set data( value:Object ):void {
    super.data = value;
    var post:FacebookPost = value as FacebookPost;
    if (post) {
        profile_img.source = Facebook.getImageUrl( post.from.id,
"square" );
    }

    if ( !updateTimer ) {
        updateTimer = new Timer( 1000 );
        updateTimer.addEventListener( TimerEvent.TIMER, onTimerTick );
        updateTimer.start();
    }
}

function onTimerTick( e:Event ):void {
    time_lbl.text = timestampToRelative( post.updated_time.
toUTCString());
}
```

With these functions integrated in our item renderer, we can change the time display of the posts from "Wednesday 1 June, 2011" to something more like the Facebook.com website, with "3 minutes ago".

Extracting and highlighting links in status updates

Another useful improvement for our item renderers is to turn plain text URL links into functional hyperlinks—which is something that we can easily render in ActionScript using the HTML capabilities of the `RichEditableText` component from the Flex framework. If we supply HTML with hyperlink code included, it will highlight the link and make it clickable, which will in turn open a new browser window.

HTML-formatted text can be set using the `TextConverter` class, with the following code:

```
TextConverter.importToFlow( htmlText, TextConverter.TEXT_FIELD_HTML_
FORMAT );
```

The content we receive from Facebook doesn't include HTML hyperlink tags; however, it's something that we'd need to add ourselves. To actually detect and extract the links, we can use regular expressions, which are described as:

> *"[...]a concise and flexible means for matching strings of text, such as particular characters, words, or patterns of characters."*

Regular expressions can be used both for matching strings and replacing or substituting other strings. An expression which we could use to identify URLs in text looks like this:

```
/((?:http|https):\/\/[a-z0-9\/\?=_#&%~-]+(\.[a-z0-9\/\?=_#&%~-
]+)+)|(www(\.[a-z0-9\/\?=_#&%~-]+){2,})/gi
```

I'm no expert with regular expressions (far from it, in fact!), so we have the Internet to thank for this particular regular expression—a post from `stackoverflow`, in fact:

`http://stackoverflow.com/questions/3722918/extracting-links-and-twitter-replies-from-a-string`

We can apply this regular expression to a plain text string by using the `RegExp.replace` method, like this:

```
override public function set data( value:Object ):void {
    super.data = value;
    typed = value as FacebookPost;
    if ( value ) {
        profile_img.source = Facebook.getImageUrl( typed.from.id,
"square" );
```

```
        time_lbl_lbl.text = timestampToRelative( typed.updated_time.
toUTCString());
        var url:RegExp = /((?:http|https):\/\/[a-z0-9\/\?=_#&%~-
]+(\.[a-z0-9\/\?=_#&%~-]+)+)|(www(\.[a-z0-9\/\?=_#&%~-]+){2,})/gi;
        var cur:String = typed.message + " ";
        var output:String = cur;
        while ( url.exec( cur ) != null ) {
            output = cur.replace( url, setUrl );
        }

        message_lbl.textFlow = TextConverter.importToFlow( output,
TextConverter.TEXT_FIELD_HTML_FORMAT );
    }
}

function setUrl( ... arguments:Array ):String {
    return " <a href=\"" + arguments[ 1 ] + "\" target=\"_blank\">" +
arguments[ 1 ] + "</a>";
}
```

Once applied to our item renderer, hyperlinks should start looking like this:

For more information on using the `RegExp` `ActionScript 3` class, see the Adobe LiveDocs:

`http://help.adobe.com/en_US/FlashPlatform/reference/actionscript/3/RegExp.html`

For more general information on regular expressions, check out the regular expression tutorials at `http://www.regular-expressions.info/`

See also

▸ *Chapter 4, Loading Graph API Connections*

Creating a status update with ActionScript

Besides using the Graph API for reading data from Facebook, we can also use it to create or delete individual objects in the Facebook ecosystem.

When a user posts something on Facebook, through the traditional web-based interface, they have a selection of different update types. Status updates are just one of those objects—whether the items are labeled **Status**, **Photo**, **Link**, or **Video**—all of the items are actually of the type **Post**.

In this recipe, we're going to use `ActionScript` to create a status update for the current user, which will be posted on their Profile feed.

Getting ready

The starting point for this recipe should be that of our previous recipe—built on top of the `ApplicationBase` class, which manages extended permissions and is already set up to load a Graph API connection containing post objects. The URL that our application should be loading is the `"me/feed"` connection.

In addition to the existing `List` component, `news_feed_list`, add a new `TextArea` component, `message_txt`, and a `Button` component, `create_post_btn`, to the application interface.

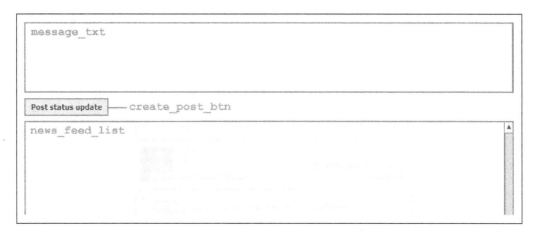

As our application needs to create objects on behalf of the current user, our application will also need the `"publish_stream"` extended permission.

How to do it...

To create a new object in the Graph API we continue to use the same URL as for reading that connection, but instead of loading that Graph API connection URL we choose to POST an object to that URL.

To change our API requests from **read** mode to **create** mode, we add an additional fourth parameter to the `Facebook.api` method call:

```
Facebook.api( "me/feed", responseFunction, params, "post" );
```

The third parameter of this method represents the parameters for our request. These parameters correspond to the Post object that we are creating (which has the parameters listed in the table on previous page).

1. To create a simple status update, posting only the `message` parameter populated, we could use the following `ActionScript`:

```
var options:Object = new Object();
options.message = "My Awesome status message";
Facebook.api( "me/feed", responseFunction, options, "post" );
```

2. This code is posting a hard-coded status message however, so now it's time to link it into our application interface. Add a click event handler function to the `create_post_btn` in MXML, by changing the highlighted MXML:

```
<s:Button id="create_post_btn" label="Post status update"
        click="postButtonClickHandler(event)" />
```

3. In this `postButtonClickHandler` function we need to extract the text property of the `TextArea` component, and use it as the `message` parameter of our options object for our request, using the following function:

```
function postButtonClickHandler(e:Event):void {
    var options:Object = new Object();
    options.message = message_txt.text;
    Facebook.api("me/feed", responseHandler, options, "post");
}
```

If our POST request is successful in creating the new status update, the response from the Graph API should be a single object, with a single parameter, the **ID**, of the newly created object as it is represented in the Graph API. Therefore, when we seek to validate whether our publish request was successful, we look for this ID parameter in the response. If it doesn't exist, then it's most likely that an error occurred in the request. With this in mind, the `responseHandler` function can look like this:

```
function responseHandler(success:Object, fail:Object):void {
    if(success && success.id) {
        // returns the id of the new link if successful
    }
}
```

The final output of this request, when seen through the `Facebook.com` website interface, would be a simple status update object; which might look like this:

James Ford
My Awesome status message
11 seconds ago via My First Application · Like · Comment

How it works...

The first thing that we have to know is what object properties are required or expected in our API post, and what the Graph connection URL will be. That information is detailed in the Graph API, Post object documentation, available online at:

`http://developers.facebook.com/docs/reference/api/post/#publishing`

Generally speaking though, Post objects can contain the parameters `message`, `picture`, `link`, `name`, `caption`, `description`, `source`, `actions`, `privacy`, and `targetting`. Status messages like those explored in this recipe are generally only concerned with the message. Start adding links or pictures to the mix and our Post objects become Links, which are covered in the next recipe.

There's more...

From a functionality point of view, the only further item we haven't explored is the privacy settings of a status update. (We'll cover posting `Links` in other another recipe).

Posting status updates to other user's walls.

In this recipe, we've been posting to the current user's profile feed (also known as their Wall). If we wanted to post an update to another Wall, whether it is that of a User, Group, Page, or an Application, all we have to do is change the URL in the API request.

To post a status update on the Facebook Platform page, for example, we could direct our API requests at the URL "`platform/feed`" instead.

Privacy settings and status updates—who can see your updates?

Privacy settings can easily become a complex subject, but in short, there are a few common privacy settings:

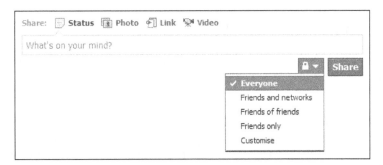

If the user chooses to customize the privacy settings of their updates, they're shown this dialog, where they can choose specific users to allow or deny access to our update:

To specify the privacy settings of a status update, we should supply an object under the `privacy` property. This is also documented online in the Facebook Developer Documentation at: `https://developers.facebook.com/docs/reference/api/post/`, but involves sending a complex JSON-encoded object as part of our API request options.

To define and add the privacy settings to our request, we could use the following code:

```
var privacyObject:Object = new Object();
privacyObject.value = "EVERYONE";

var options:Object = new Object();
options.message = update_text.text;
options.privacy = JSON.encode(privacyObject);

Facebook.api( "me/feed", responseHandler, options, "post" );
```

The Facebook developer documentation describes the options for the privacy parameter with the following block quote:

> *"[An] object containing the `value` field and optional `friends`, `networks`, `allow` and `deny` fields.*
>
> *The `value` field may specify one of the following JSON strings: EVERYONE, CUSTOM, ALL_FRIENDS, NETWORKS_FRIENDS, FRIENDS_OF_FRIENDS.*
>
> *The `friends` field must be specified if value is set to CUSTOM and contain one of the following JSON strings: EVERYONE, NETWORKS_FRIENDS (when the object can be seen by networks and friends), FRIENDS_OF_FRIENDS, ALL_FRIENDS, SOME_FRIENDS, SELF, or NO_FRIENDS (when the object can be seen by a network only).*
>
> *The `networks` field may contain a comma-separated list of network IDs that can see the object, or 1 for a user's entire network.*
>
> *The `allow` field must be specified when the `friends` value is set to SOME_FRIENDS and must specify a comma-separated list of user IDs and friend list IDs that 'can' see the post.*
>
> *The `deny` field may be specified if the `friends` field is set to SOME_FRIENDS and must specify a comma-separated list of user IDs and friend list IDs that 'cannot' see the post."*

We make use of the JSON class and the `JSON.encode` method to preserve the value of the privacy object—if we don't encode the object, it gets converted to a `String [object Object]`, which isn't any help! The JSON class makes lossless encoding and decoding possible.

Without specifying the privacy settings of the update, the default setting would take effect—which would be the privacy setting of EVERYONE. To make our update only available to friends of friends, we could use the following code:

```
var privacyObject:Object = new Object();
privacyObject.value = "FRIENDS_OF_FRIENDS";

var obj:Object = new Object();
obj.message = update_text.text;
obj.privacy = JSON.encode(privacyObject);

Facebook.api("me/feed", onPostedSuccess, obj, "post");
```

To make our update available to only ourselves and a select group of three specific users, we could use the following code:

```
var privacyObject:Object = new Object();
privacyObject.value = "CUSTOM";
privacyObject.friends = "SOME_FRIENDS";
privacyObject.allow = "100001828360986,518107684,566997770";

var obj:Object = new Object();
obj.message = update_text.text;
obj.privacy = JSON.encode( privacyObject );

Facebook.api("me/feed", onPostedSuccess, obj, "post");
```

See also

 ▸ *Loading a user's status updates*
 ▸ *Chapter 4, Creating, Editing, and Deleting Graph API objects*

Posting a link with ActionScript

As you might expect, Links make it possible for a user to publish a Link to a website to their profile feed, and these links are in turn seen by the user's connections in the 'social graph'. For this reason, links are a popular method for promoting Facebook applications, as well as for their original purpose!

Here are a couple of examples of `Link` objects, as seen on the `Facebook.com` website:

From the technical point of view, a `Link` object is simply a Graph API Post object that has more parameters than a standard status message. Specifically, a `Link` can have `name`, `caption`, `description`, and `link` parameters in addition to the `message`, `privacy`, and `actions` parameters that apply to a status message.

In this recipe, we're going to create an interface which we can use to publish a link on Facebook, which is designed to advertise and drive traffic back to our application.

Getting ready

As in our previous recipe, publishing a link to Facebook requires that our application has the `"publish_stream"` extended permission. We don't necessarily need a user interface for this recipe, although you probably want to at least create a `Button` component that can be used to manually publish these links.

How to do it...

1. When publishing a `Link` on Facebook, the parameters we can supply are `name`, `caption`, `description`, `link` and `picture`—all of which take plain text strings. The `picture` should be the URL to a publicly-accessible image, hosted on our own web server. The `link` should also be an URL—which can link to an external website, or one based on the `apps.facebook.com` domain.

```
var options:Object = new Object();
options.name = "I found a trophy";
options.caption = "Gold trophy";
```

```
options.description = "I found a Gold trophy while using My First
Application, an awesome Facebook Game for finding treasure!";
options.link = "http://apps.facebook.com/packt_facebook/";
options.picture = "http://facebook.psyked.co.uk/packt/assets/
images/gold.png";

Facebook.api("me/feed", responseHandler, options, "post");
```

2. Executing this code will create a new post on Facebook, which would look like this:

3. The response type and handler function for such a request is exactly the same as if we'd posted a basic status update:

```
function responseHandler(success:Object, fail:Object):void {
    if(success && success.id) {
        // returns the id of the new link if successful
    }
}
```

How it works...

Whichever values we submit when we create our link becomes part of the link displayed in the `Facebook.com` website. Elements like the `name`, `caption`, `description` and `message` are optional, but the `Link` is not (otherwise the post is treated as a status message). What can distinguish a Facebook `Link` from a status update are the parameters of the request. If we include only the `message` parameter, we get a `Status update`; any of the other parameters and we get a `Link` object.

There's more...

There are obvious parallels between the links that can be created through the `Facebook.com` website (or the JavaScript SDK dialogs) and our own Flash Player applications. The dialog-based Link posting method doesn't however require any extended permissions.

Publishing internal links to a Canvas application

When we intend to use a `Link` to promote our application and increase its traffic, it will help to provide direct links to the Canvas application. Finding these direct links is a matter of understanding how `Facebook.com` is able to interpret these links:

▶ A Canvas application has its own page on `Facebook.com`, such as this:

```
https://apps.facebook.com/packt_facebook/
```

▶ In addition, it also has its own source URL, such as:

```
http://facebook.psyked.co.uk/packt/
```

▶ The source of our Canvas application is hosted online, at:

```
http://facebook.psyked.co.uk/packt/ Posting_A_Link.html
```

▶ To create a direct link to a page within our Canvas application, we take what would be our non-Facebook.com URL and swap our source URL for the Canvas Page URL, producing a link like this:

```
https://apps.facebook.com/packt_facebook/Posting_A_Link.html
```

See also

▶ *Creating a status update with ActionScript*

▶ *Adding Custom Actions to Facebook Posts*

▶ *Chapter 11, Launching Facebook.com UI dialogs from ActionScript 3*

Deleting a status update with ActionScript

Deleting a status update from Facebook is achieved through the same process as deleting any other object from Facebook—all we require is the **ID** of the object and we can work out the appropriate connection URL.

In this recipe, we're going to add the delete functionality to the code from our previous recipes, and tie this in with functions that will remove the status objects from Facebook.

Getting ready

This recipe builds on what we built in the earlier recipe, *Loading a user's status updates*, and in particular the item renderers that we created to display the different types of `Post`.

To these item renderers, were going to add the ability to delete the posts that they represent. Add a `Button` component with an **ID** of `delete_btn` to either the `StatusMessageItemRenderer` or `LinkItemRenderer` component.

How to do it...

To delete an object using the Graph API, we need its **ID**, which we can use to form the URL parameter of our `Facebook.api` method call. Because the Flash Player is a browser-dependent technology, we can't make use of the REST-style `DELETE` value for our method parameter in the request, but thanks to the way that the Graph API works, we can issue a `POST` request and specify an overriding method parameter in the request options:

```
var options:Object = new Object();
options.method = "delete";
Facebook.api(post.id, responseHandler, options);
```

So how do we extend our previous examples to incorporate this delete capability?

1. The first thing we need to do is add a click handler function to the `delete_btn` component, with the following (highlighted) addition to the component's MXML:

```
<s:Button id="delete_btn" label="Delete"
          click="deleteClickHandler();" />
```

2. The `deleteClickHandler` function should pull information from the item renderer's `data` property to formulate the request, with the following function:

```
function deleteClickHandler():void {
    var options:Object = new Object();
    options.method = "delete";
    Facebook.api(post.id, deleteResultHandler, options);
}
```

3. As with any other API request, we need a return function. If the API request is successful, we should receive a very simple response—no JSON objects this time, just the values `true` or `false`, depending on whether the request was successful or not.

4. Next, we should look at handling the response from the Graph API when we make a delete request.

5. To deal with this response our handler function should be pretty simple—it should check that there's no error, and then check that the response equals `"true"`.

6. If that's the case, we need to refresh the list's data provider, or even better, remove the `ActionScript` object for the object we've just deleted from Facebook, which we can achieve with this code:

```
function resultHandler( success:Object, fail:Object ):void {
    if ( success ) {
    DataGroup(parent).dataProvider.removeItemAt(itemIndex);
    }
}
```

There's one more problem to throw in the mix, and that's permissions. Although our application is acting on the user's behalf, it is only able to delete items that it itself created—not those created by another application or by through the official Facebook.com website interface.

7. Even acting on the user's behalf, as our application is, not all updates can be removed. Ideally our application should know whether these items can be deleted by our Flash Player application, and update the user interface accordingly.

All updates created by third-party applications on Facebook have the `application` property, which contains an `id` and a `name` parameter, much like this:

```
"application": {
    "name": "My First Application",
    "id": "172944549389721"
}
```

Of course, we'd need to first know our application's App ID for Facebook (which is listed alongside the API Key on the Facebook Developer website). When we update our item renderer's interface, in the `data` setter function, we can check against the `application.id` parameter, and if the two match we disable or remove the `delete_btn` component, with code like this:

```
override public function set data(value:Object):void {
    super.data = value;
    var post:FacebookPost = value as FacebookPost;
    if (value && post) {
        message_lbl.text = post.message;
        user_name_lbl.text = post.from.name;
        profile_img.source = Facebook.getImageUrl(post.from.id,
        "square");
        var dateFormatter:DateFormatter = new DateFormatter();
        dateFormatter.formatString = "EEEE, MMM. D, YYYY at L:NN:
        QQQ A";
        time_lbl.text = dateFormatter.format(post.updated_time);
        if (post.application) {
            if (post.application.id == "[YOUR_APP_ID]") {
                delete_btn.enabled = true;
            } else {
                delete_btn.enabled = false;
            }
        } else {
            delete_btn.enabled = false;
        }
    }
}
```

How it works...

Deleting objects in the Graph API is simply a case of requesting their Graph API URL, with the parameter "method" set to a value of "post". (This is discussed further in the recipe in *Chapter 4, Creating, Editing, and Deleting Graph API objects*).

All Graph API objects should at least have an ID parameter, which we can use to construct the URL to be used in the delete request. Unfortunately, there's no real way to check in advance whether our application has permissions to delete objects. The only way for our application to pre-emptively know if a deletion is possible is by anticipating those permissions, as we do in this recipe by checking the ID of the application that originally created the update.

There's more...

What happens if you delete a status message or Link that has Comments or Likes associated with it? Well, **Comments** and **Likes** are dependant items, and are attached to the parent Graph API object, meaning that deleting a status update has the immediate effect of also removing all of the Comments associated with that object—and there's no going back—it all just disappears, effectively.

See also

▶ *Chapter 4, Creating, Editing, and Deleting Graph API objects*

Adding custom actions to Facebook posts

When we publish a link, we also have the ability to create a Custom Action for that link, which appears alongside the built-in Like and Comment actions for other Facebook users to interact with.

The aim of an Action is to provide a context-sensitive link between the published Link and our application. Often this translates into actions which provide incentives for users to interact with an application, or into actions which allow users to replicate whatever process the original poster took to publish the Link in the first place.

In this recipe, we'll be building on our earlier recipe, *Posting a Link with ActionScript* and will create an application which can publish a `Link` with custom actions. In our *There's more...* section, we're also going to look at a simple way in which we can create and handle custom actions, using query string parameters.

How to do it...

1. The first place to start is to understand how a custom action is represented in a Graph API response. The example we'll create in this recipe looks like this:

A custom action is simply two values—a **link**, and a **name** for that link. These actions must be specified in the `actions` parameter of the request's options object, and should be a JSON-encoded array of objects, with each object in that array featuring the properties `name` and `link`.

2. Building on top of the code from our earlier recipe, the basic `ActionScript` code that we'd use to create a link with custom actions could look like this (additions highlighted):

```
var action:Object = new Object;
action.name = "I want to find one too!";
action.link = "http://apps.facebook.com/packt_facebook/";

var customActions:Array = new Array();
customActions.push( action );

var options:Object = new Object();
options.name = "I found a trophy";
options.caption = "Gold trophy";
options.description = "I found a Gold trophy while using My First
Application, an awesome Facebook Game for finding treasure!";
options.link = "http://apps.facebook.com/packt_facebook/";
options.picture = "http://facebook.psyked.co.uk/packt/assets/
images/gold.png";
options.actions = JSON.encode( customActions );

Facebook.api("me/feed", responseHandler, options, "post");
```

This code creates a single object, giving it values for the name and link parameters. We then push that object into an array, and associate that array as the actions parameter of our API request's options object.

When we construct our array of custom actions, the `name` parameter corresponds directly to the text that appears in the `Facebook.com` website interface, and the `link` represents the URL that the user is directed to when they click on these actions.

How it works...

The `name` parameter for each action corresponds directly to the text that appears in the `Facebook.com` website interface, and the `link` represents the URL that the user is directed to when they click on these actions. A single link can have several custom actions, and these custom actions are stored as an array.

To give our application multiple custom actions, we simply have to create more action objects and push them into the `actions` array.

There's more...

There's a wealth of possibilities open to our application through clever use of custom actions, and in practice many of them rely on some form of server-side solution to minimize the chances of users manipulating the application.

Custom Actions rely on the URL supplied, and most of these custom actions being used by other Facebook applications rely on passing parameters in the query string of an URL, which is then read by the application if and when other users click on the custom action.

Working with query strings and responding to custom actions

In this recipe, the address that our custom action would link to is that of the Canvas URL: `http://apps.facebook.com/packt_facebook/` which means that any users that click on our custom action will be taken directly to the application itself.

For our application to know that incoming users have been referred by a custom action link, we can pass variables as part of the page's query string—which goes on the end of this URL, like this:

`http://apps.facebook.com/packt_facebook/Recipe_06_05_Custom_Action.html?trophy=bronze`

The query string parameters themselves can be open to manipulation by unscrupulous users, which is why a server-side solution is often the best for handling important data, but client-side-only solutions are perfectly usable for less critical actions, such as simple cosmetic personalization.

1. To read in values from a query string, we first have to be publishing links with query strings included in the custom action's URL. Modify the URL of the existing `Link` creation code to use an URL with a query string included, like this:

```
var action:Object = new Object;
action.name = "I want to find one too!";
action.link = "http://apps.facebook.com/packt_facebook/Recipe_06_
05_Custom_Action.html?trophy=bronze";

var customActions:Array = new Array();
customActions.push( action );

var options:Object = new Object();
options.name = "I found a trophy";
options.caption = "Gold trophy";
options.description = "I found a Gold trophy while using My First
Application, an awesome Facebook Game for finding treasure!";
options.link = "http://apps.facebook.com/packt_facebook/";
options.picture = "http://facebook.psyked.co.uk/packt/assets/
images/gold.png";
options.actions = JSON.encode( customActions );

Facebook.api("me/feed", responseHandler, options, "post");
```

2. We can obtain the URL of our Flash Player application's parent HTML page by using the following `ActionScript` code:

```
var fullUrl:String = ExternalInterface.call( "window.location.
href.toString" );
```

3. When our application starts up, we can then split the page URL into its constituent parts with the following `ActionScript` function, which returns a `Dictionary` class instance:

```
function getQueryParams():Dictionary {
    var qsValues:Dictionary = new Dictionary();
    if ( ExternalInterface.available )
    {
        var fullUrl:String = ExternalInterface.call( "window.
location.href.toString" );
        var paramStr:String = fullUrl.split( "?" )[ 1 ];
        if ( paramStr != null )
        {
```

```
        var params:Array = paramStr.split( "&" );
        for ( var i:int = 0; i < params.length; i++ )
        {
            var keyPair:Array = params[ i ].split( '=' );
            qsValues[ keyPair[ 0 ]] = keyPair[ 1 ];
        }
    }
}
    return qsValues;
}
```

4. To detect whether the current user has accessed our application directly, or has accessed it via a `Custom Action`, we need to check for a value in our dictionary instance and look for a value under a specific dictionary key—in this case, we're looking for the parameter named `"trophy"`:

```
function applicationCompleteHandler(e:Event):void {
    var params:Dictionary = getQueryParams();
    if ( params[ "trophy" ] ) {
        // the custom action has been used
    } else {
        // a custom action has not been used
    }
}
```

5. What this function does is check for the existence of any value under the `"trophy"` query string parameter. If we wanted to extract the value of this parameter, we could use some ActionScript like this:

```
message_lbl.text  = "Found a " + params[ "trophy" ] + " trophy. ";
```

And of course, we can start introducing far more parameters in our custom action URLs, such as the name of the referring user or different trophy types.

See also

▶ *Creating a status update with ActionScript*

▶ *Chapter 7, Likes and Comments*

7

Comments and "Like this"

In this chapter, we will cover:

- ▸ Loading the Comments for a Graph API object
- ▸ Adding a Comment to a Graph API object
- ▸ Deleting a Comment
- ▸ Retrieving Likes for a Graph API object
- ▸ Adding a "Like" to a Facebook Post
- ▸ Retrieving a "Like" count for a specified URL

Introduction

Comments and Likes are one of the key elements that make up the "social network" side of Facebook—without them, users are just shouting into a vacuum, but with them, they're connecting with friends and strangers alike, and voicing their opinions.

For the most part, working with Comments and Likes is little different from working with any other Graph API object—the methods and API requests are more or less the same, but it still helps to look into the specifics of working with these object types, find out where they can be applied, where they can be used, and how we can best integrate them into a Flex-based application.

Loading Comments for a Graph API object

In this recipe, we're going to load the comments for a given item on Facebook and display them using a Flex framework **List** component, using a further **Item Renderer** component to format the output, so that each comment looks more like this:

And less like this, which is what would happen without a custom Item Renderer:

[id: 200843466599829_613142, message: O RLY?]

Comments can be added to almost every Facebook object type, but for the purposes of this recipe, we're going to display the comments for a publicly-available photo object.

Because this photo is publicly available and because the comments attached to a Graph API object inherit their permissions from the object itself, there's no requirement for the user to be authenticated with Facebook in order to load the image data or the comments associated with it.

The object ID of the photo in question is 200843466599829. When loaded, this object should look like this:

Getting ready

The first thing we will want for this example is an interface. Create a new application and add three components: an **Image** component, with an ID of image_preview, a **List** component, with an ID of comments_list, and a **Label** component with an ID of comments_count_lbl.

The layout of these components should look like this:

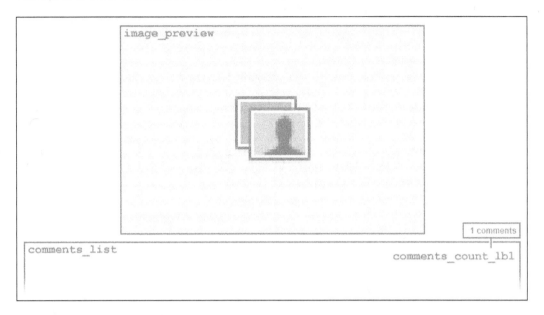

How to do it...

1. The first thing that we need to add to our application is a function that will execute automatically when our application starts up. We can do that by adding a handler for the applicationComplete Event, using this (highlighted) MXML tag:

```
<s:Application xmlns:fx="http://ns.adobe.com/mxml/2009"
               xmlns:s="library://ns.adobe.com/flex/spark"
               xmlns:mx="library://ns.adobe.com/flex/mx"
               applicationComplete="loadPhoto();"
               width="758" height="600">
```

2. We already know the ID of our photo object that we want to load—200843466599829—so we can now add some code to load the preview of the photo object, using the Facebook.getImageUrl method:

```
public function loadPhoto():void {
image_preview.source = Facebook.getImageUrl(
                  "200843466599829", "normal");
}
```

3. The comments for our photo object are available as a Graph API connection, which returns an Array of Comment objects. To request that connection, we use the `Facebook.api` method, using the connection URL `/200843466599829/comments` in our function, as follows:

```
public function loadPhoto():void {
    image_preview.source = Facebook.getImageUrl("200843466599829",
"normal");
    Facebook.api("200843466599829/comments", photoComments);
}
```

4. To use the results of the `likes` connection in our List component, we need to convert the results of this request into something that works with Flex's data binding capabilities, using ActionScript code as follows:

```
import mx.collections.ArrayCollection;
import com.facebook.graph.data.api.comment.FacebookComment;

[Bindable]
private var photoComments:ArrayCollection;

function onCommentsLoaded(success:Object, fail:Object):void {
    photoComments = new ArrayCollection();
    var results:Array = success as Array;
    if ( success && results ) {
        for ( var i:int = 0; i < feed.length; i++ ) {
            var comment:FacebookComment = FacebookComment.
fromJSON(results[ i ]);
            photoComments.addItem(comment);
        }
    }
}
```

In this code, we have an `ArrayCollection` instance, which is what we'll be using for the data binding in our List component. This `onCommentsLoaded` function takes the result of the request, interprets it as an Array, and then iterates through the results and converts the objects in the Array into strict-typed **FacebookComment** class instances.

5. For these results to be displayed in our List component, we need to attach the `photoComments ArrayCollection` instance as the `dataProvider` for the component, for which we'd need to make the (highlighted) changes in the component's MXML:

```
<s:List id="news_feed_list"
  dataProvider="{photoComments}"/>
```

If we run our application now, we should get a result that looks like this:

This doesn't display the comments very nicely, so to improve the appearance we're going to use a custom Item Renderer component.

6. Create a new MXML component that extends the Spark `ItemRenderer` class, and call it `FacebookCommentItemRenderer`. This will create a new MXML file, whose contents should look as follows:

```
<s:ItemRenderer xmlns:s="library://ns.adobe.com/flex/spark">
</s:ItemRenderer>
```

The Facebook.com website interface for comments looks like this:

To replicate this style of interface in Flex, we will need an Image and a series of Label and RichText components—enough to cover the comment text itself, the commenter's name, the time since the comment was posted, and the number of likes (if any) that a comment has received.

7. Create a new Item Renderer component, which should include an Image component with an ID of `profile_img`, a RichText component with an ID of `message_lbl`, and two Label components, with IDs of `time_lbl` and `likes_count_lbl`. These components should be laid out as follows:

8. Introduce a few strategically placed background graphics, and our Item Renderer components should look like this:

To have our Item Renderer display the appropriate information in the components, we need to override the data setter method of the Item Renderer, using the following code:

```
override public function set data(value:Object):void {
    super.data = value;
    var comment:FacebookComment = value as FacebookComment;
    if (value && comment) {
        profile_img.source = Facebook.getImageUrl( comment.from.id,
"square" );
        message_lbl.textFlow = TextConverter.importToFlow( "<b>" +
comment.from.name + "</b> " + comment.message, TextConverter.TEXT_
FIELD_HTML_FORMAT );
        time_since.text = timestampToRelative(comment.created_time.
toUTCString());
        likes_count.text = comment.likes + " like(s)";
    }
}
```

By overriding the data setter function in this Item Renderer, we can simultaneously validate the class of the inputted data, and then use the values of that input to immediately update the user interface.

> The `timestampToRelative` function is the same as the one used in the recipe in *Chapter 6, Facebook News Feeds and Status Updates*, the recipe — *Loading a users' status updates*—more information about this function and the full code itself can be found in the *There's more...* section of that recipe.

How it works...

The comments for an object are available through a Graph API connection, which gets tagged onto the end of the Graph API URL for the object. This connection is called /comments—so the final Graph API Connection URL becomes /OBJECT_ID/comments.

There's more...

There are several types of object in the Graph API, but not all of them can have comments associated with them, so...

What type of objects can have Comments?

The Graph API object types that can have comments associated with them are: **Album**, **Link**, **Note**, **Photo**, **Post**, **Status message**, and **Video**.

The objects that cannot have comments directly associated with them are those which are either explicitly private, those which represent users or groups, or those that exist as part of a larger object.

See also

> ▶ *Loading Graph API connections* in *Chapter 4, Reading and Writing Data with the Graph API*

Adding a Comment to a Graph API object

Comments for a Graph API object are linked to the object through their Graph API connection, so to add a new comment, what we need to do is post an appropriately formatted object to the object's connection URL.

In this recipe, we're going to extend our comments loading application from the previous recipe to include the ability to post a comment on to an existing Graph API object.

Getting ready

Adding objects to the Graph API on a user's behalf requires that our application be authenticated as that user, along with the `publish_stream` Extended Permission. An easy way to ensure that our application has this Extended Permission is to use the `ApplicationBase` class that we develop in the recipe *Creating the ApplicationBase class* from *Chapter 11, Bridging the Flash and Application Gap*.

To test this functionality, we'll build an interface which can be used to create new comments. In addition to the components and layout from our previous recipe, we need to create two new components: a **RichEditableText** component with an ID of `message_inpt` and a **Button** component with an ID of `add_comment_btn`.

 To retain some consistency with the Facebook.com website, we can also add additional Image and Label components—`user_img` and `user_lbl`—which we'll use to display a preview of the current user, although that's not a critical part of this recipe.

The layout of all of these components should look as follows:

```
┌──────────────────────────────────────────────┐
│ ┌──┐  ┌─ message_inpt                      │
│ │  │  ├─ user_img                          │
│ └──┘  │                                    │
│ James ├─ user_lbl                          │
│ Ford  └─          add_comment_btn ─ Add comment │
└──────────────────────────────────────────────┘
```

How to do it...

1. Comments have only one supported data field when publishing to the Graph API and that is the `message` field. The basic code to publish a comment on an object would look similar to this:

```
var options:Object = new Object();
options.message = "Your comment text here.";
Facebook.api("OBJECT_ID/comments", responseHandler, options,
"post");
```

2. For our next step, we should integrate this functionality with the value in our RichEditableText component and add it as a click event handler function for our Button component. Our ActionScript code for this function should look like this:

```
var object_id:String = "200843466599829";

function addComment(e:Event):void {
    var options:Object = new Object();
    options.message = message_lbl.text;
    Facebook.api(object_id + "/comments", responseHandler,
      options, "post");
}
```

3. And the MXML code to link this associate function should look as follows:

```
<s:Button buttonMode="true"
    click="addComment(event)"
    label="Add comment" />
```

If we run our application at this point, it should something like this:

How it works...

When we retrieve comments, the JSON object that represents individual comments should look as follows:

```
{
    "created_time": "2011-02-16T01:13:47+0000",
    "id": "200843466599829_621697",
    "message": "This is another test comment.",
    "from": {"id": "172944549389721", "name": "My First Application"}
}
```

The only unique property for a Graph API comment object is the `message`—the remaining properties: user, creation time, uid, and the likes count are all supplied by the Graph API when the object is created. The owner of a comment is the user associated with the access token that was used to publish the comment.

There's more...

Considering that we can see comments from users that we otherwise have no connection to, how does privacy work with a comment?

Comments and privacy settings

The Graph API documentation states that when a user creates a comment on a specific item, the privacy settings for that comment are inherited from the settings of the item itself, instead of the user's privacy settings, and that it's not possible to specify custom privacy settings for a comment.

This doesn't actually affect our code or how it works; it just goes towards explaining why, unlike status updates, we can't customize the privacy settings for comments that we create using the Graph API.

The official FAQ from Facebook details this behavior as:

> "The only people that can see the story about your comment are those who can see the content you commented on. For example, if you commented on a photo that only you and your friend can see, only you and your friend would be able to see the story on your Wall."

See also

▶ *Creating a Graph API object* recipe in *Chapter 4*

Deleting a Comment

Deleting a comment on Facebook is much the same process as for deleting any other Graph API object with the same restrictions.

In this recipe, we're going to take the end result from the previous recipe, which uses a List component and item renderers to present the comments for a Graph API object and to these Item Renderers we'll add functionality to delete comments.

Getting ready

To introduce the delete capability to our application, we should add a Button component to the `FacebookCommentItemRenderer` class with an ID of `delete_btn`.

How to do it...

To delete the comment from the Graph API, we make a request with the comment's ID, with a request options object that includes the property `method` with the value of `'delete'`, as follows:

```
var option:Object = new Object();
option.method = "delete";
Facebook.api(COMMENT_ID, responseHandler, option, "post");
```

1. Into our existing Item Renderer, we should add a click event handler for the `delete_btn` component, which makes this request:

```
function delete_comment_clickHandler(e:Event):void {
    var option:Object = new Object();
    option.method = "delete";
    Facebook.api(comment.id, responseHandler, option, "post");
}
```

2. In the response handler function, we need to check if the delete request was successful. If it is, we can immediately remove the comment from the List component's `dataProvider`, using the following function:

```
function responseHandler(success:Object, fail:Object):void {
    if (success) {
        (this.owner as List).dataProvider.removeItemAt(itemIndex);
    }
}
```

How it works...

Deleting a comment is a similar process as for deleting any other Graph API object.

For this recipe to work, our application must have a valid access token for the current user, must have the `publish_stream` Extended Permission, and the original comment must have been created by our own application.

 More information about deleting an object in the Graph API can be found in the recipe in *Chapter 4—Creating, editing, and deleting Graph API objects.*

There's more...

When it comes to deleting comments or rather *attempting* to delete comments, we'll find that we can (obviously) only actually delete the comments posted by the current user (unless they are in fact the administrator of a Page, which is a different story).

Attempting to delete a comment you're not allowed to delete will throw the following error back from the Graph API:

```
{
    "error": {
        "type": "OAuthException",
        "message": "(#200) Users can only delete their own comments"
    }
}
```

This leads us to...

Knowing which comments can be deleted by the current user

The current user can always delete their own comments, so one simple expansion to our current code would be to check the `uid` of the currently authenticated user against the `uid` of the comment's owner, and remove the delete button if they don't match.

The following code snippet can help us do just that, while keeping our Item Renderer re-usable for all users:

```
if (comment.from.id == Facebook.getSession().uid) {
    delete_comment.includeInLayout = true;
    delete_comment.visible = true;
} else {
    delete_comment.includeInLayout = false;
    delete_comment.visible = false;
}
```

This will probably be enough information for most users, but users can also be administrators for objects in the Graph API, such as a Fan page, which gives them additional privileges when it comes to deleting objects.

See also

▶ *Creating, editing, and deleting Graph API objects* recipe in *Chapter 4*

Retrieving Likes for a Graph API object

In this recipe, we're going to load a list of users who have 'liked' a publicly-available object in Facebook. The object we're going to load is one that comes as an example in the Facebook Developer Documentation, and will return a list of objects containing the Facebook user name and user id of those that have 'Liked' the object we're querying.

Getting ready

As the object we will be loading in this recipe is publicly-accessible, all of its Likes and Comments will also be publicly available, which means that we don't have to worry about authentication with the Graph API.

How to do it...

The ID of the object that we'll be loading is 98423808305, which is again a publicly-accessible photo object in the Graph API, and one of the samples listed in the Developer Documentation.

1. Likes are available as a Graph API connection, so the path that we'll be supplying to the Facebook.api method is 98423808305/likes:

```
Facebook.api("98423808305/likes", responseHandler);
```

2. To parse handle this result, we cast the return object as an Array and then loop through the objects in that Array, convert them into FacebookUser class instances, and store them in another Array instance in our application:

```
function responseHandler(success:Object, fail:Object):void {
    var photoLikes:Array = new Array();
    var results:Array = success as Array;
    if (success && results) {
        for (var i:int = 0; i < results.length; i++) {
            var user:FacebookUser = FacebookUser.
fromJSON(results[i]);
            photoLikes.push(user);
        }
    }
}
```

How it works...

When we request the data for this Graph API connection, we should receive JSON-formatted data that looks a little something like this:

```
[
    {"id": "589116860", "name": "Alan McConnell"},
    {"id": "1217422578", "name": "Armando Orrala Gonzalez"},
    {"id": "100000554048206", "name": "Marco Manenti"},
    {"id": "100001785018693", "name": "Johanka Veli☐ková"},
    {"id": "100000694883125", "name": "Andrei Nede"},
    {"id": "548018728", "name": "Cindirellas Delia"},
]
```

It's not overly informative, but it's concise and all we can get from the `/likes` connection alone.

Comments, **Notes**, **Photos**, **Pages**, **Posts**, and **Status messages** are all objects in the Graph API that can all be 'liked' by a user, according to the Developer Documentation.

A **Like** doesn't really have its own object type in the Graph API—the only properties it has are the user's `name` and user's `id`, but these same properties exist in the `FacebookUser` class, so we can swap the two without issue—so long as we don't want to request any of the empty parameters of that instance.

There's more...

Loading the Likes for an object, or instead loading the Likes for the *correct* object, can be a little problematic.

No Likes? Make sure you're using the object ID

The six object types (Comments, Notes, Photos, Pages, Posts, and Status messages) for which the `/likes` connection applies can all be 'liked' by a user—either through the Graph API or through the Facebook website.

The key to loading any Graph API connection is in getting the correct id of the object in the API, and it's all too easy to confuse something like the `aid` property of an album with the `object_id` of the album, and to make it worse, confusing the two properties won't actually throw any errors in the Graph API, so we might end up none the wiser.

  ▶ *Loading Graph API connections* recipe in *Chapter 4*

Adding a "Like" to a Graph API object

As we explored in the previous recipe, there are many Graph API object types within Facebook that can be 'liked' by a user. A Post object is one of these, and can represent any of the four update types present in Profile or News Feeds—which are Status, Link, Photo, and Video objects.

In this recipe, we're going to build on the recipe *Loading Graph API connections* from *Chapter 4*, and create an application that will allow us to 'Like' updates in a user's News Feed, with some simple adjustments to the Item Renderer components.

Getting ready

As with any other action that creates objects with the API, we will need to be authenticated with Facebook to allow us access to non-public data. We'll be reading from the current user's News Feed, so we'll need the `read_stream` Extended Permission, and we'll also require the `publish_stream` permission to be able to add data to the Graph API.

How to do it...

The ideal starting point for this recipe is the final code from the aforementioned. This gives us an application which loads status updates for the current user, and displays the results in a Flex List component and uses Item Renderers to display the individual posts.

1. Inside the Item Renderers used in this List, we need to add a Button component, with and ID of `like_btn`, which the user can use to 'like' that update, and a Label component, `like_count_lbl`, which we can use to display a count of the total number of Likes for that post.

    When the `like_btn` component is clicked, we want to post data to the Graph API connection, and we do that with the usual `Facebook.api` method. The `data` property of our Item Renderer is an instance of the `FacebookPost` class, so we can use the `id` property of this value to construct our URL for the request.

2. Inside each of Item Renderers, we can add the following function:

```
function likeClickHandler():void {
    var post:FacebookPost = data as FacebookPost;
    Facebook.api(post.id + "/likes", responseHandler, null,
"post");
}
```

3. And this function is tied to our `like_btn` in the usual manner, using MXML:

```
<s:Button id="like_btn" label="Like this"
    click="likeClickHandler();"/>
```

Providing all goes well with the request, the result we receive from the Graph API will simply say `true` and likewise a failed response will say `false`.

4. Once we have this successful result, we will want to update the Item Renderer interface to reflect the options now available to the user, by incrementing the 'Likes' count and changing the behavior and text of the 'Like this' button:

```
function responseHandler(success:Object, fail:Object):void {
    if (success) {
        data.likes++;
        like_count_lbl.text = typed.likes + " likes";
        like_btn.enabled = false;
    }
}
```

How it works...

Adding Likes in the Graph API is actually a really simple process, because it doesn't require anything more than visiting a specific URL with a valid access token—no additional parameters required. The Facebook ActionScript 3 SDK takes care of the access token management for us, so all we need to do is generate the request's URL from the object ID and the connection URL.

There's more...

Of course, our code so far assumes that the user hasn't already 'liked' the current post, but we're obviously going to want a slightly different interface if the user has already 'liked' the post in question.

The easiest way to work out if the user has liked the post already is to make sure that we're requesting the `likes` data field in our original request, and then we can cross-check the IDs in the request with the ID of the current user—which we can get through querying the `Facebook.getSession().uid` property in ActionScript.

Removing a Like from Graph API object

To remove a Like from our Post object, we need to call the API again with the value of `delete` in the method parameter, which would look as follows:

```
var options:Object = new Object();
options.method = "delete";
Facebook.api(post.id + "/likes", responseHandler, options, "post");
```

One way to adapt our Item Renderer further and allow for both adding and deleting Likes, is to swap the Button component for a ToggleButton component, and treat Likes as something that can be toggled on and off.

The following ActionScript code would enable this behavior, alternating between calling the post and delete versions of the API request, based on the selected property of the button component:

```
function likeClickHandler():void {
    if (like_btn.selected) {
        var options:Object = new Object();
        options.method = "delete";
        Facebook.api(post.id + "/likes", responseHandler, options,
"post");
    } else {
        Facebook.api(post.id + "/likes", responseHandler, null,
"post");
    }
}

function responseHandler(success:Object, fail:Object):void {
    if (success) {
        if (like_btn.selected) {
            post.likes--;
            like_btn.label = "Like this";
        } else {
            post.likes++;
            like_btn.label = "Unlike this";
        }
        like_count_lbl.text = post.likes + " likes";
        like_btn.selected != like_btn.selected;
    }
}
```

These functions make use of the built-in selected property to keep track of the 'Like' state on Facebook and change the label of the button to appropriately reflect the action they will perform when activated.

See also

> ▸ *Loading a user's status updates* recipe in *Chapter 6*
> ▸ *Creating, editing, and deleting Graph API objects* recipe in *Chapter 4*

Retrieving a "Like" count for a specified URL

Our recipes so far have dealt with the assumption that we know the ID of an object on Facebook, and even that there is an object in the Graph API that represents what we want to show a 'Like' counter for, but that's not necessarily the case.

What we need is a way to retrieve statistics for an URL, without knowing the ID for the object in the Graph API.

In this recipe, we'll develop an interface which can do just that—take any user-specified URL as its input, load and then display statistics from Facebook about that URL.

 The statistics for 'Likes' are anonymous and the URLs we can query are not governed by any privacy settings, so we don't need to worry about Facebook authentication in this recipe.

How to do it...

There are two ways to retrieve information about URLs from Facebook—using the Graph API and using FQL queries. The Graph API method is good for a quick overview, but the results from FQL are more verbose, so we'll look at both methods in this recipe.

Retrieving URL statistics with the Graph API

The Graph API has a simple method for returning URL stats, whereby we simply supply a full URL (`http://` included) to the Graph API subdomain. To retrieve statistics for the URL `http://www.packtpub.com/`, we would make the following request to the Graph API: `https://graph.facebook.com/http://www.packtpub.com/`.

This will return basic statistics about the URL, which consists of the total number of 'shares' of that URL on Facebook, which corresponds to the number of times an object has been promoted on Facebook (a combination of Likes, Comments, and Links posted to News Feeds).

A request such as the one aforementioned would return data similar to the following:

```
{
    "id": "http://www.packtpub.com/",
    "shares": 116
}
```

1. To make this request using the Facebook ActionScript 3 SDK, we'd first make our request using the following ActionScript code:

    ```
    Facebook.api("http://www.packtpub.com/", responseHandler);
    ```

2. And to handle the response, we'd use the following function:

```
function responseHandler(success:Object, fail:Object):void {
    if (success && success.shares) {
        trace("Number of shares = " + success.shares);
    } else {
        trace("No stats found for URL: http://www.packtpub.com/");
    }
}
```

If all goes as planned, we should get the following output in the Flash Builder debugger console (although the actual values may change somewhat):

```
Number of shares = 116
```

That's all well and good, but it's not _technically_ a Likes count for that URL; it's a count of the number of times that URL is discussed on Facebook, as a whole.

Retrieving URL statistics with FQL

To retrieve a better breakdown of the 'shares' figure, we can use FQL queries. By querying the link_stat table, we are able to see exactly how many Likes, Comments, and Shares (times the URL has been used in a Profile Feed Post) make up the overall total.

1. The FQL query to retrieve this information would look like this:

```
SELECT url,share_count,like_count,comment_count,total_count
   FROM link_stat
   WHERE url = 'http://www.packtpub.com/'
```

2. And executing it will return JSON-encoded data that should look similar to this:

```
[
    {
        "total_count": 116,
        "like_count": 14,
        "url": "http://www.packtpub.com/",
        "comment_count": 40,
        "share_count": 62
    }
]
```

3. To execute this FQL query with the Graph API, we'd use the following ActionScript code:

```
Facebook.fqlQuery("SELECT url, share_count, like_count, comment_
count, total_count FROM link_stat WHERE url='http://www.packtpub.
com/'", responseHandler);
```

4. To parse the results, our response handler function needs to be a little different to that of the standard Graph API, and would look as follows:

```
function responseHandler(success:Object, fail:Object):void {
    var results:Array = success as Array;
    if (success && results && results.length) {
        for (var i:int = 0; i < results.length; i++) {
            var item:Object = results[i];
            trace("Number of likes = " + item.like_count);
            trace("Number of comments = " + item.comment_count);
            trace("Number of shares = " + item.share_count);
            trace("Total shares = " + item.total_count);
        }
    } else {
        trace("No stats found for URL: http://www.packtpub.com/");
    }
}
```

5. Run this code in debug mode and the following should be outputted to your console:

```
Number of likes = 14
Number of comments = 40
Number of shares = 62
Total shares = 116
```

The Developed Documentation for the FQL `link_stat` table that we're using in this recipe is available online at the URL:

`http://developers.facebook.com/docs/reference/fql/link_stat/`

How it works...

Although we normally work with an object's Graph API object ID, Facebook actively promotes itself to the wider Web through the 'Like this' functionality, which is in turn based around URLs.

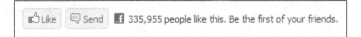

It is obviously advantageous to both ourselves and Facebook to keep the number of API data requests for commonly-accessed statistics down to a minimum, hence the Graph API making URL-based queries so readily available and FQL offering a `url` as an indexable field for its 'link statistics' table.

The statistics we're gathering in this recipe are completely anonymous as far as identifying users goes—we can find the number of comments, likes, and shares, but without being able to extract Graph API object IDs from these URLs, we're unable to query deeper into the API to retrieve the specific instances where those URLs were originally shared.

There's more...

As you might expect, the URLs for an object have to be exact—a query using the URL `http://google.co.uk` will return different results than one based on `http://www.google.co.uk/`, even though the page content may be the same.

Requesting statistics for the current page URL

To request information about the current page, we can use a simple JavaScript function to return the current page URL, and use that in our requests (instead of using a text input component or hardcoded value).

To get the current page URL, we can use the `ExternalInterface` class and have it execute a line of JavaScript in the containing page, returning the result back to our Flash Player movie.

This code will return the current page location, synchronously into our Flash movie:

```
ExternalInterface.call("window.location.href.toString");
```

Our ideal code for requesting information about the current URL location with the Graph API would therefore look as follows:

```
if (ExternalInterface.available) {
    var currrentURL:String = ExternalInterface.call("window.location.
href.toString");
    Facebook.api(encodeURIComponent(currentURL), responseHandler);
}
```

Requesting statistics for multiple URLs

Website URLs and page IDs are interchangeable in the Graph API and we can retrieve information about multiple URLs simultaneously using the technique discussed in the recipe from *Chapter 4*, the recipe *Loading multiple Graph API objects in a single request*.

For example, a Graph API request for multiple URLs might look like this:

```
https://graph.facebook.com/?ids=http://www.facebook.com/
platform,http://www.google.co.uk/,http://www.packtpub.com/
```

And this request would return JSON-formatted data that looks something like this:

```json
{
    "http://www.google.co.uk/": {
        "id": "http://www.google.co.uk/",
        "shares": 73601
    },
    "http://www.facebook.com/platform": {
        "id": "http://www.facebook.com/platform",
        "shares": 1522312
    },
    "http://www.packtpub.com/": {
        "id": "http://www.packtpub.com/",
        "shares": 123
    }
}
```

We can also use FQL, not just the standard Graph API, to retrieve this information. The same (or similar) request expressed in FQL could look like this:

```sql
SELECT url,share_count,like_count,comment_count,total_count
    FROM link_stat
    WHERE url
    IN ('http://www.facebook.com/platform', 'http://www.google.co.uk/',
    'http://www.packtpub.com/')
```

And this request would return data in the following format:

```json
[
    {
        "url": "http://www.facebook.com/platform",
        "total_count": 2244391,
        "like_count": 2243861,
        "comment_count": 55,
        "share_count": 475
    },
```

```
{
    "url": "http://www.google.co.uk/",
    "total_count": 115168,
    "like_count": 29441,
    "comment_count": 37669,
    "share_count": 48058
},
{

    "url": "http://www.packtpub.com/",
    "total_count": 200,
    "like_count": 49,
    "comment_count": 48,
    "share_count": 103
}
]
```

Ensuring correct URL encoding for the Graph API

In this recipe, there is one further item to highlight and that is in the URLs for the Graph API version of the code. Because of the way query strings work with URLs, it is important to ensure that any query strings in the URL we're supplying are properly encoded. If they're not, the query strings are lost.

So if we want to retrieve stats for the URL:

`http://www.facebook.com/apps/application.php?id=172944549389721`

And we mistakenly supply that request as:

`https://graph.facebook.com/http://www.facebook.com/apps/application.php?id=172944549389721`

The actual request that gets sent to the API is:

`http://www.facebook.com/apps/application.php`

Which is of course, missing the `?id=172944549389721` section. To actually send the full address, query string included, we need to properly encode the request URL with the `encodeURIComponent` method of ActionScript 3.

See also

- *Loading multiple Graph API objects in a single request* recipe in *Chapter 4*
- *Using logical operators in FQL requests* recipe in *Chapter 5*

8
Working with Photos, Albums, and Tags

In this chapter, we will cover:

- ▸ Retrieving Photo and Album information from Facebook
- ▸ Loading and displaying Photo Tags
- ▸ Creating an Album with the Graph API
- ▸ Uploading Photos to Facebook

Introduction

Besides the text-based communication methods in Facebook, one of the major connections between users is the Photos they can upload and view. Using the Facebook ActionScript 3 SDK, we are able to access information about publicly-accessible Albums and Photos, and of course the Tags, Comments, and Likes associated with all of those objects.

With our application authorized as a user, granted the required Extended Permissions and interacting with the Graph API on their behalf, we are able to load information about the Photos and Albums that the current user—or the current user's friends—have created. When it comes to creating a Photo on behalf of the user, we are able to upload both existing image files and generated images, thanks to the image data capabilities of the Flash Platform.

In this chapter, we're going to cover some of the image-related capabilities of Facebook and the Graph API, specifically loading the Albums and Photos information of the current user and their friends.

We'll also look specifically at displaying the Tags information for existing Photos on Facebook. Unfortunately, tagging an existing Photo isn't a capability offered by the Graph API, but we can use it to create new Photos and Albums, as we'll explore in the latter two recipes in this chapter.

Retrieving Photo and Album information from Facebook

In this recipe, we're going to build an interface which allows us to load the Album's information for a User or a User's friends, and then load the Photos within that Album, displaying the content as thumbnails in a Flex framework List component.

When completed, our application should look a little like this:

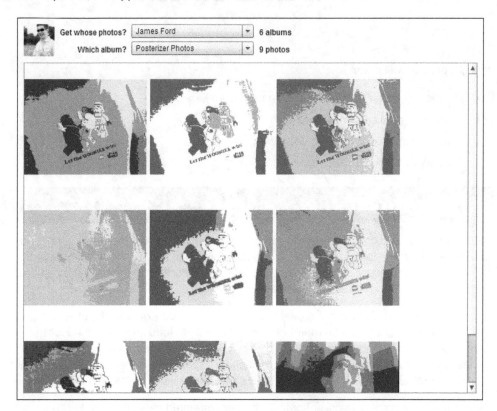

Getting ready

We're going to be loading information about the current user and displaying Photo and Album information from the user and their friends, so we will need to include authentication code which ensures that our application has the necessary user_photos and friend_ photos Extended Permissions. To do that we can build our application on top of the ApplicationBase class detailed in the recipe *Creating the ApplicationBase class* from *Chapter 11, Bridging the Flash and Application Gap* and include the following function:

```
override protected function get requiredPermissions():Array {
    return [ExtendedPermission.USER_PHOTOS,
            ExtendedPermission.FRIENDS_PHOTOS];
}
```

The first step for our application is to create the user interface—we're going to include two DropDownList components—friends_list and album_list—with one for listing the Facebook Users and another for Photo Albums of the selected user. Once an Album has been selected, we'll display the Photos in a List component, photos_list, using an Image component as the item renderer to show the Photo data itself.

The layout of these components should look like this:

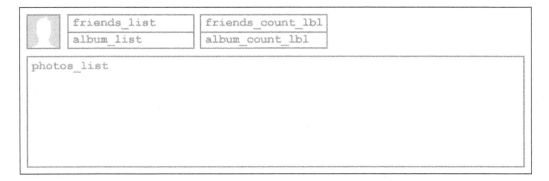

How to do it...

Before we get into creating event listeners or attaching data providers to components, we need to define the variables that will be available to our entire application.

1. There are three sets of data that will be shown in the user interface—friends, albums, and users. To display that information in our Flex components, we'll use `ArrayCollection` instances, with the `[Bindable]` metadata tag. These instances should be named `friendsArrayCollection`, `albumsArrayCollection`, and `photosArrayCollection` respectively. With three `ArrayCollection` variables defined, the contents of the `fx:Script` tag should look like this:

```
import mx.collections.ArrayCollection;

[Bindable]
var albumsArrayCollection:ArrayCollection;

[Bindable]
var friendsArrayCollection:ArrayCollection;

[Bindable]
var photosArrayCollection:ArrayCollection;
```

    Friends are a Graph API Connection so the basic code we would execute to retrieve a list of the user's friends from Facebook would look like this:

```
Facebook.api("me/friends", responseHandler);
```

    Because our application is developed on top of the `ApplicationBase` class we can override the `facebookReady` method, which will be executed automatically once our application authenticates with the Graph API.

2. Add this code into the `facebookReady` function, and the ActionScript should look like this:

```
override public function facebookReady():void {
    Facebook.api("me/friends", friendsResponseHandler);
    showLoader();
}
```

3. Once a response is received from the Facebook Graph API, we should hide the modal loading animation, parse the results from the request into `FacebookUser` class instances and insert them into the `ArrayCollection` called `friendsArrayCollection`.

    In addition to the results from the API request, we also want to include the current user in the list of available users, and we can include that by manually adding inserting `currentUser` value, which again comes as part of the `ApplicationBase` class.

The following code will achieve all of this—instantiating the `friendsArrayCollection ArrayCollection` and populating it with new `FacebookUser` instances parsed from the results of the API request:

```
function friendsResponseHandler(success:Object,
                                fail:Object):void {
    hideLoader();
    friendsArrayCollection = new ArrayCollection();
    var results:Array = success as Array;
    if (success && results) {
        friendsArrayCollection.addItem(currentUser);
        for (var i:int = 0; i < results.length; i++) {
            var postUpdate:FacebookUser = FacebookUser.
fromJSON(results[i]);
            friendsArrayCollection.addItem(postUpdate);
        }
    }
}
```

4. To display these objects in the `DropDownList` component, we can simply set the `dataProvider` property of the `friends_list` component, with the `labelField` parameter set to `name`, like so:

```
<s:DropDownList id="friends_list"
 dataProvider="{friendsArrayCollection}"
 labelField="name" />
```

5. Next, we want to load details about the selected user's Albums on Facebook. Before we do that, we need to add a listener for the change event of the `friends_list` component, which we can achieve with the addition of the `change` property in the MXML tag:

```
<s:DropDownList id="friends_list"
 change="friendsListChangeHandler(event)"
 dataProvider="{friendsArrayCollection}"
 labelField="name" />
```

6. Then when we change the `DropDownList` component's selected index, we need to make another API request, this time to the `/albums` connection.

   To construct this request we extract the ID of the selected item in the `DropDownList` component, and combine it with the `/albums` connection URL. As we make this API request, we also display another modal loading animation, again by invoking the built-in `showLoader` method.

```
function friendsListChangeHandler(e:IndexChangeEvent):void {
    showLoader();
    Facebook.api((friends_list.selectedItem as FacebookUser).id +
"/albums", albumsResponseHandler);
}
```

7. Once a response is received from the Albums request, we need to hide the modal loading animation once more, and this time parse the results of the request into strict-typed `FacebookAlbum` class instances, inserting them into the `albumsArrayCollection` instance.

```
function albumsResponseHandler(success:Object,
                                    fail:Object):void {

    hideLoader();
    albumsArrayCollection = new ArrayCollection();

    var results:Array = success as Array;
    if (success && results) {
        for (var i:int = 0; i < results.length; i++) {
            var postUpdate:FacebookAlbum = FacebookAlbum.
fromJSON(results[i]);
            albumsArrayCollection.addItem(postUpdate);
        }
    }
}
```

8. Next, we need to attach the `albumsArrayCollection` instance as the `dataProvider` for the `album_list` component, along with a change event handler linked to a function which will start loading the Photos from that selected Album. This would require the following additions to the component's MXML tag:

```
<s:DropDownList id="album_list"
                change="albumListChangeHandler(event)"
                dataProvider="{albumsArrayCollection}"
                labelField="name" />
```

9. The process for loading Photo details from an Album is more or less the same as it was previously, with minor changes to Graph API connection URL, the object type that the results are parsed into, and the variable that they are parsed into—which means that the code for our change event handler and the API response handler should look like this:

```
function albumListChangeHandler(e:IndexChangeEvent):void {
    showLoader();
    Facebook.api((album_list.selectedItem as FacebookAlbum).id +
"/photos", photosResponseHandler);
}

function photosResponseHandler(success:Object,
                                    fail:Object):void {

    hideLoader();
    photosArrayCollection = new ArrayCollection();
```

```
        var results:Array = success as Array;
        if (success && results) {
            for (var i:int = 0; i < results.length; i++) {
                var postUpdate:FacebookPhoto = FacebookPhoto.
fromJSON(results[i]);
                photosArrayCollection.addItem(postUpdate);
            }
        }
    }
```

10. Attaching the `photosArrayCollection` instance as the `dataProvider` of our `photos_list` component will display a text-based representation of the results, looking somewhat similar to this:

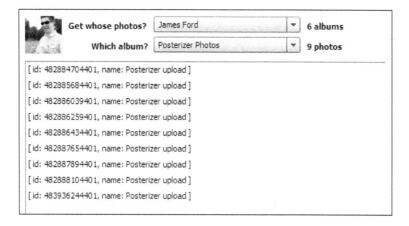

    To display the actual image data, we need to give our `List` component a custom item renderer. Using the `Image` component as an item renderer, we are able to display the Photo content itself instead of this text-based representation.

11. In this instance, we should pass the source URL to the `Image` component, telling it where to load image data from, which is available as the `source` property of our `FacebookPhoto` instance.

    We can achieve all of this in MXML, with the following tags:

```
<s:List id="photos_list" width="100%" height="100%"
    dataProvider="{photosArrayCollection}">
    <s:layout>
        <s:TileLayout columnWidth="200" rowHeight="200" />
    </s:layout>
    <s:itemRenderer>
        <fx:Component>
            <mx:Image horizontalAlign="center"
```

```
                            source="{data.source}"
                            verticalAlign="middle" />
            </fx:Component>
        </s:itemRenderer>
    </s:List>
```

12. Finally, as a little bit of decoration for our application, we have two `Label` components, which we will use to display a count of the items available under each heading. These will be useful for helping us tell whether our application is working correctly!

We can use the data binding capabilities of Flex to get these components to display the total number of items in each collection with the following MXML:

```
<s:Label text="{albumsArrayCollection.length} Albums" />
<s:Label text="{photosArrayCollection.length} Photos" />
```

That's it! What we should now have is an interface which loads the current user's profile, and populates a list of themselves and their Facebook friends. When a user is selected from the first drop-down, a list of their Albums will be loaded, with the total number of Albums displayed next to the drop-down list. When an Album is selected, the number of Photos will be updated, and the Photos within those Albums will be loaded in the larger list component at the bottom of the stage.

How it works...

By building our application on top of the `ApplicationBase` class we are able to easily authenticate with the Graph API, and ensure that we have the required `user_photos` and `friend_photos` Extended Permissions, before we start making any API requests. Of course, if we were looking for only publicly-available Photos, we wouldn't have to worry about these permissions.

A lot of the interface in this example relies on the data binding capabilities of the Flex framework components and classes like `ArrayCollection`. Neither is required of course, but it abstracts some of the complexity of updating and refreshing data, and makes our examples shorter.

 Every Facebook User has at least one Album, even if it's just a *Profile Pictures* Album, which is created automatically, and which cannot be deleted.

Often users will have more than one Album, especially if they've uploaded any images to Facebook—as every image they upload must be placed into an Album. Each Photo can only have one parent Album. If an Album doesn't exist, a new one gets created for the uploaded Photo (more on this in the later recipe, *Uploading Photos to Facebook*).

When it comes to actually displaying a Photo from the data received from the Graph API, we don't actually get any of the raw bytes of the image data returned; instead we get references to where the images can be loaded from, elsewhere on the Facebook network. This isn't a problem for our example, as the `Image` component within Flex accepts everything from a `String` to `ByteArray` data as its input `source` parameter, making it easy to load remote images into our interface.

An example response object from the Graph API for a Photo might look like this:

```
{
        "link": "http://www.facebook.com/photo.php?pid=8172018&id=526
534401",
        "from": {"id": "526534401", "name": "James Ford"},
        "id": "10150145474699402",
        "images": [{
          "source":    "http://a4.sphotos.ak.fbcdn.net/hphotos-ak-
snc6/184351_10150145474699402_526534401_8172018_3360392_n.jpg",
            "height":    324,
            "width":    576
        }, {
          "source":    "http://photos-d.ak.fbcdn.net/hphotos-ak-
snc6/184351_10150145474699402_526534401_8172018_3360392_a.jpg",
            "height":    101,
            "width":    180
        }, {
          "source":    "http://photos-d.ak.fbcdn.net/hphotos-ak-
snc6/184351_10150145474699402_526534401_8172018_3360392_s.jpg",
            "height":    73,
            "width":    130
        }, {
          "source":    "http://photos-d.ak.fbcdn.net/hphotos-ak-
snc6/184351_10150145474699402_526534401_8172018_3360392_t.jpg",
            "height":    42,
            "width":    75
        }],
            "position": 2,
            "source": "http://a4.sphotos.ak.fbcdn.net/hphotos-ak-
snc6/184351_10150145474699402_526534401_8172018_3360392_n.jpg",
            "width": 576,
            "created_time": "2011-02-20T22:26:44+0000",
            "height": 324,
            "icon": "http://b.static.ak.fbcdn.net/rsrc.php/v1/yz/r/
StEh3RhPvjk.gif",
```

```
            "picture": "http://photos-d.ak.fbcdn.net/hphotos-ak-
snc6/184351_10150145474699402_526534401_8172018_3360392_s.jpg",
            "updated_time": "2011-02-20T22:26:45+0000"
}
```

This object contains the URLs of our Photo objects, with the locations supplied to us being ones from the **Facebook Content Delivery Network** (**CDN**). Each of the properties `source`, `picture` and `icon` contain the URL of the image on this CDN, and the `images` parameter contains details of the various size versions of the Photo, versions which are generated by Facebook when the image is initially uploaded.

In this recipe we've used the `source` parameter as the input for our Image component item renderer, which gives the URL of the *highest* resolution version of the image available. Not the most optimal choice, admittedly. An alternative choice for our thumbnails could be to use the `picture` or `icon` parameters, although they return comparably very low resolution images.

Another alternative for retrieving different sized images, now that we have the Graph API ID of the Photo, would be to use the `Facebook.getImageUrl` method, with the size specified in the second parameter—`small`, `medium` or `large`—like this:

```
Facebook.getImageUrl("10150145474699402", "medium");
```

And of course, the final alternative is to use the values from the `images` property of the response, although currently speaking, such data is not retained by the Facebook ActionScript 3 SDK's `fromJSON` parsing method of the **FacebookPhoto** class—so we'd instead have to reference these elements via the `rawResult.images` property of our class instances.

There's more...

Albums and Photos exist for more than just Users, but also for Groups, Pages, and Applications, and they're not only accessible through such a linear fashion, thanks to FQL and other Graph API connections.

Loading Photos, without selecting an Album first

When we consider loading Photos, it's not actually necessary for us to load the Albums at all, because both the Graph API and FQL make it possible to retrieve information about Photos without first specifying the Album they come from.

And failing to know the containing Album in advance is no great loss to the organization of the Photos themselves, as each even has a reference to that parent Album, which could assist us in establishing Photo grouping from a bottom-up perspective.

For example, we could remove the `albums_list` component from the interface entirely, make a few changes to our ActionScript code and build an interface which sought to load all Photos featuring the User, regardless of the Album which they reside within.

Such changes would involve changing the Graph API Connection from /albums to /photos, and changing the response handler to point at the photosResponseHandler function, like so:

```
function friendListChangeHandler(e:IndexChangeEvent):void {
    showLoader();
    Facebook.api((friends_list.selectedItem as FacebookUser).id + "/
photos", photosResponseHandler);
}
```

Whether it is better to navigate primarily through Albums or Photos depends largely on the purpose of an application—Albums help with organization and categorization, acting as a filter, in turn helping to keep the length and number of data requests down, helping them load faster, and generally keep your application in Facebook's good books.

> The /PROFILE_ID/photos connection isn't a simple replacement for our
> Albums and Photos duo however, as the data it returns does not come from
> the same sources. The results of this /photos Graph API connection are
> retrieved based on Photos in which the user has been tagged, rather than
> Photos which they themselves have uploaded.

See also

▸   _Chapter 11, Creating the ApplicationBase class recipe_

Loading and displaying Photo Tags

Photos on Facebook can be 'tagged' by users—either the user that uploaded the original image, or by their friends (or any other user that has access to the Photo, such as a Group member).

A Tag is essentially a link between a portion of the Photo and another Facebook User, and exists as an object with x and y position properties, a name to display at that location, and usually—but not always—a Facebook id property.

In the Facebook website a Tag is represented by a small interactive area on a Photo which, when the user rolls over the area, displays their name as part of an overlay. In this recipe we're going to go partway in recreating this interface, loading the Tags information for the Photo and displaying the Tags as a permanent overlay on top of the Photo's image preview.

Getting ready

In this recipe, we're building on top of our previous recipe, *Retrieving Photo and Album information from Facebook*, which means that the MXML interface and ActionScript code used in that recipe should be the starting point for this one.

In addition to the `user_photos` and `friend_photos` permissions that our application already requests, we will also need the `user_photo_video_tags` and `friend_photo_video_tags` Extended Permissions.

How to do it...

Our application already has image previews in the `photos_list` component, but we now need to expand this to introduce custom overlay graphics. Instead of retaining the existing `Image` component as the item renderer for this component, we're going to create our own custom item renderer which will display an overlay, with a marker for each individual Tag.

1. To make this item renderer, create a new MXML file; name it `TaggedImage` and save it in the `itemrenderer` package.

    Creating a new `ItemRenderer` class in Flash Builder creates an MXML file with the root element of type `ItemRenderer`, and a single child element of type `Label`.

2. Delete that Label tag and add an `Image` and `UIComponent` tag, both with `width` and `height` properties of `100%`, and with `ids` of `image_preview` and `image_overlay` respectively. The basic MXML for this item renderer component should look like this:

```
<s:ItemRenderer xmlns:mx="library://ns.adobe.com/flex/mx"
                xmlns:s="library://ns.adobe.com/flex/spark">

    <mx:Image id="image_preview" height="100%"
              trustContent="true"
              width="100%" />

    <mx:UIComponent height="100%" id="image_overlay"
                    width="100%" />
</s:ItemRenderer>
```

This gives us an `Image` component, into which we will display an image preview, and a `UIComponent` instance, which will be the container into which we can draw graphics using the basic ActionScript 3 drawing API.

3. To use this new item renderer component in our application, we need to switch back to the main application file and change the `itemRenderer` property of our `photos_list` component—removing the existing nested MXML tags and replacing them with the value `itemrenderer.TaggedImage`:

```
<s:List id="photos_list" width="100%" height="100%"
        dataProvider="{photosArrayCollection}"
        itemRenderer="itemrenderer.TaggedImage">
    <s:layout>
        <s:TileLayout columnWidth="200" rowHeight="200" />
    </s:layout>
</s:List>
```

4. Returning to the `TaggedImage` MXML file, we're now going to add an ActionScript function that will draw overlay graphics representing each of the Photo's Tags.

5. Inside the `fx:Script` MXML tag of the item renderer (create one if it doesn't already exist), we should introduce the following code:

```
import com.facebook.graph.data.api.photo.FacebookPhoto;

var photo:FacebookPhoto;

override public function set data(value:Object):void {
    if (super.data != value) {
        super.data = value;
        photo = value as FacebookPhoto;
    }
}
```

This will create and update an additional variable—a strict-typed version of the `data` property, which we've called `photo`. Adding this property gives us better code completion and compile-time checking in Flash Builder.

6. To display the image of each `FacebookPhoto` object we can extend the `data` setter function, so that it changes the source parameter of the `image_preview` component whenever the data is changed, with the following code:

```
override public function set data(value:Object):void {
    if (super.data != value) {
        super.data = value;
        photo = value as FacebookPhoto;
        image_preview.source = photo.source;
    }
}
```

This code is only replicating what we previously achieved with MXML data binding. What we actually want to be focusing on in this item renderer is displaying the Tags as an overlay for our image. And the way we're going to achieve this is by using the `image_overlay` UIComponent as a basic drawing container, and creating and drawing to a new `Sprite` instance for each Tag.

7. As soon as the data setter function has been called, we want to create new marker graphics for each Tag, and we can do that with the introduction of the `createTagMarkers` function, with the following code:

```
import com.facebook.graph.data.api.photo.FacebookPhoto;
import com.facebook.graph.data.api.photo.FacebookPhotoTag;

var photo:FacebookPhoto;

override public function set data(value:Object):void {
    if (super.data != value) {
        super.data = value;
        photo = value as FacebookPhoto;
        image_preview.source = photo.source;
    createTagMarkers();
        }
    }
}


function createTagMarkers(e:Event = null):void {
    if (photo && photo.tags) {
        for (var j:int = 0; j < photo.tags.length; j++) {
            var item:FacebookPhotoTag = photo.tags[j] as
            FacebookPhotoTag;
            addTag(item);
        }
    }
}
```

The x and y values of each Tag can contain a value from 0 to 100, which represents the location across the image as a percentage. So to work out the actual location on a full size image we'd need to draw our object on to the stage; take the image width and height and then multiply it by the x or y value (treating it as a percentage), using code similar to this:

```
var xPos:int = image_preview.contentWidth * (tag.x / 100);
var yPos:int = image_preview.contentHeight * (tag.y / 100);

var p:Point = new Point(xPos, yPos);
```

The positioning of these markers depends on the dimensions of our loaded image, so calling this function whenever the `data` property of our item renderer is changed is simply not enough to position the marker correctly, working on the assumption that our images will not be loaded the moment that the property is set, and therefore the `contentWidth` and `contentHeight` properties will be inaccurate.

In addition, the positioning of our markers in the `addTag` function is currently only based on the full dimensions of the image, but our item renderer is currently scaling down and repositioning previews of the Photos.

8. To cope with these changes of the position and size, we would need some code similar to this, which works out the scaling ratio and adapts and offsets the marker position accordingly:

```
var xMax:int;
var yMax:int;
var ratio:Number = image_preview.contentWidth / image_preview.
contentHeight;
if (ratio > 1) {
    xMax = image_preview.width;
    yMax = image_preview.width / ratio;
} else {
    xMax = image_preview.height * ratio;
    yMax = image_preview.height;
}
var hDiff:int = (image_preview.width - xMax) / 2;
var vDiff:int = (image_preview.height - yMax) / 2;
var p:Point = new Point(((tag.x / 100) * xMax) + hDiff,
                        ((tag.y / 100) * yMax) + yMax);
```

9. Alongside this ActionScript, we will also need to make the following changes to the `image_preview` component's MXML tag, where we specify the image alignment, using the `horizontalAlign` and `verticalAlign` properties:

```
<mx:Image id="image_preview" height="100%"
          horizontalAlign="center"
          verticalAlign="middle"
          width="100%" />
```

By this point, our code should be correctly working out the position at which the tag is located on our scaled-down image preview, so now we need to actually draw that overlay.

10. Our tag overlay will consist of a single `TextField` component, added to a `Sprite` instance, which is added to our `image_overlay` `UIComponent`. Added to the existing `addTag` function, our code should look like this:

```
function addTag(tag:FacebookPhotoTag):void {
    if (image_preview.content) {
```

```
        var xMax:int;
        var yMax:int;
        var ratio:Number = image_preview.contentWidth /
          image_preview.contentHeight;
        if (ratio > 1) {
            xMax = image_preview.width;
            yMax = image_preview.width / ratio;
        } else {
            xMax = image_preview.height * ratio;
            yMax = image_preview.height;
        }
        var hDiff:int = (image_preview.width - xMax) / 2;
        var vDiff:int = (image_preview.height - yMax) / 2;
        var p:Point = new Point(((tag.x/100) * xMax) + hDiff,
                                ((tag.y/100) * yMax) + yMax);
```

```
    var marker:Sprite = new Sprite();
    var textFormat:TextFormat = new TextFormat("_sans");

    var tf:TextField = new TextField();
    tf.x = p.x;
    tf.y = p.y - 20;
    tf.text = tag.name;
    tf.selectable = false;
    tf.textColor = 0xffffff;
    tf.background = true;
    tf.backgroundColor = 0x000000;
    tf.setTextFormat(textFormat);
    tf.autoSize = TextFieldAutoSize.LEFT;
    marker.addChild(tf);
    image_overlay.addChild(marker);
    }
}
```

11. Item renderers get reused and they may also get resized during the course of our application, so we'll also need to be able to reliably remove and recreate all of those Tags that we create.

12. We're going to have to start keep track of the **Sprites** that we create, and introduce functions that will remove or reset any existing markers. We can keep track of them by creating a new Array called `markers` and pushing the Sprites that we create into this Array, with the following additions to our ActionScript code:

```
var markers:Array;

function addTag(tag:FacebookPhotoTag):void {
    if (image_preview.content) {
        var xMax:int;
        var yMax:int;
```

```
    var ratio:Number = image_preview.contentWidth /
    image_preview.contentHeight;
    if (ratio > 1) {
        xMax = image_preview.width;
        yMax = image_preview.width / ratio;
    } else {
        xMax = image_preview.height * ratio;
        yMax = image_preview.height;
    }
    var hDiff:int = (image_preview.width - xMax) / 2;
    var vDiff:int = (image_preview.height - yMax) / 2;
    var p:Point = new Point(((tag.x/100) * xMax) + hDiff,
                            ((tag.y/100) * yMax) + yMax);

    var marker:Sprite = new Sprite();
    var textFormat:TextFormat = new TextFormat("_sans");

    var tf:TextField = new TextField();
    tf.x = p.x;
    tf.y = p.y - 20;
    tf.text = tag.name;
    tf.selectable = false;
    tf.textColor = 0xffffff;
    tf.background = true;
    tf.backgroundColor = 0x000000;
    tf.setTextFormat(textFormat);
    tf.autoSize = TextFieldAutoSize.LEFT;
    marker.addChild(tf);
    image_overlay.addChild(marker);

    markers.push(marker);
    }
}
```

We also need to be able to remove these Sprites—an easy task now that we're keeping track of those that exist, which requires the following changes in our code:

```
function createTagMarkers(e:Event = null):void {
    removeTagMarkers();
    if (photo && photo.tags) {
        for (var j:int = 0; j < photo.tags.length; j++) {
            var item:FacebookPhotoTag = photo.tags[j] as
            FacebookPhotoTag;
            addTag(item);
        }
```

```
            }
        }

        function removeTagMarkers():void {
            if (markers) {
                while (markers.length) {
                    image_overlay.removeChild(markers.pop());
                }
            }
            markers = new Array();
        }
```

13. Finally, to further improve the positioning of the markers, we should also call this `createTagMarkers` function when the image preview is loaded and if/when the preview is resized, which we can achieve by adding it as an **init** and **resize** event handler in MXML:

```
<mx:Image height="100%" horizontalAlign="center"
        id="image_preview"
        init="createTagMarkers(event)"
        resize="createTagMarkers(event)"
        trustContent="true" verticalAlign="middle"
        width="100%" />
```

Finally, when we run our application, it is should look a little like this:

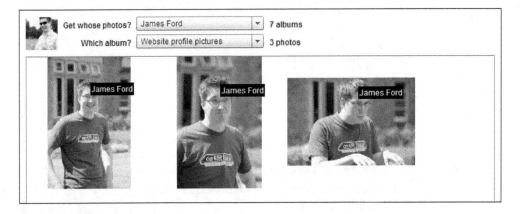

How it works...

When a Photo is tagged, it creates an array of objects containing x and y coordinates, along with id and name properties, as detailed in this snippet from the Facebook Developer Documentation:

Name	Description	Permissions	Returns
tags	The tagged users and their positions in this photo	Available to everyone on Facebook by default	An array of JSON objects, the x and y coordinates are percentages from the left and top edges of the photo, respectively

When we use the `fromJSON` method to parse a `FacebookPhoto` object, we get these Tag objects parsed into `FacebookPhotoTag` objects, and that's what we're using as the basis for our Tags display.

 A Photo Tag always features an x and y coordinate, in contrast to a Video Tag, which doesn't contain any coordinates, only the basic `id` and `name` properties. Tags will always have a name, but they won't always have an `id` property.

The key element to displaying Photo Tags in our application is being able to translate the percentage representation of a Tag's location into actual pixel-oriented coordinates, and we achieve this by multiplying the image dimensions by the x and y values of the Tag object, like this:

```
var xPos:int = image_preview.contentWidth * (tag.x / 100);
var yPos:int = image_preview.contentHeight * (tag.y / 100);
```

Of course, we can't always use the full dimensions of the Image component's content, because the content is shrunk or scaled down. To cope with that detail, we can use the following code, which works out the coordinates when the image is shrunk down to a maximum dimension (being the `image_preview` component's width or height):

```
var xMax:int;
var yMax:int;
var ratio:Number = image_preview.contentWidth / image_preview.
contentHeight;
if (ratio > 1) {
    xMax = image_preview.width;
    yMax = image_preview.width / ratio;
} else {
    xMax = image_preview.height * ratio;
    yMax = image_preview.height;
}
```

With our image component using centered vertical and horizontal alignment, and our own code not accounting for this alignment, we need to work out how much difference will there be between the position that the image appears and the location that the markers originate from. To work that out, we compare the bounds of our `image_preview` component's content and the actual `image_preview` component, like this:

```
var hDiff:int = (image_preview.width - xMax) / 2;
var vDiff:int = (image_preview.height - yMax) / 2;
```

And all of this combined gives us the `addTag` function and its calculations from this recipe.

There's more...

Creating or removing Tags would be the next logical step for this recipe, but unfortunately, we're currently not able to perform either of those actions over the Facebook Graph API. Creating or editing Photo Tags on Facebook can only be done by users on the official Facebook.com website.

Creating an Album with the Graph API

Every Photo object that is added to Facebook must be placed in an Album—there is no such thing as a Photo without an Album. If a Facebook application uploads an image without specifying a target Album, one is automatically created, following a naming convention comprised of the application name and 'Photos'; such as **My First Application Photos**:

Although individual users are able to use the Facebook website to manage their Photos and Albums, we're unable to edit or delete Albums using the Graph API once they've been created. So in order to upload our Photos to a custom-named Album, we need to create that Album separately, before attempting to upload our images.

In this recipe, we're going to create an interface which demonstrates how we could create a new Album using the Graph API. We won't be adding any Photos to this new Album, but are simply creating the Album itself.

Our final interface should look like this, which gives us both a list of the existing Albums on Facebook, and an interface for creating a new Album, with a specified name and description for the Album.

My existing albums:	7 *albums*	Create a new Album:
create album test		Album Name:
My First Application Photos		Album description:
04 February 2011		
Posterizer Photos		
Profile Pictures		
Website profile pictures		
Bowling (2/11/2007)		
		Reset Create Album

Getting ready

The base for this recipe will be the `ApplicationBase` class, which handles basic authentication and permissions checking with the Graph API. The `ApplicationBase` class is discussed in depth in the recipe *Creating the ApplicationBase class* in *Chapter 11*.

The Extended Permissions that we will need for this recipe are `user_photos` and `publish_stream`, which give us the ability to view the current user's Photos and Albums, and the ability to create new objects, respectively.

We'll need a variety of components on the stage for this recipe—to start with, a **List** component, `albums_list`, which will display all of the user's existing Albums; a **TextInput** component, `album_name_inpt`; a **TextArea** component, `album_description_inpt`; and two **Button** components, `create_btn` and `reset_btn`. The layout of these components should look like this:

My existing albums:	Create a new Album:
`albums_list`	Album Name: `album_name_inpt`
	Album description:
	`album_description_inpt`
	`reset_btn` `create_btn`

How to do it...

Before we move on to creating new Albums, we should first retrieve details of the existing Albums and display them in our `List` component. Doing so will help our users by allowing them to avoid giving their Album a duplicate name, and will also help us, by making it possible to refresh the interface after our post request is executed.

1. To retrieve details about the current user's Albums, we can use the following code, which automatically retrieves details of the current user's Albums—in a similar manner to our previous recipes.

```
import com.facebook.graph.Facebook;
import com.facebook.graph.data.api.album.FacebookAlbum;

import mx.collections.ArrayCollection;

[Bindable]
var albumsArrayCollection:ArrayCollection;

override public function facebookReady():void {
    Facebook.api("me/albums", albumsResponseHandler);
    showLoader();
}

function albumsResponseHandler(success:Object,
                                fail:Object):void {
    hideLoader();
    albumsArrayCollection = new ArrayCollection();
    var results:Array = success as Array;
    if (success && results) {
        for (var i:int = 0; i < results.length; i++) {
            var album:FacebookAlbum = FacebookAlbum.
fromJSON(results[i]);
            albumsArrayCollection.addItem(album);
        }
    }
}
```

2. To display the retrieved Albums information in the interface, we need to attach our `albumsArrayCollection` instance to the components, which we can do with these highlighted changes to the MXML:

```
<s:List id="albums_list"
    dataProvider="{albumsArrayCollection}"
    labelField="name" />
```

At this point, we should be able to run our application, and see that a listing of the current user's Albums and their names are displayed in the left side of our screen.

3. Next we're actually going to add the code that allows us to create an Album. There are two properties that can be used when creating an Album—the `name` and `message` (which appears as the Album description or caption), and we're going to pull that information out of the `TextInput` component and `TextArea` components on stage.

   To execute our request when the **Create Album** is clicked, add the following function:

```
function createClickHandler(e:Event):void {
    showLoader();
    var options = new Object();
    options.name = album_name_input.text;
    options.message = album_description_input.text;
    Facebook.api("me/albums", createAlbumHandler, options,
"post");
}
```

4. Once a response is received from the Graph API, we want to refresh the interface, which we can achieve by executing the initial `facebookReady` method once again, which will in turn reload the list of Albums.

```
function createResponseHandler(success:Object,
                                fail:Object):void {
    facebookReady();
}
```

5. Next we need to link this function to the `create_btn` component, by adding this `createClickHandler` function under the `click` property in MXML:

```
<s:Button id="create_btn" label="Create Album"
    click="createClickHandler(event)" />
```

6. To clear and reset the interface, both in response to clicks on the **Reset** button and when a response is received from the Graph API, make the following changes:

```
function resetInterface(e:Event = null):void {
    album_description_input.text = "";
    album_name_input.text = "";
}

function createResponseHandler(success:Object,
                                fail:Object):void {
    facebookReady();
    if (success) {
        resetInterface();
    }
}
```

7. Finally, in the MXML tag for the `reset_btn`, we should attach this `resetInterface` function, using the following code:

```
<s:Button id="reset_btn" label="Reset"
    click="resetInterface(event)" />
```

That's it for this recipe—we can use the two text input components to enter the name and description for a new Album, press the button component to create this Album, and once the request has finished the list of Albums for the current user, we will refresh.

How it works...

Most of the code for this recipe actually goes into creating the interface. To create an Album on Facebook, we need to make a POST request to the `/PROFILE_ID/albums` connection, with the property `name`, as we created in the function `createClickHandler` from this recipe.

There's more...

Unfortunately, we can't create an interface that makes it possible to edit or delete existing Albums—that functionality is currently not supported by the Graph API (as of version 1.6), so the only way to administer these Albums is through the actual Facebook.com website.

The same goes for specifying the cover image in an Album—it simply takes the first Photo uploaded to the Album as the cover, and can only be changed through the official website interface.

Uploading Photos to Facebook

We can use the Graph API to upload an image file to Facebook by either sending the raw file bytes data or the bitmap data of the image to a Graph API Connection—which itself can be either a specific Album, `/ALBUM_ID/photos`, or a User's Photos connection, `/PROFILE_ID/photos`.

In this recipe, we're going to build a Flash Player-based application which leverages Flash Player 10+ `FileReference` class to build an application that can upload an image file from the user's local machine to either a new or existing Facebook Album.

In this recipe, we will be creating an interface which looks like this:

Such an interface allows us to upload Photos to either a user's existing Album or to the user's profile.

Getting ready

As with our previous recipe, we're going to develop our application on top of the `ApplicationBase` class, which handles the authentication process and validates that the current user has granted our application the required Extended Permissions; the permissions that we would need for this recipe are `user_photos` and `publish_stream`.

For this recipe we will need three **Button** components: `select_btn`, `cancel_btn`, and `upload_btn`; two **RadioButton** components: `profile_select` and `album_select`; an **Image** component: `image_preview`; and a **DropDownList** component: `album_list`.

These components should be arranged on the stage like this:

In this layout the `select_btn` and `image_preview` components are positioned over the top of each other—with only one visible at a time. In addition, the `cancel_btn` component should be initially hidden, and our `RadioButton` components will need to be assigned to the same `RadioButtonGroup`, using MXML much like this:

```
<fx:Declarations>
    <s:RadioButtonGroup id="radiogroup1" />
</fx:Declarations>
```

```
<s:RadioButton id="profile_select" groupName="radiogroup1"
               label="Upload to profile (creates a new album)"
               />

<s:RadioButton id="album_select" groupName="radiogroup1"
               label="Upload to album" />
```

How to do it...

To make it possible for a user to select an image from their computer, we're going to use the Flash Player 10+ `FileReference` class. Using this class, our ActionScript code will open the native file browse dialog, and once the user has selected a file, load the selected file's raw byte data. Once loaded, we have access to this raw byte data, which can be interpreted in the same fashion as a remote file would be—in this case, displaying it as a preview in an `Image` component.

1. Inside an `fx:Script` tag (create one if it doesn't exist), add the following code, which achieves this browse, selection and loading process, followed by passing the file byte data into the `image_preview` component:

```
var fr:FileReference;

function onSelectClick(e:Event):void {
    fr = new FileReference();
    fr.addEventListener(Event.SELECT, fileReferenceSelectHandler);
    fr.addEventListener(Event.COMPLETE,
fileReferenceLoadCompleteHandler);
    fr.browse();
}

function fileReferenceSelectHandler(e:Event):void {
    fr.load();
    cancel_btn.visible = true;
}

function fileReferenceLoadCompleteHandler(e:Event):void {
    image_preview.source = fr.data;
    select_btn.visible = false;
    upload_btn.enabled = true;
}
```

Also added to this code are lines which deal with changing the visibility of the `select_btn` and `cancel_btn` components.

2. The next step is to create and add a click handler function to our image selection button, which we can achieve with this addition to the MXML:

```
<s:Button id="select_btn"
          label="Select an image from local file system"
          click="onSelectClick(event)" />
```

With this ActionScript and MXML code in place, we should be able to launch a native file browser dialog, similar to this:

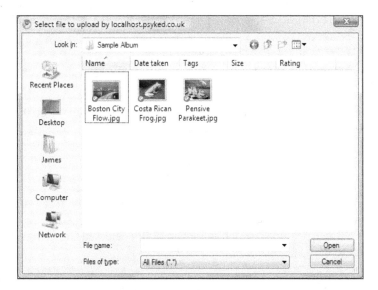

And once an image is loaded, we should see our interface change to show a preview of that selection, like this:

3. Of course, just because we're expecting users to select an image, doesn't mean that they actually will. The image formats that our code will support are `JPEG`, `GIF`, and `PNG`, so to limit the file types that a user can select, we need to go back to our click handler function and add a **FileFilter** to our `FileReference.browse` method:

```
new FileFilter("Images", "*.jpg;*.jpeg;*.gif;*.png");
```

Apply this file filter to our `onSelectClick` function; it should look like this:

```
function onSelectClick(e:Event):void {
    var filters:Array = new Array(new FileFilter("Images",
    "*.jpg;*.jpeg;*.gif;*.png"));
    fr = new FileReference();
    fr.addEventListener(Event.SELECT, fileReferenceSelectHandler);
    fr.addEventListener(Event.COMPLETE,
    fileReferenceLoadCompleteHandler);
    fr.browse(filters);
}
```

4. Next, we need to upload the selected image to the Graph API. To do that, we need to make a post request in the Facebook ActionScript 3 SDK, passing three specific variables in the options object—`fileName`, `image`, and `contentType`, which contain the file name as a `String`, image as `ByteArray` data, and image mime-type `String` respectively.

The filename and bytes data can be easily extracted from the `FileReference` instance, but the mime-type of the image needs to be supplied by our code. We can assume mime-types from the file extension of the selected file, using an ActionScript switch statement like this:

```
switch (fileExtension) {
    case "gif":
        contentType = "image/gif";
        break;
    case "png":
        contentType = "image/png";
        break;
    case "jpeg":
    case "jpg":
        contentType = "image/jpeg";
        break;
}
```

5. The function we'd use to upload selected images to the current user (rather than a specified Album) would be like this:

```
function uploadClickHandler(e:Event):void {
    showLoader();
    var options:Object = new Object();
```

```
        options.fileName = fr.name;
        options.image = fr.data;
        var fileExtension:String = fr.name.split(".")[fr.name.
split(".").length - 1];

        switch (fileExtension) {
            case "gif":
                options.contentType = "image/gif";
                break;
            case "png":
                options.contentType = "image/png";
                break;
            case "jpeg":
            case "jpg":
                options.contentType = "image/jpeg";
                break;
        }

        Facebook.api("me/photos", uploadCompleteHandler, options,
"post");
    }
```

6. To link this function with our button in MXML, add the highlighted code:

```
<s:Button id="upload_btn" label="Upload Photo"
        click="uploadClickHandler(event)" />
```

We're only able to upload to the /me/photos location at the moment, because we don't have any information about any Albums.

7. To enable uploading to specific Albums, we should override the facebookReady function, which is executed when the user is authenticated with Facebook, and have it make an API request for the current user's Albums, parsing and storing the results in an ArrayCollection.

```
[Bindable]
private var albumsArrayCollection:ArrayCollection;

override public function facebookReady():void {
    Facebook.api("me/albums", albumsResponseHandler);
    showLoader();
}

function albumsResponseHandler(success:Object,
                                fail:Object):void {
    hideLoader();
    albumsArrayCollection = new ArrayCollection();
```

```
        var results:Array = success as Array;
        if (success && results) {
            for (var i:int = 0; i < results.length; i++) {
                var postUpdate:FacebookAlbum = FacebookAlbum.
fromJSON(results[i]);
                albumsArrayCollection.addItem(postUpdate);
            }
            album_list.selectedIndex = 0;
        }
    }
```

8. We can use data binding to attach this `ArrayCollection` to our `DropDownList` component, with the following changes:

```
<s:DropDownList id="album_list"
                dataProvider="{albumsArrayCollection}"
                labelField="name" />
```

With the `album_list` component containing a selection of `FacebookAlbum` instances, we can now retrieve the ID fragments we need for our Graph API requests, in order to upload to specific Albums instead of a default Album.

9. To switch the upload location depending on the selected radio button (`album_select` or `profile_select`), and the Album selected from the `album_list` component, make the highlighted changes to the `uploadClickHandler` function:

```
function uploadClickHandler(e:Event):void {
    showLoader();
    var options:Object = new Object();
    options.fileName = fr.name;
    options.image = fr.data;
    var fileExtension:String = fr.name.split(".")[fr.name.
    split(".").length - 1];

    switch (fileExtension) {
        case "gif":
            options.contentType = "image/gif";
            break;
        case "png":
            options.contentType = "image/png";
            break;
        case "jpeg":
        case "jpg":
            options.contentType = "image/jpeg";
            break;
    }
```

```
    if (album_list.selectedIndex && album_select.selected) {
        Facebook.api((album_list.selectedItem as FacebookAlbum).id
+ "/photos", uploadCompleteHandler, options, "post");
    } else {
        Facebook.api("me/photos", uploadCompleteHandler, options,
"post");
    }
}
```

We should now be able to actually upload image data to Facebook, but there are few interface changes that we can add to our application, to allow our users to cancel uploads and reset the interface.

10. Our image selection button is already hiding itself and showing the cancel button when the user clicks it, so the logical starting point is to attach a reset function to this MXML button:

```
<s:Button id="cancel_btn" label="Cancel"
            click="cancelImageSelectHandler(event)"
            visible="false" />
```

11. This button is linked to the `cancelImageSelect` function and by extension the `resetInterface` function, which should look like this:

```
function cancelImageSelectHandler(e:Event):void {
    resetInterface();
}

function resetInterface():void {
    image_preview.unloadAndStop();
    image_preview.source = null;
    select_btn.visible = true;
    upload_btn.enabled = false;
}
```

12. Finally, there's the `uploadCompleteHandler` function, which looks like this:

```
function uploadCompleteHandler(success:Object, fail:Object):void {
    hideLoader();
    resetInterface();
    if (success) {
        // upload is complete
    } else {
        // upload failed
    }
}
```

This function doesn't actually display a confirmation of the success or failure of the upload, but it does reset the interface and hide the loading animation.

How it works...

Here's what the Facebook Developer Documentation has to say about uploading Photos through the Graph API:

> *To publish a photo, issue a POST request with the photo file attachment as* `multipart/form-data`.

Uploading file data in an URL request is a little more of a complex process than simply supplying plain-text values—internally it requires three values: the file name, the file type (as a mime-type value), and the actual file byte data. These properties must be supplied to the Facebook ActionScript 3 SDK under the properties, `fileName`, `contentType`, and `image` respectively, and they are used to create the multipart POST request required for the Graph API. In contrast, any other properties supplied as options for another Graph API request are used almost as-is to formulate the query string parameters of the URL request.

Not all image uploads have to be done using the `ByteArray` data of an image. In fact, there are three types of input type that are accepted by the Facebook ActionScript 3 SDK—`ByteArray`, `BitmapData`, and `Bitmap`. Each of these classes is relatively interchangeable, but different inputs suit different use-cases better.

When supplying either `BitmapData` or `Bitmap` content, we are only required to supply the `fileName` and `image` properties of our API request options object—the `contentType` is automatically inputted as `image/png`, and the image data is sent in a completely uncompressed format to the Graph API.

What about the upload locations? Again, we have this information from the Developer Documentation:

> *"You can publish an individual photo to a user profile with a POST to* `http://graph.facebook.com/PROFILE_ID/photos`. *We automatically create an album for your application if it does not already exist. All Photos from your application will be published to the same automatically created album.*
>
> *You can publish a photo to a specific, existing photo album with a POST to* `http://graph.facebook.com/ALBUM_ID/photos`."

This simply says that, as we've seen in this recipe, uploading to an existing Album connection puts the resulting Photo in that same Album. Whereas uploading to a profile connection creates a default Album for your application, if it doesn't already exist, and then places your upload into that new Album.

To actually have control over the name of an Album, we need to create a new Album, and then specifically upload to it. For more information on creating Albums, see the recipe *Creating an Album with the Graph API* in this chapter.

There's more...

There are a few further options available to us when we upload images to the Graph API—captions, tags, and generated images, rather than ones coming from existing files.

Uploading Webcam or generated images to Facebook

With the flexibility that the Facebook ActionScript 3 SDK gives us, it is almost trivial to upload something that we can draw in Flash to the Graph API. There are plenty of ways to retrieve a `Bitmap` or `BitmapData` of any visual element in Flash. To create a `BitmapData` representation of the current Flash Player stage for example, we could use `ImageSnapshot` Flex class, with this code:

```
import mx.graphics.ImageSnapshot;

ImageSnapshot.captureBitmapData(stage);
```

And this would create a `BitmapData` snapshot of our entire application.

Alternatively, to retrieve a snapshot image from a Webcam, we can add the following MXML components to our application:

```
<mx:VideoDisplay height="240" id="webcam_display"
                 width="320" x="10" y="10" />
```

Then use the following ActionScript to attach a Webcam to this `VideoDisplay` component:

```
function applicationCompleteHandler(e:Event):void {
    webcam_display.attachCamera(Camera.getCamera());
}
```

And when the **Upload Photo** button is clicked, we can use this ActionScript code to take a `BitmapData` snapshot of the Webcam feed, and then use that in our `uploadClickHandler` function from earlier in this recipe:

```
function uploadClickHandler(e:Event):void {
    showLoader();
    var options:Object = new Object();
    options.fileName = "webcam.png";
    options.image = ImageSnapshot.captureBitmapData(webcam_display);

    if (album_list.selectedIndex && album_select.selected) {
        Facebook.api((album_list.selectedItem as FacebookAlbum).id +
"/photos", uploadCompleteHandler, options, "post");
    } else {
        Facebook.api("me/photos", uploadCompleteHandler, options,
"post");
    }
}
```

Adding a message to uploaded images

We can also supply a message with images that we upload, which becomes their caption and possibly the message that appears in the user's News Feed; although the latter is controlled almost entirely by Facebook, with the visibility depending on the volume of other updates in the user's News Feed.

To add a message, add a parameter `message` to the options object during API requests, like so:

```
var options:Object = new Object();
options.fileName = fr.name;
options.image = fr.data;
options.contentType = "image/png";
options.message = "This is my message.";

Facebook.api("me/photos", uploadHandler, options, "post");
```

The rules around messages are practically the same rules as for creating a status update, meaning plain text content only, and less than 420 characters in length.

See also

▶ *Chapter 8, Creating an Album with the Graph API*

9
Working with Groups and Events

In this chapter, we will cover:

- ▶ Retrieving Facebook Group information
- ▶ Retrieving Group membership information
- ▶ Retrieving Facebook Event information
- ▶ Plotting Events on a Map
- ▶ Loading Event RSVP statuses
- ▶ Changing current user's RSVP status
- ▶ Creating an Event on the user's behalf
- ▶ Inviting friends to an Event

Introduction

Exactly what a Facebook Group or a Facebook Event actually is should hopefully, to anyone who's used Facebook, be self-explanatory. But essentially, a Group is a loose association of Facebook users. Any user can create a Group, and depending on the sign-up process specified by the owner for that Group, anyone can join. Similarly, any user can create an Event and invite other users.

Both Groups and Events have a basic set of information—name, description, and picture. Events are obviously time- and location-sensitive, although they don't automatically disappear after they've occurred, and Groups are a more long-term collection of users, with no specific venue, geographical location, or prior connection between the members.

Information about Facebook Groups in general, and a web interface that can be used to create a new Group, can be found on the Facebook.com website, at the URL: http://www.facebook.com/groups, and the same goes for Events, which are similarly available from: http://www.facebook.com/events.

In this chapter, we're going to explore the basics of retrieving information about Groups and Events, their members, and in the case of Events the RSVP status for those users. We will see how we can create and respond to an Event on the user's behalf, and we will use the Legacy REST API to invite our friends to an Event.

Retrieving Facebook Group information

In this recipe, we're going to create an interface which can search for publicly-accessible Facebook Groups by name and then display their basic information.

As the groups we're going to be loading are publicly-available, we won't need to have our application authenticate with the APIs, so the base class for this recipe can be the normal Flex Application tag.

At the end of this recipe, we will be able to search for publicly-accessible Facebook Groups, and present the results of that search in an interface similar to this:

Getting ready

Our first step is to construct the user interface. A wireframe outline of our application and the placement of its constituent components should look like this:

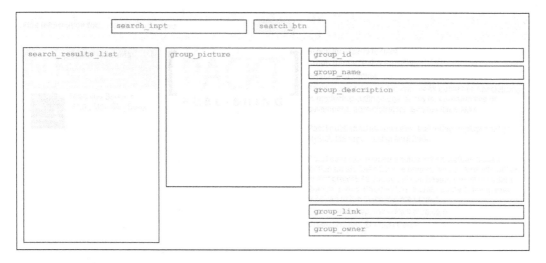

Create this basic user interface in MXML, using a **TextInput** component (**search_inpt**), a **Button** component (**search_btn**), a **List** component (**search_results_list**), an **Image** component (**group_picture**), and five **RichText** components (**group_id**, **group_name**, **group_description**, **group_link**, and **group_owner**).

This gives us a component where the user can input their search query, a button to click on to start the search, a component to display the search results, and appropriate components to display the details of the currently selected Facebook Group.

How to do it...

1. The logical place to start adding our ActionScript code is in the click event handler for the search_btn button.

    To do that, we first need to add a reference to our click handler function in the click parameter of the component's MXML declaration:

    ```
    <s:Button click="searchClickHandler(event)"
            id="search_btn" label="Search" />
    ```

2. Then create a new function called searchClickHandler, which can accept an Event as a parameter:

    ```
    function searchClickHandler(e:Event = null):void {
        // your code will go here...
    }
    ```

    Within this function, we will make a request to the Facebook Graph API using the /search URL to search for publicly-available items by name, rather than by association to other specific Graph API objects.

In the request itself we will need to specify (at least) three parameters: type, q, and fields. The type of the search will be group and the query (q) will be whatever value is currently in our search_inpt component. We specify the fields because we want to retrieve information about a Group that isn't returned as part of the default Graph API response (more on this in the *How it works...* section).

3. The fields that we want to retrieve from this request are the Group id, name, description, owner, and link. With this request and its parameters, our searchClickHandler function should look like this:

```
function searchClickHandler(e:Event = null):void {
    var options:Object = new Object();
    options.type = "group";
    options.q = search_inpt.text;
    options.fields = new Array(FacebookGroupField.ID,
                              FacebookGroupField.NAME,
                              FacebookGroupField.DESCRIPTION,
                              FacebookGroupField.OWNER,
                              FacebookGroupField.LINK
                              ).toString();
    Facebook.api("search", searchResponseHandler, options);
}
```

4. When we receive a response from the Graph API, it will come as an array of objects, which we can parse using the following basic function:

```
function searchResponseHandler(success:Object,
                              fail:Object):void {
    hideLoader();
    var results:Array = success as Array;
    if (success && results) {
        for (var i:int = 0; i < results.length; i++) {
            var item:FacebookGroup = FacebookGroup.
fromJSON(results[i]);
        }
    }
}
```

We can easily take the results from this request and display them in our interface by leveraging the data binding capabilities of the Flex framework—in short, we copy these results into an instance of an ArrayCollection (which is a class that supports data binding) and then set the dataProvider property on our search_results_list component.

5. The following (highlighted) changes to our `ActionScript` function will copy the results of our search query into an `ArrayCollection`:

```
[Bindable]
var groupSearchResults:ArrayCollection;

function searchResponseHandler(success:Object,
                                    fail:Object):void {
    hideLoader();
    groupSearchResults = new ArrayCollection();
    var results:Array = success as Array;
    if (success && results) {
        for (var i:int = 0; i < results.length; i++) {
            var item:FacebookGroup = FacebookGroup.
fromJSON(results[i]);
            groupSearchResults.addItem(item);
        }
    }
}
```

6. To associate this `groupSearchResults ArrayCollection` instance with our `search_results_list` **List** component, that component's MXML declaration would look something like this:

```
<s:List id="search_results_list"
        dataProvider="{groupSearchResults}" />
```

If we run our application at this point, we should see the **List** component populating with search results, which appear like this:

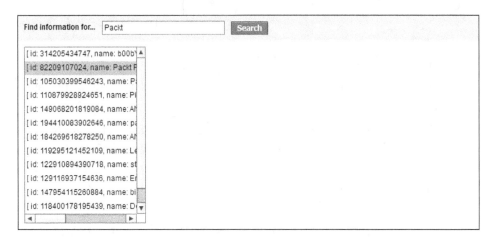

The appearance of the search results list is not ideal, because by default each `FacebookGroup` instance is displaying a text-based representation of the `Group` object, drawn from the `toString` method built-in to the `Group` class.

7. To make the results appear a little bit nicer, we can add a custom item renderer to our **List** component, consisting of an **Image** and **RichText** component.

    To display the name of the Group, we can use the following MXML in our item renderer:

    ```
    <s:RichText height="50" text="{data.name}" width="100%" />
    ```

8. To display the thumbnail of the Group in an `Image` component, we can use the following MXML:

    ```
    <mx:Image height="50" width="50"
              source="{Facebook.getImageUrl(data.id,'square')}" />
    ```

    With an item renderer applied, our application should look more like this:

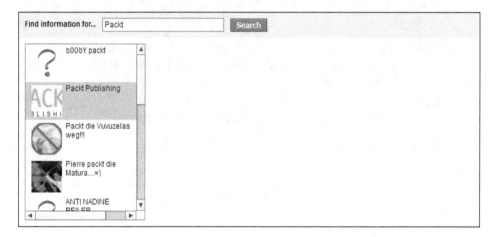

At this point, we've already got all of the data that we're going to use in this recipe available in our application.

9. To actually display the details of the currently selected `FacebookGroup` in the rest of our interface, we will need to attach a selection change handler function in our MXML:

    ```
    <s:List dataProvider="{groupSearchResults}"
            change="listSelectionChangeHandler(event)"
            id="search_results_list"
            itemRenderer="itemrenderers.GroupNameItemRenderer" />
    ```

10. The following function will extract the appropriate values from the selected item and copy them into the components in our interface.

```
function listSelectionChangeHandler(e:IndexChangeEvent):void {
    var selectedGroup:FacebookGroup = search_results_list.
selectedItem as FacebookGroup;
    group_picture.source = Facebook.getImageUrl(selectedGroup.id,
'large');
    group_id.text = selectedGroup.id;
    group_name.text = selectedGroup.name;
    group_description.text = selectedGroup.description;
    group_link.text = selectedGroup.link;
    group_owner.text = selectedGroup.owner.name;
}
```

How it works...

The key elements that make up this recipe are:

- Searching for objects within the Graph API
- Requesting specific data fields from the Graph API
- Parsing the results into strict-typed `ActionScript` class instances

Detailed information and explanations for these elements can be found as part of the recipes in _Chapters 4_ and _Chapters 5_ of this cookbook.

When searching for Groups, the only field that the search query checks against is the text-based query (q) field, as opposed to being able to filter the search results with multiple fields or even locations. Should we want to filter results by searching based on more than one parameter, we would have to switch to constructing our requests with FQL, or simply filter the search results manually with `ActionScript`, rather than relying on the Graph API.

Without manually specifying the data fields to return for a search query, the result we get back from a request like this would look like this:

```
{
"id": "82209107024",
"name": "Packt Publishing"
}
```

As you can see, this response only contains the `name` and `id` properties of a Group, and we want our request to include additional information, specifically the `description`, `link` and `owner` fields. By adding the JSON-encoded array of fields in to our request, the results from the Graph API will instead look like this:

```
{
"link": "http://www.PacktPub.com",
  "owner": {
```

```
            "id": "596491430",
            "name": "Damian Packt"
        },
    "name": "Packt Publishing",
    "updated_time": "2009-11-26T14:40:02+0000",
    "description": "Packt is a modern, IT focused book publis...",
    "id": "82209107024"
}
```

Because of the way that the Facebook ActionScript 3 SDK is designed, the existence or absence of specific data fields has no effect on the success of parsing the loosely-typed API response objects into actual strict-typed ActionScript class instances.

There's more...

The additional data fields that are available for a Group, but that we've chosen to not include in the API request for this recipe, are `updated_time`, icon, and privacy settings. The updated time and icon we've omitted because we're simply not displaying that data in our interface, and privacy we're leaving out because it has no bearing on our results—without being authenticated we can't receive results that are `hidden` or `private`, only `public` groups.

Of course, searching is far from the only way to locate a Group on Facebook. Graph API connections, such as a user's /PROFILE_ID/groups connection, returns a list of Groups that the user has joined. Similar connections also exist for other objects, like /PAGE_ID/groups or /APPLICATION_ID/groups.

Loading the current user's Groups

To switch from simply searching through publicly-available available Groups and onto loading information about the Groups that a user is a member of, we would need to change the initial API request URL from a `/search` request to a more specific Graph API connection request such as `/me/groups`, which would return Facebook Group objects.

With our application authenticated with the Graph API and acting on behalf of a user, we can use the following code to request information about the current user's Groups.

```
Facebook.api("me/groups", searchResponseHandler);
```

A request such as this requires the `user_groups` extended permission, and returns the details of all of the Groups that our current user is associated with.

See also

▸ *Chapter 4*, Loading specific data fields in a Graph API request

▸ *Chapter 4*, Loading a Graph API object connection

Retrieving Group membership information

Just as we can retrieve information about specific a user's Groups through the Graph API `/PROFILE_ID/groups` connection, we can also retrieve information about the members of a Group through the `/GROUP_ID/members` connection.

In this recipe, we're going to expand upon our previous recipe and include a display of users associated with the currently-selected Group. Our final result should look a little like this:

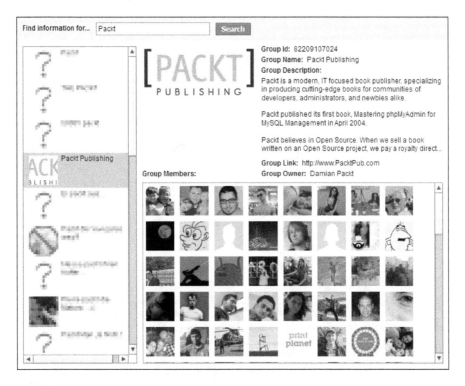

Getting ready

Access to the `/GROUP_ID/members` connection is only permitted when our application is authenticated with Facebook, meaning that we will have to have to ask the user to be logged in to proceed. To do that, we will need to build our application on top of the `ApplicationBase` class, which is detailed in the recipe, *Creating the ApplicationBase class*, from *Chapter 11*.

The basic structure of our application is almost the same as in our previous recipe, with an additional **List** component, `group_members`, added to the interface. The layout of these components should look like this:

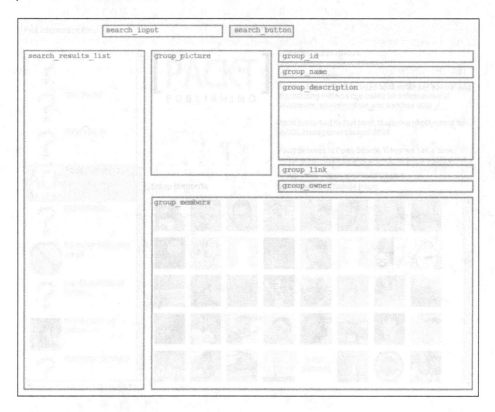

How to do it...

1. Group membership information is available through a Graph API connection, so we're going to have to make a new request to the Graph API whenever the currently-selected Group in our interface is changed.

    We already have a change handler function that reacts to a change in the selection of the current Group, so to make this new request we should make the following (highlighted) change to our existing `listSelectionChangeHandler` function:

```
function listSelectionChangeHandler(e:IndexChangeEvent):void {
    var selectedGroup:FacebookGroup = search_results_list.
selectedItem as FacebookGroup;
    group_picture.source = Facebook.getImageUrl(selectedGroup.id,
'large');
    group_id.text = selectedGroup.id;
    group_name.text = selectedGroup.name;
```

```
        group_description.text = selectedGroup.description;
        group_link.text = selectedGroup.link;
        group_owner.text = selectedGroup.owner.name;
        Facebook.api(selectedGroup.id + "/members",
        groupMembershipResultHandler);
    }
```

2. This additional API request will of course require its own result handler function, which we'll call `groupMembershipResultHandler`. The results of this connection will be Graph API user objects, which we will transform into `FacebookUser` class instances.

   This Graph API response handler function should look like this:

```
function groupMembershipResultHandler(success:Object,
                                        fail:Object):void {
    var results:Array = success as Array;
    if (success && results) {
        for (var i:int = 0; i < results.length; i++) {
            var item:FacebookUser = FacebookUser.
fromJSON(results[i]);
        }
    }
}
```

3. We want to display these results in our `group_members` **List** component, and the way we can achieve this is by putting the parsed `FacebookUser` instances into an `ArrayCollection` instance.

4. To do this, we need to make a new `ArrayCollection` instance available in our application—in this case, with the name `selectedGroupMembers`, and integrate it with the `groupMembershipResultHandler` function:

```
[Bindable]
var selectedGroupMembers:ArrayCollection;

function groupMembershipResultHandler(success:Object,
                                        fail:Object):void {
    var results:Array = success as Array;
    selectedGroupMembers = new ArrayCollection();
    if (success && results) {
        for (var i:int = 0; i < results.length; i++) {
            var item:FacebookUser =
                FacebookUser.fromJSON(results[i]);
            selectedGroupMembers.addItem(item);
        }
    }
}
```

5. Once those `FacebookUser` objects are in our `selectedGroupMembers` instance, we use that `ArrayCollection` as the `dataProvider` for our `group_members` component:

```
<s:List dataProvider="{selectedGroupMembers}" />
```

With these changes in place, once we run our application it should look like this:

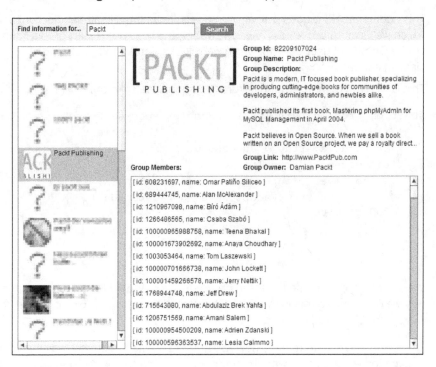

6. Finally, to get our application to display a nice thumbnail version of the user's profile picture, we'll change the item renderer of the `group_members` component to use a custom item renderer, containing an `Image` component, and using Flex's data binding capabilities to integrate with the `Facebook.getImageUrl` method:

```
<s:List dataProvider="{selectedGroupMembers}">
    <s:layout>
        <s:TileLayout columnWidth="60" horizontalGap="0"
                      rowHeight="60" verticalGap="0" />
    </s:layout>
    <s:itemRenderer>
        <fx:Component>
            <s:ItemRenderer>
                <fx:Script>
                    <![CDATA[
                        import com.facebook.graph.Facebook;
```

```
                    ]]>
                </fx:Script>
                <mx:Image height="50" horizontalCenter="0"
             source="{Facebook.getImageUrl(data.id,'square')}"
                        toolTip="{data.name}"
                        verticalCenter="0" width="50" />
            </s:ItemRenderer>
          </fx:Component>
        </s:itemRenderer>
    </s:List>
```

Save your changes, test the application, and it should appear very similar to the image shown in the introduction for this recipe.

How it works...

Group membership is really just a normal Graph API connection. The users that are shown in the result depend on the membership privacy settings for the Group itself, and we can't affect or circumvent the permissions settings for this membership connection.

For this recipe, the information we're using is simply the `id`, which along with the `name` of the user is always publicly available.

We can—of course—always request extra data fields, but unless the users returned in the request have made that information publicly available, or are connected to the currently authenticated user in another manner such as being friends, that additional data requested won't be returned.

There's more...

The extent of the membership information we can retrieve for a Group depends completely on the Group and User's individual privacy settings, but by default Groups have an open membership list—meaning that we can at least see a complete list of the group members, and in turn all of the publicly-available information.

Other permission levels for Groups include a completely or partially hidden list of members—in some cases returning a fixed number of randomly-selected members, but never the full list.

More information on Privacy for groups—including Group Membership – can be found online at: `http://www.facebook.com/help/?faq=220336891328465`.

See also

▶ *Chapter 4, Loading a Graph API connection*

Retrieving Facebook Events information

A Facebook Event is an object which is aimed at storing time- and location-based information, so in addition to the usual name, description, and attendee information, it also has details of the time, duration, and physical location of an Event.

For this recipe, we'll be looking to adapt our earlier recipe *Retrieving Facebook Group information* to have it load publicly-available Events information instead. There is a fair amount of overlap between the information available for an Event and for that of a Group, so what we will also focus on particularly in this recipe is interpreting date information received from Facebook, and where location data is available, plotting that information on a map.

The completed application for this recipe should look a little like this:

Getting ready

Our application layout for this recipe is quite similar to that of our previous recipe, although the components themselves differ a little thanks to the differences in the data we'll be loading. The components we'll need for this recipe are: a **TextInput** component, `search_inpt`; a Button, `search_btn`; a **List**, `search_results_list`; and eight **RichText** components, `event_id`, `event_name`, `event_start_time`, `event_end_time`, `event_location`, `event_street`, `event_city`, and `event_description`.

The layout of these components should look like this:

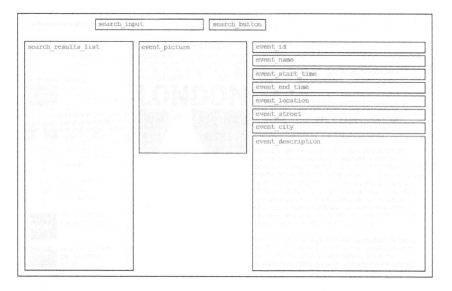

How to do it...

1. As we saw in the previous recipe, *Retrieving Facebook Group information*, the search capabilities of the Graph API allow us to search for objects by name and filter the results to a single object type, with a request like this:

```
function searchClickHandler(e:Event):void {
    var options:Object = new Object();
    options.type = "group";
    options.q = search_inpt.text;
    options.fields = new Array(FacebookGroupField.ID,
                                FacebookGroupField.NAME,
                                FacebookGroupField.DESCRIPTION,
                                FacebookGroupField.OWNER,
                                FacebookGroupField.LINK
                                ).toString();
    Facebook.api("search", searchResponseHandler, options);
}
```

2. To change this request and have it search for an Event, and retrieve the data fields that we're going to display in our application, we would need to make the following changes to our `searchClickHandler` function:

```
function searchClickHandler(e:Event):void {
    var options:Object = new Object();
    options.type = "event";
    options.q = search_inpt.text;
    options.fields = new Array(FacebookEventField.ID,
                               FacebookEventField.NAME,
                               FacebookEventField.DESCRIPTION,
                               FacebookEventField.START_TIME,
                               FacebookEventField.END_TIME,
                               FacebookEventField.VENUE,
                               ).toString();
    Facebook.api("search", searchResponseHandler, options);
}
```

3. To parse the results of this request and put them into a `Bindable` `ArrayCollection` instance, we would need the following function:

```
[Bindable]
var eventSearchResults:ArrayCollection;

function searchResponseHandler(success:Object,
                               fail:Object):void {
    eventSearchResults = new ArrayCollection();
    if (success) {
        var results:Array = success as Array;
        for (var i:int = 0; i < results.length; i++) {
            var item:FacebookEvent = FacebookEvent.
fromJSON(results[i]);
            eventSearchResults.addItem(item);
        }
    }
}
```

4. We can then use the `eventSearchResults ArrayCollection` as the `dataProvider` for our `search_results_list` component, with the following addition to our MXML:

```
<s:List id="search_results_list"
        dataProvider="{eventSearchResults}">
```

5. When a Facebook Event is selected in our `search_results_list` component, we want to display the details of that Event in our application. To achieve that, we create a new selection change handler function, called `listSelectionChangeHandler`, and link it to our **List** component with the following change in MXML:

```
<s:List id="search_results_list"
        change="listSelectionChangeHandler(event)"
        dataProvider="{eventSearchResults}">
```

6. And to display all of the selected Event's properties into our components onscreen, we can use the following function:

```
function listSelectionChangeHandler(e:IndexChangeEvent):void {
    var selectedEvent:FacebookEvent = search_results_list.
selectedItem as FacebookEvent;

    event_id.text = selectedEvent.id;
    event_name.text = selectedEvent.name;
    event_description.text = selectedEvent.description;
    event_picture.source = Facebook.getImageUrl(selectedEvent.id,
'large');
    event_start_time.text = selectedEvent.start_time.toString();
    event_end_time.text = selectedEvent.end_time.toString();
    event_location.text = selectedEvent.location;

    if (selectedEvent.venue) {
        event_street.text = selectedEvent.venue.street;
        event_city.text = selectedEvent.venue.city;
    } else {
        event_street.text = "";
        event_city.text = "";
    }
}
```

This function first casts the selected item as a `FacebookEvent` instance (which it already is, but the compiler doesn't know that at this point) and then sets the text or source properties of each of our interface components in turn to display the information for the selected Event.

How it works...

Much of the logic for this example is the same as our earlier recipe, _Retrieving Facebook Group information_, which searches for Facebook Groups. The difference between this recipe and that one is in the data types received from Facebook.

A Facebook Event can have properties for the `id`, `name`, `description`, `owner`, `start_time`, `end_time`, `location`, `privacy`, `updated_time` and `venue`; a venue can be broken down further into street, city, state, country, latitude and longitude information. Of all of these properties, only the name and `start_time` are compulsory.

Why does an Event have both a location and venue? It's because the location is actually a descriptive name for a location, such as 'Gary's house', rather than the actual specifics of a location, such as the postal address or geolocation.

There's more...

When it comes to displaying the optional properties, like `end_time` or location, it may be the case that those properties are blank, in which case nothing will be displayed. If the venue is empty, and we try to access its sub-properties, we'll get a run time error, which is why we've wrapped the street and city information in an `IF` statement—the street and city information will only be updated if there is a venue object returned for the selected Event.

Understanding and formatting time information from Facebook

The Event start time and end time information that we receive as part of these requests comes in ISO-8601 format, according to the Facebook developer documentation.

 More information on the **ISO-8601** Date/ Time format can be found online at:
`http://www.iso.org/iso/support/faqs/faqs_widely_used_`
`standards/widely_used_standards_other/date_and_time_`
`format.htm`

In practical terms, means that the raw response looks like:

```
"start_time": "2011-10-21T20:00:00"
```

When we convert the response objects into `FacebookEvent` class instances with the `fromJSON` method, this information is converted into a built-in `ActionScript` `Date` class instance. The code we are currently using relies on the `toString` method built into the `Date` class to convert this `Date` into a text-based representation, which then looks like this:

```
Fri Oct 21 20:00:00 GMT+0100 2011
```

A more user-friendly way to display this information would be to use a Flex Date formatter, which we could do by adding the following code:

```
var formatter:DateFormatter = new DateFormatter();
formatter.formatString = "EEEE, D MMM, YYYY at L:NN A";

event_start_time.text = formatter.format(selectedEvent.start_time);
event_end_time.text = formatter.format(selectedEvent.end_time);
```

This would instead convert this date into one that appears like this:

```
Friday, 21 October, 2011 at 8:00 PM
```

 Detailed information about the `DateFormatter` class and the formats that you can specify are available from the Adobe ActionScript 3 LiveDocs, available online at:

```
http://help.adobe.com/en_US/FlashPlatform/reference/
actionscript/3/mx/formatters/DateFormatter.html
```

Plotting Events on a Map

Some Events actually have precise geolocation coordinates associated with them, so wouldn't it be good to display those locations on a map?

This recipe builds directly on top of the final result of our previous recipe—adding only a Map component to the interface.

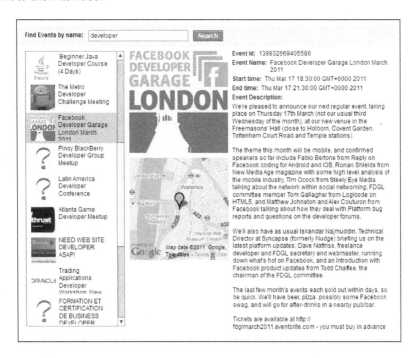

Getting ready

Using the Google Maps components for Flash is covered in more detail in the next chapter, *Working with Facebook Places*, but for the purposes of a quick recipe, download the Flex Google Maps SWC from its repository at:

```
http://code.google.com/apis/maps/documentation/flash/
```

Add this downloaded SWC to your Flash Builder project, which will make the Maps components available to our Flash Builder application.

How to do it...

1. To make the Map components available to our Flash Builder application, we need to add the maps namespace to our application, with a value of com.google.maps.*, like this:

   ```
   <s:Application height="600" width="758"
                  xmlns:fx="http://ns.adobe.com/mxml/2009"
                  xmlns:maps="com.google.maps.*"
                  xmlns:mx="library://ns.adobe.com/flex/mx"
                  xmlns:s="library://ns.adobe.com/flex/spark">
   ```

2. Next, use the following MXML to add a Maps component to the application's interface:

   ```
   <maps:Map height="200" id="map" key="YOUR_API_KEY"
             width="200" />
   ```

3. Whenever an Event has a venue, and that venue has geolocation coordinates (latitude and longitude), we can display this as a map marker and center the map on these coordinates.

   When there aren't coordinates, we'll hide the map altogether. The following additions to our listSelectionChangeHandler function will be needed to achieve this behavior:

   ```
   import com.google.maps.LatLng;
   import com.google.maps.overlays.Marker;

   var selectedMarker:Marker;

   function listSelectionChangeHandler(e:IndexChangeEvent):void {
       var selectedEvent:FacebookEvent = search_results_list.
   selectedItem as FacebookEvent;
       event_id.text = selectedEvent.id;
       event_name.text = selectedEvent.name;
       event_description.text = selectedEvent.description;
       event_picture.source = Facebook.getImageUrl(selectedEvent.id,
   'large');
       event_start_time.text = selectedEvent.start_time.toString();
   ```

```
    event_end_time.text = selectedEvent.end_time.toString();
    event_location.text = selectedEvent.location;
    if (selectedEvent.venue) {
        event_street.text = selectedEvent.venue.street;
        event_city.text = selectedEvent.venue.city;
    } else {
        event_street.text = "";
        event_city.text = "";
    }
    if (selectedMarker) {
        map.removeOverlay(selectedMarker);
        selectedMarker = null;
    }
    if (selectedEvent.venue && !isNaN(selectedEvent.venue.
latitude) && !isNaN(selectedEvent.venue.longitude)) {
        var latlng:LatLng = new LatLng(selectedEvent.venue.
latitude, selectedEvent.venue.longitude);
        var marker:Marker = new Marker(latlng);
        map.addOverlay(marker);
        selectedMarker = marker;
        map.setCenter(latlng, 14);
        map.visible = true;
    } else {
        map.visible = false;
    }
}
```

Not all Events have specified venues, and not all venues have location data—especially location data that includes the longitude and latitude coordinates—which is why we've taken care to validate that the Events have venues and valid (non-NaN) coordinates.

How it works...

Key to this recipe is the fact that the locations for Facebook Events are stored under the venue parameter, with widely-recognized latitude and longitude values. These same values can be passed straight into a new instance of the LatLng class, a key element of the Google Maps components, and from that into a Marker instance, to be displayed on the Map itself.

There's more...

Coordinates for Facebook Events generally have one of the three points of origin: they can be specified by the user through the drag-and-drop interface on the Facebook.com website, they can be automatically geolocated by the Facebook servers based on the venue's supplied address, or they can be taken from location-aware devices such as mobile phones.

> ▸ *Retrieving Facebook Events information*

> ▸ *Chapter 10, Downloading and integrating the Google Maps API*

Loading Event RSVP statuses

Details of those users that have been invited and have responded to an Event are available to us as a Graph API connection, with an individual Graph API connection specifying each status type—attending, unsure, not attending, or not responded.

In this recipe, we're going to build on the application from our previous recipe—which loads and displays the details for a specific Event—and expand it to display a list of users and their attendance statuses for that Event.

In this recipe, we're going to build an interface that allows us to retrieve details of the current user's Events—those that the user has either created themselves or responded to, and then we can see which other Facebook users have also been invited or have responded to the same Event.

Our final application for this recipe could look like this:

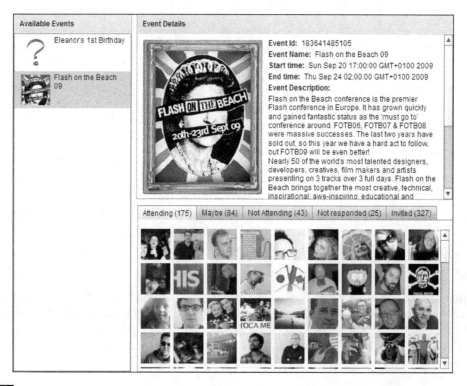

Getting ready

This recipe builds on the final result of the previous recipe, _Retrieving Facebook Events information_, so we'll use that as our starting point. Retrieving any attendee information—even for publicly-available Events—requires a valid access token, which means that our application will have to authenticate with Facebook. To do that, our application should be built on top of the `ApplicationBase` class, detailed in the recipe _Creating the ApplicationBase class_ from _Chapter 11_.

To ensure that we can read the Events connection for the current user, we will need our application to request the `user_events` extended permission.

The layout of our application will also need to change, as it introduces a tabbed component. This component contains five tabs—one for each Graph API connection, and within each of those we have a **List** component. To use multiple instances of these components in the same location onscreen we can use the Flex framework's `TabbedNavigator` component, with nested `NavigatorContent` components containing these **List** instances, using the basic MXML structure shown here:

```
<mx:TabNavigator>
    <s:NavigatorContent height="100%" width="100%"
                label="Attending">
        <s:List height="100%" width="100%" />
    </s:NavigatorContent>

    <s:NavigatorContent height="100%" width="100%"
                    label="Maybe">
        <s:List height="100%" width="100%" />
    </s:NavigatorContent>

    <s:NavigatorContent height="100%" width="100%"
            label="Not Attending">
        <s:List height="100%" width="100%" />
    </s:NavigatorContent>

    <s:NavigatorContent height="100%" width="100%"
            label="Not responded">
        <s:List height="100%" width="100%" />
    </s:NavigatorContent>

    <s:NavigatorContent height="100%" width="100%"
                    label="Invited">
        <s:List height="100%" width="100%" />
    </s:NavigatorContent>
</mx:TabNavigator>
```

How to do it...

Details of the attendees for an Event are available through a series of Graph API connections: `/invited`, `/attending`, `/maybe`, `/declined`, and `/noreply`. To request information for all of these connections, we're going to make five separate API requests once an Event is selected, and parse the results in five different result handlers.

1. To store the results of these requests, we'll need five separate `Bindable` `ArrayCollection` instances, which we'll use as `dataProviders` for our **List** components. These instances are created by adding the following `ActionScript` code:

```
[Bindable]
var attendingUsers:ArrayCollection;

[Bindable]
var invitedUsers:ArrayCollection;

[Bindable]
var maybeUsers:ArrayCollection;

[Bindable]
var notAttendingUsers:ArrayCollection;

[Bindable]
var unrepliedUsers:ArrayCollection;
```

2. To connect these variables with our MXML **List** components, we could use the following code:

```
<mx:TabNavigator>
    <s:NavigatorContent height="100%" width="100%"
                label="Attending ({attendingUsers.length})">
        <s:List height="100%" width="100%"
                dataProvider="{attendingUsers}"/>
    </s:NavigatorContent>

    <s:NavigatorContent height="100%" width="100%"
                label="Maybe ({maybeUsers.length})">
        <s:List height="100%" width="100%"
                dataProvider="{maybeUsers}"/>
    </s:NavigatorContent>

    <s:NavigatorContent height="100%" width="100%"
            label="Not Attending ({notAttendingUsers.length})">
        <s:List height="100%" width="100%"
```

```
                        dataProvider="{notAttendingUsers}"/>
            </s:NavigatorContent>

            <s:NavigatorContent height="100%" width="100%"
                    label="Not responded ({unrepliedUsers.length})">
                <s:List height="100%" width="100%"
                        dataProvider="{unrepliedUsers}"/>
            </s:NavigatorContent>

            <s:NavigatorContent height="100%" width="100%"
                        label="Invited ({invitedUsers.length})">
                <s:List height="100%" width="100%"
                        dataProvider="{invitedUsers}"/>
            </s:NavigatorContent>
        </mx:TabNavigator>
```

3. Into the `selectedEventChangeHandler` function (which fires once an Event is selected in the `search_results_list` component), add the following ActionScript code, which will make a request to each of the five Graph API connections:

```
attendingUsers = new ArrayCollection();
unrepliedUsers = new ArrayCollection();
maybeUsers = new ArrayCollection();
notAttendingUsers = new ArrayCollection();

Facebook.api(selectedEvent.id + "/invited", invitedHandler);
Facebook.api(selectedEvent.id + "/attending", attendeesHandler);
Facebook.api(selectedEvent.id + "/noreply", noReplyHandler);
Facebook.api(selectedEvent.id + "/maybe", maybeHandler);
Facebook.api(selectedEvent.id + "/declined", notAttendingHandler);
```

4. The responses from these requests each go to a different function, but that's only so that the results can be parsed and then easily placed in the correct `ArrayCollection` instance.

   Each response handler function should be similar to this:

```
function attendeesHandler(success:Object, fail:Object):void {
    attendingUsers = new ArrayCollection();
    var results:Array = success as Array;
    if (success && results) {
        for (var i:int = 0; i < results.length; i++) {
            var user:FacebookUser = FacebookUser.
fromJSON(results[i]);
            attendingUsers.addItem(user);
        }
    }
}
```

We will actually need to create five variants of that same function, with each parsing the results into a different `ArrayCollection`. With these functions in place, we can populate each of the Lists in our interface with Facebook Users. Reusing the same item renderers for these Lists as we developed for our earlier recipe *Retrieving Group membership information*, we can easily display thumbnail images of the Facebook users for each of these RSVP categories.

How it works...

There are five Graph API connections concerning the RSVP status of users, but only four possible states for their response. Responses of a specific type are available from the connections /attending, /maybe, /declined, and /noreply.

The /invited connection provides us with an overall view of users that have associated themselves or been associated with an Event. This connection contains all of the results of the other four connections combined, and by default, the response objects contain three parameters—the attendees' id, name, and rsvp_status:

```
{
    "picture": "http://profile.ak.fbcdn.net/hprofile-ak-snc4/195436_
526534401_2125283_q.jpg",
    "rsvp_status": "attending",
    "id": "526534401"
}
```

There's more...

Looking at the documentation, rsvp_status is not a property that appears as a standard property for any Graph API object, it's one that is specific to an Event connection. The biggest problem with this property is that when we convert the response object into an instance of a FacebookUser class the non-standard properties in the response are not copied into our strict-typed object.

As luck would have it however, as of version 1.6 of the Facebook ActionScript 3 SDK, the original response object is retained and can still be referenced through the rawResult property of the FacebookUser class. Therefore, accessing the rsvp_status property for a FacebookUser class instance would look like this:

```
var status:String = item.rawResult.rsvp_status;
```

See also

▶ *Chapter 4, Loading a Graph API connection*

Changing current user's RSVP status

To change the current user's Event RSVP status, we simply need to make a publish request on their behalf to the appropriate Graph API connection URL.

As we saw in our earlier recipe, we can retrieve information about the Events that a user has already responded to by using the `/PROFILE_ID/events` connection URL. However, unless we want to only be able to edit the status of those Events which already have a response, that `/events` connection isn't going to be very useful.

In this recipe, we're going make use of FQL, which has the important ability to retrieve information about Event invitations that a user has **not** already responded to, and then we'll use the Graph API to post back an RSVP response on the user's behalf.

When finished, our application should look like this:

Getting ready

This recipe builds on top of our previous recipe, *Loading Event RSVP statuses*. To RSVP to an Event on behalf of a user, our application will now require the `rsvp_event` extended permission, in addition to the `user_events` permission that we already have.

At this point our application only loads in the Events which our current user hasn't responded to, although outwardly it doesn't look any different to our previous recipe—yet.

To the existing interface, we need to add three new `Button` components, with IDs of `im_attending_button`, `maybe_button`, and `no_button`, to create an interface which looks like this:

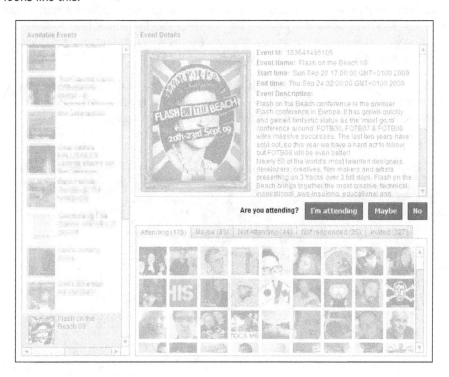

How to do it...

1. To retrieve details of Events that a user has been invited to, including those that they haven't already responded to, we will have to use an FQL query.

   This FQL query would have to initially look at the `event_member` table, to retrieve details of all Events associated with a specified user, and then go onto the main `event` table, to retrieve the detailed data for the `Event` object.

   To retrieve basic Event details—similar to those we'd get from the `/events` connection—using FQL, we'd need to use an FQL request like this:

```
SELECT eid,name,description,start_time,end_time,venue
    FROM event
    WHERE eid
    IN (
        SELECT eid
```

```
        FROM event_member
        WHERE uid = me()
    )
```

2. To narrow these results down to only those results that the current user hasn't responded to, we add the following (highlighted) additional clause:

```
SELECT eid,name,description,start_time,end_time,venue
    FROM event
    WHERE eid
    IN (
        SELECT eid
            FROM event_member
            WHERE uid = me()
            AND rsvp_status = 'not_replied'
    )
```

3. To make this FQL request in `ActionScript` we can use the following code, replacing the existing contents of our `facebookReady` function:

```
override public function facebookReady():void {
    var query:String = "SELECT eid,name,description,start_
time,end_time,venue FROM event WHERE eid IN (SELECT eid FROM
event_member WHERE uid = me() AND rsvp_status = 'not_replied')";
    Facebook.fqlQuery(query, responseHandler);
    showLoader();
}
```

Our response handler function is, for the most part, the same as it was for our previous Graph API response. The exception is the `id` value of our response—with the results coming from an FQL query rather than the Graph API, the `id` is returned under the parameter `eid`, which consequently means that this property isn't correctly parsed into our typed `FacebookEvent` object.

4. To properly convert the responses from this FQL request into the `FacebookEvent` class instances, we need to make the following addition to the `responseHandler` function:

```
function responseHandler(success:Object, fail:Object):void {
    hideLoader();
    if (!eventSearchResults) {
        eventSearchResults = new ArrayCollection();
    }
    eventSearchResults.removeAll();
    var results:Array = success as Array;
    if (success && results) {
        for (var i:int = 0; i < results.length; i++) {
```

```
                          var item:FacebookEvent = FacebookEvent..
            fromJSON(results[i]);
                      item.id = results[i].eid;
                      eventSearchResults.addItem(item);
                  }
              }
          }
```

Our existing `List` component's data binding and selection change handlers take care of selecting Events and populating the interface components.

5. Our three new Button components need to respond to click events, with each one triggering a slightly different Graph API request. We can set this up by making the following changes in the component's MXML declarations:

```
<s:Button id="im_attending_button" label="I'm attending"
          click="attendingClickHandler(event)" />
<s:Button id="maybe_button" label="Maybe"
          click="maybeClickHandler(event)" />
<s:Button id="no_button" label="No"
          click="notAttendingClickHandler(event)" />
```

6. To change the RSVP status for a user, we need to make a post request to the appropriate Event's Graph API connection. The click handler functions for our newly created buttons should look like this:

```
function attendingClickHandler(e:Event):void {
    showLoader();
    var selectedEvent:FacebookEvent = search_results_list.
selectedItem as FacebookEvent;
    Facebook.api(selectedEvent.id + "/attending",
                 rsvpResponseHandler, null, "post");
}


function maybeClickHandler(e:Event):void {
    showLoader();
    var selectedEvent:FacebookEvent = search_results_list.
selectedItem as FacebookEvent;
    Facebook.api(selectedEvent.id + "/maybe",
                 rsvpResponseHandler, null, "post");
}


function notAttendingClickHandler(e:Event):void {
    showLoader();
    var selectedEvent:FacebookEvent = search_results_list.
selectedItem as FacebookEvent;
    Facebook.api(selectedEvent.id + "/declined",
                 rsvpResponseHandler, null, "post");
}
```

Each of these functions makes a call to the Graph API, but the response that we get from any of these requests is either `true` or `false`, depending on the success of the request.

7. Once we retrieve the response of this request, we should refresh the interface, which we can do using the following response handler function:

```
function rsvpResponseHandler(success:Object,
                            fail:Object):void {
    hideLoader();
    facebookReady();
    if (success) {
        trace("Changing RSVP status successful!");
    } else {
        trace("Failed to change RSVP status.");
    }
}
```

How it works...

When logged in as a user, a post request can be made on their behalf, which registers the user as attending, unsure, or definitely not attending that Event. If a user doesn't respond, they simply appear as having made no response to that invitation.

A user can respond to any Event that they can view, regardless of whether or not they've been invited to that Event by another user. This means that if an Event is public, a user can RSVP to that Event. If the Event is hidden, then similarly a user can only see it if they're actually able to RSVP to that Event—meaning they've actively been invited to the Event previously.

See also

- ▶ *Chapter 4, Posting data to the Graph API*
- ▶ *Chapter 5, Loading data with FQL*

Creating an Event on the user's behalf

Using the Graph API, we can create a new Event on the user's behalf. Events are essentially just Graph objects, and as such, they can be created through a Graph API POST request.

In this recipe, we're going to build an interface that is able to create Events on Facebook, and we'll look specifically at how properties like the start time, end time, location, and Event photo can be supplied by our ActionScript code to the Graph API.

Our final application for this recipe should look like this:

Getting ready

Creating Events requires an authenticated user, and that user having granted our Facebook application the `create_event` extended permission. As in our other recipes that require authentication, our application is going to be built on top of the `ApplicationBase` class, detailed in the recipe *Creating the ApplicationBase class*, from Chapter 11.

Our application should consist of three `Button` components; `add_photo_btn`, `create_event_btn`, and `cancel_btn`; an `Image` component: `picture_img`; two `DateField` components, `start_time_inpt`, and `end_time_inpt`; a **TextArea** component, c and four **TextInput** components, `name_inpt`, `location_inpt`, `street_inpt`, and `city_inpt`, laid out like so:

	Basic Event settings:
	Name: `name_inpt`
	Description:
add_photo_btn & picture_img	`description_inpt`
cancel_btn	

Start time: `start_time_inpt` End time: `end_time_inpt`
Location: `location_inpt`
Street: `street_inpt`
City: `city_inpt`

`create_event_button`

In this interface we have two overlapping elements—`picture_img` and `add_photo_btn`. The components `cancel_btn` and `picture_img` should be hidden by default, and overlaid by the component `add_photo_btn`. Once an image has been selected we'll then swap the visibility of both groups of components, improving our user experience.

How to do it...

To create an Event, we need to make a `POST` request to the Graph API `/events` connection—in the case of those Events created on behalf of a user, to the `/PROFILE_ID/events` connection.

1. The first step for our application is to attach a click handler function to our `create_event_btn` component, with the following MXML:

```
<s:Button id="create_event_btn" label="Create Event"
        click="createEventClickHandler(event)" />
```

Now we need to create our click handler function that will actually send this information to the Graph API. For the text-based properties like `name` and `description`, this is as simple as extracting the `text` property from the appropriate components.

2. The click handler function which supplies all of the plain text-based properties for our new Event should look like this:

```
function createEventClickHandler(e:Event):void {
    var options:Object = new Object();
    options.name = name_inpt.text;
    options.description = description_inpt.text;
    options.start_time = start_time_inpt.text;
    options.end_time = end_time_inpt.text;
    options.street = street_inpt.text;
    options.city = city_inpt.text;
    options.location = location_inpt.text;
    Facebook.api("me/events", eventPostHandler, options, "post");
}
```

3. The `start_time` and `end_time` properties of our new Event need to be specified in a format which the Graph API understands, and we extract the selected date using the `text` property of our `DateField` components. To make sure that the format of these dates are suitable to use in our request, we should also be sure to set the `formatString` parameter of the `DateField` component's MXML, like this:

```
<mx:DateField id="start_time_inpt"
              formatString="YYYY-MM-DD 00:00Z" />

<mx:DateField id="end_time_inpt"
              formatString="YYYY-MM-DD 00:00Z" />
```

We're only dealing with the text-based elements at the moment, so our next step is to add the ability to upload images with our request.

4. To start with, we want to add click handlers to the `cancel_btn` and `add_photo_btn` components' MXML:

```
<s:Button id="cancel_btn" label="Remove image"
          click="cancelClickHandler(event)"
          visible="false" />

<s:Button id="add_photo_btn" label="Add image"
          click="addPhotoClickHandler(event)" />
```

5. To allow the user to select a local image file and use it in our request, add the following new functions and `ActionScript` code:

```
var fileReference:FileReference;

function addPhotoClickHandler(e:Event):void {
    var filters:Array = new Array(new FileFilter("Images",
"*.jpg;*.jpeg;*.gif;*.png"));
    fileReference = new FileReference();
```

```
    fileReference.addEventListener(Event.COMPLETE,
fileReferenceCompleteHandler);
    fileReference.addEventListener(Event.SELECT,
fileReferenceSelectHandler);
    fileReference.browse(filters);
}

function cancelClickHandler(e:Event):void {
    picture_img.source = null;
    fileReference = null;
    add_photo_btn.visible = true;
    cancel_btn.visible = false;
}

function fileReferenceCompleteHandler(e:Event):void {
    picture_img.source = fileReference.data;
    add_photo_btn.visible = false;
}

function fileReferenceSelectHandler(e:Event):void {
    fileReference.load();
    cancel_btn.visible = true;
}

function createEventClickHandler(e:Event):void {
    var options:Object = new Object();
    options.name = name_inpt.text;
    options.description = description_inpt.text;
    options.start_time = start_time_inpt.text;
    options.end_time = end_time_inpt.text;
    options.street = street_inpt.text;
    if (fileReference) {
        options.fileName = fileReference.name;
        options.image = fileReference.data;
        var fileExtension:String = fileReference.name.
split(".")[fileReference.name.split(".").length - 1];
        switch (fileExtension) {
            case "gif":
                options.contentType = "image/gif";
                break;
            case "png":
                options.contentType = "image/png";
                break;
            case "jpeg":
```

```
                    case "jpg":
                        options.contentType = "image/jpeg";
                        break;
                }
            }
            options.city = city_inpt.text;
            options.location = location_inpt.text;
            Facebook.api("me/events", eventPostHandler, options, "post");
            showLoader();
        }
```

Once the result has been sent by us and received by Facebook, we will get a response which, if successful, contains the Graph API ID of our new Event.

6. The final step for our recipe can be to receive this response, and for our own testing purposes, to open this new Event in the main Facebook website.

   In our response handler function we can use an `Alert` component to display the success of the result and create an URL link to our Event in a new browser window:

```
function eventPostHandler(success:Object, fail:Object):void {
    hideLoader();
    if (success) {
        trace(success);
        var alert:Alert = Alert.show("Open Event on Facebook
website?", "Event creation successful", Alert.YES | Alert.NO,
this, closeHandlerFunction);
    } else {
        trace(fail);
    }

    function closeHandlerFunction(e:CloseEvent):void {
        if (e.detail == Alert.YES) {
            navigateToURL(new URLRequest("http://www.facebook.com/
event.php?eid=" + success.id), "_blank");
        }
    }
}
```

How it works...

The properties that can be passed to an Event are `name`, `description`, `start_time`, `end_time`, `street`, `city`, `location`, and `picture`.

The name, description, street, and location are all easy enough—they can be free text strings. The start and end times should be date-time strings, either an **ISO-8601** String (such as `2011-03-21 09:34:23`) or a **UNIX timestamp** (such as `1300718063`).

For the picture itself, we can supply the raw byte data for the image file—which, with the ActionScript 3 SDK, means supplying either `ByteArray`, `Bitmap`, or `BitmapData` under the `image` property, along with a `fileName` and `contentType` property.

Finally, there's the `city` parameter of our request. Technically this is a free-text String, but in fact, this value has to correspond to a valid Facebook Place name. If your request doesn't supply a valid place in exactly the correct format, your entire POST request will be rejected.

There's more...

When Events are created using the Graph API, they are created on behalf of both the active Facebook User and the Application that created the Event, meaning that the Event will always have a reference back to our application.

Of course, that doesn't stop you from removing the original owner from the list of attendees for an Event in subsequent API requests; it literally just means that to initially create Events; our application actually has to be authenticated as a user and acting on their behalf.

See also

 ▶ *Changing a user's Event RSVP status*

Inviting friends to an Event

In our earlier recipes, we've looked at how we can view, respond to, and create Events in Facebook using the Graph API. In this recipe, we're going to look at inviting users to an Event, and build an interface that allows us to do just that.

Invites to an Event can only be sent through use of the **Legacy REST API**, rather than the Graph API. To call the Legacy REST API, we need to make a request to the `Facebook.callRestAPI` method, passing in the name of the REST API method and the options for that request.

Working from our previous recipe, *Retrieving Facebook Events information* we have an application which is able to load the `/events` connection for the current user—returning those Events that a user has RSVP'd to and displaying the detailed information for those Events. In this recipe, we're going add new components which show a list of the current user's friends who are not attending the selected Event, and add a functionality to invite those users.

Getting ready

To invite other users to an Event, our application will require the `create_event` and `user_events` extended permissions. In addition, the current user will require some friends to invite and some Events, which the current user has either created themselves or has responded to an invitation to attend.

The starting point for this recipe is the final status of our earlier recipe, *Retrieving Facebook Events information*, and on top of this we will add a **List** component, `friends_list`; a **TextArea** component, `personal_message_inpt`; and a **Button** component, `invite_friends_btn`.

The layout of these new components should look like this:

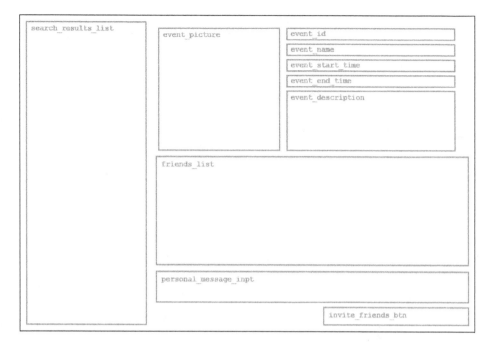

How to do it...

1. The first task is to retrieve details of the current user's friends, that aren't already invited to the current Event.

    We can't specifically request this information in a single API request, so we have to make it a two-part request and compare the results. The first portion of this process is to retrieve a list of the current user's friends, which we can achieve with the following (highlighted) additional variables, handler functions, and changes to the facebookReady function:

    ```
    [Bindable]
    private var friends:ArrayCollection;

    override public function facebookReady():void {
        var options:Object = new Object();
        options.fields = [FacebookEventField.ID,
                         FacebookEventField.NAME,
                         FacebookEventField.DESCRIPTION,
                         FacebookEventField.OWNER,
                         FacebookEventField.START_TIME,
                         FacebookEventField.END_TIME,
                         FacebookEventField.VENUE].toString();
    ```

```
        Facebook.api("me/events", searchResponseHandler, options);
        var friendsOptions:Object = new Object();
        friendsOptions.fields = ["id", "picture"].toString();
        Facebook.api("me/friends", gotFriendsHandler, friendsOptions);
        showLoader();
    }

    function gotFriendsHandler(success:Object, fail:Object):void {
        friends = new ArrayCollection();
        var results:Array = success as Array;
        if (success && results) {
            for (var i:int = 0; i < results.length; i++) {
                var user:FacebookUser = FacebookUser.
fromJSON(results[i]);
                friends.addItem(user);
            }
        }
    }
```

2. To display the results of this request in our application, add the following property to the `friends_list` **List** component:

```
    <s:List allowMultipleSelection="true"
            borderVisible="false" height="100%"
            dataProvider="{friends}"
            id="friends_list" width="100%">
```

Our application should now display all of the user's friends in our **List** component. It's quite possible however, for users to already be invited to an Event, and so to avoid re-inviting those users, we can make another Graph API request against the Event's `/invited` connection and compare and filter the friends list to only show users who are not already invited to that Event.

3. To receive the results of the user's friends and filter them down to just the users which are not attending the Event, we can add or modify the following `ActionScript` functions in our application:

```
    [Bindable]
    private var invitedUsers:ArrayCollection;

    function listSelectionChangeHandler(e:IndexChangeEvent):void {
        selectedEvent = (e.currentTarget as List).selectedItem as
    FacebookEvent;

        ...
        fetchInvited();
    }

    function fetchInvited():void {
        var options:Object = new Object();
        options.fields = new Array("id", "picture");
        Facebook.api(selectedEvent.id + "/invited", invitedHandler,
    options);
```

```
    }

    function invitedHandler(success:Object, fail:Object):void {
        invitedUsers = new ArrayCollection();
        var results:Array = success as Array;
        if (success && results) {
            for (var i:int = 0; i < results.length; i++) {
                var user:FacebookUser = FacebookUser.
fromJSON(results[i]);
                invitedUsers.addItem(user);
            }
            friends.filterFunction = filterFriends;
            friends.refresh();
        }
    }

    function filterFriends(obj:Object):Boolean {
        var rtn:Boolean = true;
        if (invitedUsers && friends) {
            for each (var item:FacebookUser in invitedUsers) {
                if (item.id == obj.id) {
                    rtn = false;
                    break;
                }
            }
        }
        return rtn;
    }
```

Now we have components that allow us to select both users and Events; we actually want to add the functionality to invite those selected users to those Events.

4. To invite users to an Event, we need to make a request to the legacy REST API. The API method name to call is `events.invite`, and the request accepts the parameters `eid` and `uids`, with an optional `personal_message`.

The function we'd need to construct our API request would look like this:

```
function inviteFriendClickHandler(e:Event):void {
    var ids:Array = new Array();
    var len:int = friends_list.selectedItems.length;
    for (var i:int = 0; i < len; i++) {
        ids.push(friends_list.selectedItems[i].id);
    }
    Facebook.callRestAPI("events.invite", invitesHandler, {eid:
selectedEvent.id, uids: JSON.encode(ids), personal_message:
personal_message_inpt.text});
    showLoader();
}
```

5. Next, we should add this function as a click handler for the `invite_friends_btn` Button component:

```
<s:Button buttonMode="true"
          click="inviteFriendClickHandler(event)"
          height="30" id="invite_friends_btn"
          label="Invite Selected friends to this Event"
          skinClass="skins.GreyButton" />
```

6. Finally, our REST API request needs its callback function, which will go on to refresh our application interface once it receives a response:

```
function invitesHandler(success:Object, fail:Object):void {
    hideLoader();
    fetchInvited();
    if (success) {
        trace("Success");
    } else {
        trace("Fail");
    }
}
```

How it works...

To invite users to an Event, you either have to be the original creator of, or must have already responded to an invitation to attend that Event.

As of the Graph API, version 1.6, it's not possible to send invites to users with the Graph API, which means that we will have to rely upon the Legacy REST API instead. Eventually this functionality will be superseded by an equivalent capability in the Graph API, but for the foreseeable future, the Legacy REST API will be around for us to work with.

Documentation of the `events.invite` method used in this recipe can be found in the developer documentation, at:

`http://developers.facebook.com/docs/reference/rest/events.invite/`

10
Checkins and Facebook Places

In this chapter, we will cover:

- ▶ Downloading and integrating the Google Maps API
- ▶ Retrieving Checkin information for the current user and their friends
- ▶ Finding Facebook Places near a specific location
- ▶ Integrating the HTML5 Geolocation capabilities, Maps, and Facebook Places
- ▶ Creating new Checkins at an existing Facebook Place

Introduction

In this chapter, we're going to look at the location-oriented features of the Graph API, namely **Places** and **Checkin**s.

These two elements are intrinsically linked—**Places** are objects in the Graph API which link to real-world geolocation coordinates, existing as locations where a user can register their visit, for a fleeting moment, as a **Checkin**.

Checkins are different than Events, in that they have much more momentary significance—there's not the same level of forward-planning and formal attendance with a Checkin as there is with an Event. Likewise, Places are unusual in that they don't really have their own fixed object type in the Graph API. They exist, but as sub-objects of Checkin objects.

Checkins to Facebook Places are made primarily through mobile or location-aware devices, such as, but not exclusively, mobile phones or tablet computers. With the Facebook ActionScript 3 SDK, we are able to retrieve and create Checkins on the user's behalf.

With the Graph API methods available to our Flash Platform applications, we are able to retrieve information about Places and user's Checkins, plot them on a map, and create new Checkins on the user's behalf.

With the recipes in this Chapter being very location-aware, we're going to require some mapping capabilities in our applications.

Downloading and integrating the Google Maps API

There are, of course, a wide variety of mapping components available for use in the Flash Player, but we're going to make use of the Google Maps component.

Why use the Google Maps component?

Aside from it being a well-supported component, it's freely available. The API makes it easy to plot locations and add overlays, there are versions for both Flash and Flex applications, and although Bing is technically the official supplier of the map functionality for the Facebook website, Bing doesn't have a Flash Player-oriented component (that I'm aware of).

How to do it...

The Google Maps Flex component source files can be downloaded from its Google Code repository: http://code.google.com/apis/maps/documentation/flash/.

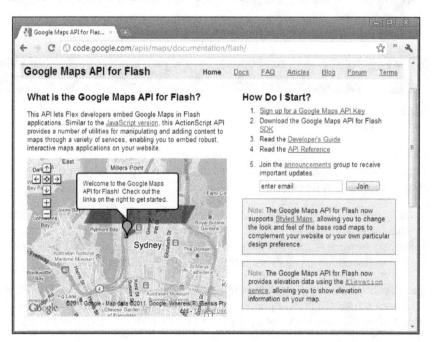

Follow the instructions on that page to obtain a Google Maps API Key, and download the SWC file (which currently is `map_flex_1_20.swc`).

1. To use the Google Maps classes in our Flash Builder applications, add that SWC file to your project's `libs` folder or modify the project's `Flex Build Path | Library path` properties to include the SWC.

2. With the SWC file included in our project, we will be able to create new Map components with MXML, like the following:

```
<maps:Map height="400" id="map"
          key="[YOUR_GOOGLE_MAPS_API_KEY]"
          sensor="true" width="400" />
```

   Of course, we should replace the `[YOUR_GOOGLE_MAPS_API_KEY]` key in the preceding code with the one that we receive after completing the sign-up process. If we don't, or if we use an invalid API Key for the application's domain, we'll get an error message instead of the Map.

3. Finally, if Flash Builder doesn't add the Google Maps XML namespace automatically to our application's root MXML tag, add the following path `com.google.maps.*`:

```
<s:Application height="600" width="758"
               xmlns:fx="http://ns.adobe.com/mxml/2009"
               xmlns:maps="com.google.maps.*"
               xmlns:mx="library://ns.adobe.com/flex/mx"
               xmlns:s="library://ns.adobe.com/flex/spark">
```

Retrieving Checkin information for the current user and their friends

In this recipe, we're going to retrieve Checkins information for a single specific user, who will be selected from a `DropDownList` component containing a list of the current user and their friends. Once we have retrieved that Checkins information, which comes as a Graph API connection, we will plot the location of those Checkin on our map component.

By the end of this recipe, we should have an application which looks a little like this:

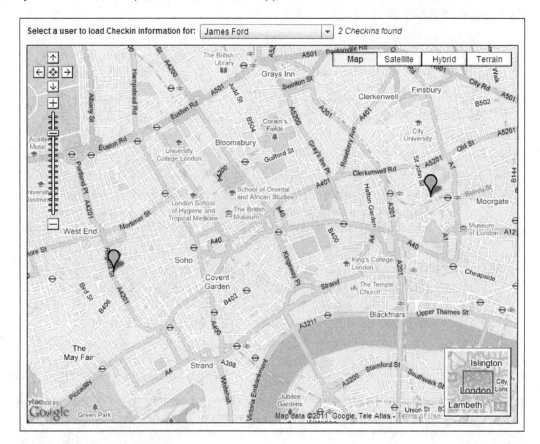

Getting ready

The `/PROFILE_ID/checkins` connection contains protected information, so our application will need to be able to authenticate with the Facebook API as a user, and will require the `user_checkins` and `friend_checkins` Extended Permissions.

To simplify the authentication process, the base class of our application should be the `ApplicationBase` class, detailed in the recipe *Creating the ApplicationBase class*, in *Chapter 11, Bridging the Flash and Application Gap*.

The visible structure of our application will contain three main components: a **DropDownList** component with the ID `users_list`, a **Map** component, with an ID of `map`, and a **Label** component, which for the sake of brevity we'll just use with Flex's data binding (no need to give it a specific ID).

1. The first step for our application (which is not directly related to this recipe) is to retrieve details of the current user's friends, which we display in the `users_list` component.

    To retrieve and parse that information into an `ArrayCollection` instance, we would use the following ActionScript code:

```
[Bindable]
Var friendsArrayCollection:ArrayCollection;

override public function facebookReady():void {
    Facebook.api("me/friends", friendsResponseHandler);
}

function friendsResponseHandler(success:Object,
                                fail:Object):void {
    friendsArrayCollection = new ArrayCollection();
    var results:Array = success as Array;
    if (success && results) {
        friendsArrayCollection.addItem(currentUser);
        for (var i:int = 0; i < results.length; i++) {
            var user:FacebookUser = FacebookUser.
fromJSON(results[i]);
            friendsArrayCollection.addItem(user);
        }
        users_list.selectedIndex = 0;
        users_list.dispatchEvent(new IndexChangeEvent(IndexChangeE
vent.CHANGE, false, false, -1, 0));
    }
}
```

2. And to display that information in our `users_list` component, we would add the following MXML properties:

```
<s:DropDownList id="users_list"
                dataProvider="{friendsArrayCollection}"
                labelField="name" />
```

How to do it...

Our application interface now includes a `DropDownList` component populated with a list of the user's friends, and our Google Maps component.

1. With a `DropDownList` of viable users ready to be selected, we add a selection change event handler function to our `users_list` component:

```
<s:DropDownList id="users_list"
                change="usersListChangeHandler(event)"
                dataProvider="{friendsArrayCollection}"
                labelField="name" />
```

Checkin information for a user can be retrieved through their `/PROFILE_ID/ checkins` connection, with a `Facebook.api` request such as this:

```
Facebook.api(user.id + "/checkins", checkinsResponseHandler);
```

2. When the current selection in `users_list` component changes, the `usersListChangeHandler` function is triggered, which requests the selected user's `/checkins` connection, like so:

```
function usersListChangeHandler(e:IndexChangeEvent):void {
    var user:FacebookUser = (users_list.selectedItem as
FacebookUser);
    Facebook.api(user.id + "/checkins", checkinsResponseHandler);
}
```

3. As with all other Graph API connections, a successful response consists of an Array of Objects; using the fromJSON method we should iterate those Objects into strict-typed FacebookCheckin class instances, using the following code:

```
function checkinsResponseHandler(success:Object,
                                 fail:Object):void {
    var results:Array = success as Array;
    if (success && results) {
        for (var i:int = 0; i < results.length; i++) {
            var checkin:FacebookCheckin = FacebookCheckin.
fromJSON(results[i]);
        }
    }
}
```

By default, the Graph API returns an object containing the properties `created_ time`, `place`, `id`, `from`, and `application`, similar to the following object:

```
{
    "created_time": "2011-01-18T13:41:40+0000",
    "place": {
        "location": {
            "city": "Uppingham",
            "zip": "LE15 9NY",
            "street": "1A Uppingham Gate, Ayston Road",
            "longitude": -0.72281,
            "country": "United Kingdom",
            "latitude": 52.58999
        },
        "id": "144796688910339",
```

```
    "name": "MMT Digital"
    },
    "id": "10150126003639402",
    "from": {"id": "526534401", "name": "James Ford"},
    "application": {"id": "6628568379",
    "name": "Facebook for iPhone"}
}
```

To place a Marker on our Google Maps component, we first need to extract the Checkin coordinates and use them to create a new `LatLng` class instance. We can then use that instance to create a new `Marker`, and then add that marker to our `Map` component:

```
var latlng:LatLng = new LatLng(checkin.place.location.latitude,
checkin.place.location.longitude);
var marker:Marker = new Marker(latlng);
map.addOverlay(marker);
```

Of course, we can't simply constantly keep adding new Markers to our map component every time the selected user is changed.

There are many ways to manage markers, but one easy way to do it is to keep track of the active markers by adding them to an Array when they're created, and before adding a new batch of markers, iterate through that Array and remove the old markers.

4. To better manage the Google Map Markers in our application, add a new application-wide variable called `currentMakers`; a new function, `removeMakers`; and introduce the highlighted code to the existing `checkinsResponseHandler` function:

```
var currentMarkers:Array;

function removeMarkers():void {
    if (currentMarkers) {
        for (var i:int = 0; i < currentMarkers.length; i++) {
            map.removeOverlay(currentMarkers[i]);
        }
    }
    currentMarkers = new Array();
}

function checkinsResponseHandler(success:Object,
                                 fail:Object):void {
    var results:Array = success as Array;
    if (success && results) {
        removeMarkers();
        for (var i:int = 0; i < results.length; i++) {
```

```
                var checkin:FacebookCheckin = FacebookCheckin.
        fromJSON(results[i]);
                var latlng:LatLng = new LatLng(checkin.place.location.
        latitude, checkin.place.location.longitude);
                var marker:Marker = new Marker(latlng);
                map.addOverlay(marker);
                currentMarkers.push(marker);
            }
        }
    }
```

5. We're almost finished—for our final step we want to adjust the position and scale of the map to focus on those new Markers.

We can do that with the help of the `LatLngBounds` class, which calculates the required map center point and zoom level needed to display all of the Markers.

The process for this is to first create an instance of the `LatLngBounds` class, and then use the `LatLngBounds.extend` method to pass in a series of `LatLng` instances. As we do this, the dimensions of the `LatLngBounds` class automatically extend to visually encapsulate the coordinates we pass in. Once we've passed in all of the Markers, we can use the `Map.setCenter` method in conjunction with that `LatLngBounds` instance to change the map center and zoom level to appropriate values. To do all of this, we need to make the following (highlighted) changes to the `checkinsResponseHandler` function:

```
function checkinsResponseHandler(success:Object,
                                 fail:Object):void {
    var results:Array = success as Array;
    if (success && results) {
        removeMarkers();
        var bounds:LatLngBounds = new LatLngBounds();
        for (var i:int = 0; i < results.length; i++) {
            var checkin:FacebookCheckin =
                FacebookCheckin.fromJSON(results[i]);
            var latlng:LatLng = new LatLng(checkin.place.location.
                latitude, checkin.place.location.longitude);
            var marker:Marker = new Marker(latlng);
            map.addOverlay(marker);
            bounds.extend(latlng);
            currentMarkers.push(marker);
        }
        map.setCenter(bounds.getCenter(),
                      map.getBoundsZoomLevel(bounds));
    }
}
```

How it works...

The default visibility of a user's /checkins connection restricts access to those Checkins to only that user's friends, which is why we go through the process of retrieving friends initially—few users go through the process of changing their settings to make their Checkins *more* publicly available, in my experience.

Plotting Facebook Checkins on a Map is a simple process because the coordinate system of the Checkins matches the coordinates system used by our Google Maps component. The coordinates themselves are not actually the coordinates that the user was physically at when they checked in, but rather the coordinates of the *Facebook Place* that they checked into, which don't necessarily have to be the same.

What's included in the /PROFILE_ID/checkins connection?

The /PROFILE_ID/checkins connection contains a combination of the Checkins that the user has actually created themselves, and other Checkins that have been made on their behalf (for example, when they are tagged at a location by one of their friends). As far as inclusion in the Graph API connection goes, there is no distinction between being tagged by others and being the instigator of the Check in.

There's more...

Like all other Graph API connections, we can narrow the scope of our request using options such as limit or since, such as when we want to find the most recent location.

Finding the user's most recent Checkin

The Checkins connection naturally returns data with the most recent items being first in the list of responses. So to find the user's most recent Checkin, we can simply add a limit parameter with a value of 1 to our request, like this:

```
var options:Object = new Object();
    options.limit = 1;
    Facebook.api(users_list.selectedItem.id + "/checkins",
    checkinsResponseHandler, options);
```

If we use this limit in conjunction with the rest of the code in this recipe, we'll see that our application now pinpoints the user's last known location, and centers the map around it, selecting the highest-available zoom level for the map at that location.

Exploring Checkins at a specific Place

In addition to exploring a specific user's Checkins, we can also explore Checkins from users at a specific location with the `/PAGE_ID/checkins` connection, although the same data access restrictions apply to this connection—meaning that unless the current user is a friend of the user who has checked in at that location, we won't see the details of their Checkin.

We can still retrieve a total Checkin count for a Facebook Place through that Place's `checkins` property, but without being friends with at least one of the users that has checked in to that location, or one of those checked-in users having made all of their Checkins publicly-available by default, the Graph API connection will always return empty results.

Finding Facebook Places near a specific location

In this recipe, we're going to create an application which can search for Facebook Places within a certain distance of specific location coordinates.

Our application will combine the current location of a map component's viewport with the Graph API's Place search capabilities: reading in the current center of the map, constructing a nearby Places search query, parsing the results of that query, and using markers to plot those Places on our map component.

At the end of this recipe, we should have an application which looks a little like this:

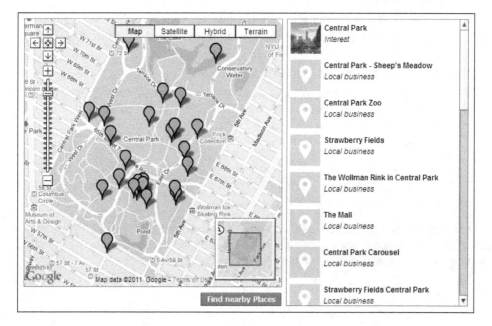

Getting ready

The layout of our components for this recipe will be rather simple, consisting of only three components—a **List** component with an **id** of `place_results`; a **Button** component, `load_button`; and a **Map** component, with an **id** of `map`.

Requesting Places data from the Graph API requires that our application be authenticated with the Graph API, so to simplify the authentication process, the base class of our application should be the `ApplicationBase` class, as detailed in the recipe _Creating the ApplicationBase class_, from _Chapter 11_, although we don't actually need any specific Extended Permissions from Facebook—just the authentication and the `access_token` it gives our application.

1. Before we begin searching for nearby Places, we're going to specify the center point of our map component, using following ActionScript function, which will center our map on the location `40.767983, -73.976999` (which corresponds to Central Park, Manhattan):

```
function onMapReady(e:MapEvent):void {
    var location:LatLng = new LatLng(40.767983, -73.976999);
    map.setCenter(location, 14, MapType.NORMAL_MAP_TYPE);
}
```

2. We can link this function to our MXML component declaration using the following code:

```
<maps:Map id="map" key="[YOUR_API_KEY]"
          mapevent_mapready="onMapReady(event)"
          sensor="true" />
```

The center point of the map doesn't actually matter—it's just going to be easier to specify a location than pick the default map location, which points at the middle of an ocean!

How to do it...

The complete Graph API request URL that we would need to generate in order to search for Places around a geolocation might look like this:

```
http://graph.facebook.com/search?type=place&center=40.767983,-
73.976999
```

This essentially boils down to a search across the entire Graph API, for objects of type 'place', within the default 1000 m of the center of Central Park.

1. We can construct this request with the following ActionScript code, which uses the value `search` as the request URL, and the data for the parameters `type` and `center` in the request options:

```
function mapClickHandler(e:Event = null):void {
    var location:LatLng = map.getCenter();
    var options:Object = new Object();
    options.type = "place";
    options.center = location.lat() + "," + location.lng();
    Facebook.api("search", placeSearchResponseHandler, options);
}
```

   As the name of this function—`mapClickHandler`—implies, this code should be the click handler function for our `load_button` component. In our application, the user can use the integrated controls to Pan and Zoom their way around the map and, once they've focused on a location, click that button to search for nearby places.

2. We can associate the `load_button` component with this click handler function in MXML, like so:

```
<s:Button id="load_button" label="Find nearby Places"
        click="mapClickHandler(event)" />
```

3. To parse the responses from this request we would use the following code, which creates an `ArrayCollection` instance, populated by `FacebookPlace` class instances:

```
[Bindable]
private var placeResults:ArrayCollection;

function placeSearchResponseHandler(success:Object,
                                     fail:Object):void {
    placeResults = new ArrayCollection();
    var results:Array = success as Array;
    if (success && results) {
        for (var i:int = 0; i < results.length; i++) {
            var place:FacebookPage = FacebookPage.
fromJSON(results[i]);
            placeResults.addItem(place);
        }
    }
}
```

To create a marker for a location in the `map` component, we first define the marker's coordinates using a `LatLng` class instance, and then create an instance of type `Marker`, which is added to the `map` component, using the following code:

```
var location:LatLng = new LatLng(40.736072, -73.992062);
var marker:Marker = new Marker();
map.addOverlay(marker);
```

4. Add this code to our existing `placeSearchResponseHandler` function and it should look like this:

```
[Bindable]
var placeResults:ArrayCollection;

function placeSearchResponseHandler(success:Object,
                                    fail:Object):void {
    placeResults = new ArrayCollection();
    var results:Array = success as Array;
    if (success && results) {
        for (var i:int = 0; i < results.length; i++) {
            var place:FacebookPage = FacebookPage.
fromJSON(results[i]);
            var latlng:LatLng = new LatLng(
                place.location.latitude, place.location.longitude);
            var marker:Marker = new Marker(latlng);
            map.addOverlay(marker);
            placeResults.addItem(place);
        }
    }
}
```

5. As before, we can't keep constantly adding new Markers to our map component every time the user clicks the `load_button` component. We'll follow the same marker management practice as in our previous recipe, and add a new variable to the application called `currentMakers`; a new function, `removeMakers`; and then make the code changes highlighted in the following code to the existing `placeSearchResponseHandler` function:

```
var currentMarkers:Array;

function removeMarkers():void {
    if (currentMarkers) {
        for (var i:int = 0; i < currentMarkers.length; i++) {
            map.removeOverlay(currentMarkers[i]);
        }
    }
}
```

```
                currentMarkers = new Array();
        }


        function placeSearchResponseHandler(success:Object,
                                            fail:Object):void {
            placeResults = new ArrayCollection();
            removeMarkers();
            var results:Array = success as Array;
            if (success && results) {
                for (var i:int = 0; i < results.length; i++) {
                    var place:FacebookPage = FacebookPage.
        fromJSON(results[i]);
                    var latlng:LatLng = new LatLng(place.location.
        latitude, place.location.longitude);
                    var marker:Marker = new Marker(latlng);
                    map.addOverlay(marker);
                    currentMarkers.push(marker);
                    placeResults.addItem(place);
                }
            }
        }
```

This ensures that each time a search is performed, the old markers are removed and a new set of map markers are created, removing any potential for erroneous or duplicated markers.

6. Finally, it would be useful to change the center and zoom level of our Map component to focus better on the Markers we've added. Add the following lines of code to the results parsing function, `placeSearchResponseHandler`:

```
        function placeSearchResponseHandler(success:Object,
                                            fail:Object):void {
            placeResults = new ArrayCollection();
            removeMarkers();
            var results:Array = success as Array;
            if (success && results) {
                var bounds:LatLngBounds = new LatLngBounds();
                for (var i:int = 0; i < results.length; i++) {
                    var place:FacebookPage =
                    FacebookPage.fromJSON(results[i]);
                    var latlng:LatLng = new LatLng(place.location.
                    latitude, place.location.longitude);
                    var marker:Marker = new Marker(latlng);
                    map.addOverlay(marker);
                    currentMarkers.push(marker);
                    placeResults.addItem(place);
                    bounds.extend(latlng);
```

```
            }
        map.setCenter(bounds.getCenter(), map.getBoundsZoomLevel(b
    ounds));
        }
    }
```

As with our previous recipe, with these additions, we're creating an instance of the `LatLngBounds` class, looping through the locations and with each successive location we're calling the `LatLngBounds.extend` method, which extends the dimensions of that `LatLngBounds` instance, if it's necessary to do so. Once we've iterated through all of the locations returned by our API request, we move and focus the center of the Map component using the `setCenter` method.

How it works...

A Facebook **Place** is an odd object to classify—in the Graph API documentation you'll see that there is in fact no standalone 'Place' object, although there are **Checkin** objects, which then have places listed as a sub-object of the Checkin. Yet within the FQL documentation, there is a dedicated `place` table available to query for information.

 General information about the purpose and scope of Facebook Places can be found online, at the URL: `http://www.facebook.com/places`

Typically, a Place comes into existence on Facebook as a result of either a location-based Check in from one of the official Facebook mobile device applications or from a Check in from the Facebook mobile-optimized website. They can also be created by extending a standard user-created Facebook Page, but again only by using the official Facebook.com website.

There's more...

There's one outstanding option that we haven't discussed with our Places search, and that's the `distance` parameter.

Searching for Places within a specific distance

In addition to the `location` and `type` parameters of our search, we can also manually specify a distance from the location, in units of metres, which the results have to be within.

Performing such a search is simply a case of adding a `distance` property to the request's options Object, such as this:

```
var location:LatLng = map.getCenter();
var options:Object = new Object();
options.type = "place";
```

```
options.center = location.lat() + "," + location.lng();
options.distance = 100;
Facebook.api("search", placeSearchResponseHandler, options);
```

If we omit the `distance` parameter from our request, it defaults to a value of 1 km, giving us a potentially huge number of results (although these will of course be limited by the standard Graph API response length limits).

Creating and using custom Map Markers for our Places

We don't have to use the standard Google Map Markers in our application—instead we can choose to display custom Flash or Flex components, by changing the initial options we supply when we create that marker.

Particularly useful for this recipe, we can use these custom Markers to display a Place's image thumbnail and name, such as this:

A Map Marker can be any class which extends the `DisplayObject` class. In this case, we're going to combine the familiar workings of the Flex framework's `ItemRenderer` class and use that as the basis for our Markers.

1. Create a new MXML component, call it `PlaceSummaryMarker`, and into it add an `Image` and a `Label` component, with IDs of `place_pic` and `place_name` respectively.

2. Into this component, add the following ActionScript function, which we can use to supply a `FacebookPlace` class instance, and immediately update the component's image thumbnail and place name:

```
public function setPlace(value:FacebookPlace):void {
    place_pic.source = Facebook.getImageUrl(value.id);
    place_name.text = value.name;
}
```

3. When we're creating new map marker instances, we can use this component instead of the default, and we can supply it a `FacebookPlace` instance at the point of its creation, like the following:

```
var markerIcon:PlaceSummaryMarker = new PlaceSummaryMarker();
    markerIcon.setPlace(place);
```

4. To use a custom marker in on our map component, we supply a `MarkerOptions` instance as the second parameter of our `Marker` class instance, like this:

```
var markerOptions:MarkerOptions = new MarkerOptions();
var marker:Marker = new Marker(latlng, markerOptions);
```

We supply a reference to this marker through the `MarkerOption` instance's `icon` property, setting the `iconOffset` property to specify the relative center point of our marker, like so:

```
var markerIcon:PlaceSummaryMarker = new PlaceSummaryMarker();

var markerOptions:MarkerOptions = new MarkerOptions();
    markerOptions.icon = markerIcon;
    markerOptions.iconOffset = new Point(-30, -69);
var marker:Marker = new Marker(latlng, markerOptions);

map.addOverlay(marker);
```

If we supply a Marker `icon` without the `iconOffset` parameter, the point of origin for our marker is the top-left corner of the component. We supply an instance of the `Point` class to act as a relative offset for this top corner—in this case `-30` and `-69`—which tells the Google Maps component to position the component 30 pixels left and 69 pixels upwards of the actual point on the map, aligning the tip of the component's background graphic with the location on the map.

> More complete information about Map Markers, and their options, is best found online in the official documentation for the Google Maps for Flash API:
>
> `http://code.google.com/apis/maps/documentation/flash/intro.html`

See also

▸   *Chapter 4, Using the search capabilities of the Graph API*

Integrating with HTML5 geolocation capabilities, Maps, and Facebook Places

Modern desktop browsers, like Google Chrome 5+, Firefox 3.5+, Safari 5+, and Internet Explorer 9+ can have scarily-accurate geolocation capabilities, even without an actual, physical GPS unit attached to your machine. These capabilities are now standardized into HTML5, and with some clever JavaScript and ExternalInterface usage our Flash Player application can hook directly in to the browser's geolocation data capabilities.

In this recipe we're going to build on our earlier recipe, *Finding Facebook Places near a specific location*, and move the center of our map component—and in turn, the center point for our Facebook Places search—based on the location data returned by the user's web browser.

Getting ready

The starting point for this application should be the end result of our previous recipe, *Finding Facebook Places near a specific location*. We'll also need to be using a browser that supports the HTML5 geolocation API, such as one of those listed in the previous paragraph.

How to do it...

The format of the basic JavaScript code that we would need to execute to request geolocation data from the web browser is standardized in HTML5, and looks like this:

```
navigator.geolocation.getCurrentPosition(success, failure, options);
```

This method asynchronously requests geolocation information from the web browser, supplying a function to call if the request is successful (`success`), a function to call if the request fails (`failure`) and an object of options (`options`) which control the caching and the accuracy requirements of the request.

> Further information about the HTML5 Geolocation specification can be found online, at the URL: `http://www.w3.org/TR/geolocation-API/`

1. Our first step for this recipe is to create our ActionScript response handler function, which will receive an Object from the JavaScript environment which conforms to the W3C **Geolocation Position** specification—meaning that the response object it receives will have (at least) two parameters—`timestamp` and `coords`.

   We can extract the coordinate values from this response object and use them to create an instance of the Google Map's `LatLng` class with the following code, which simply copies the values directly from the response position `Object` instance and into a new `LatLng` class instance:

   ```
   var location:LatLng = new LatLng(position.coords.latitude,
                                    position.coords.longitude);
   ```

   Our complete Geolocation response handler function should look like this:

   ```
   function geolocationResponseHandler(position:Object):void {
       var location:LatLng = new LatLng(position.coords.latitude,
   position.coords.longitude);
       map.setCenter(location, map.getMaxZoomLevel(map.
   getCurrentMapType(), location));
   }
   ```

As with our previous recipe, this `geolocationResponseHandler` function uses our new `LatLng` class instance (`location`) to adjust the center point and zoom level of the map component on that location.

2. The next step is to make this ActionScript function available to be called by the external JavaScript environment, which we do through use of the `ExternalInterface.addCallback` method, like so:

```
ExternalInterface.addCallback("jsResponseHandler",
                            geolocationResponseHandler);
```

The first parameter supplied to the `addCallback` method is the name under which our ActionScript function will be available in JavaScript, and the second parameter is a reference to the actual ActionScript function itself.

> More information about the `ExternalInterface` class, which is so integral to integrating the JavaScript and ActionScript environments together, is available from the URL:
> `http://help.adobe.com/en_US/FlashPlatform/reference/actionscript/3/flash/external/ExternalInterface.html`

We should call this code as soon as our application starts up, in our existing `facebookReady` function.

3. With our callback function set up and accessible to JavaScript, we should now request Geolocation information from the browser using the `navigator.geolocation.getCurrentPosition` method and the `ExternalInterface` class.

The `getCurrentPosition` method accepts one, two, or three parameters. We're actually only going to supply information for the first parameter—the callback function for successful requests—and into that we pass an anonymous JavaScript function which will in turn forward the response object back into our Flash Player application.

The ActionScript code for this request should look like this:

```
ExternalInterface.call("navigator.geolocation.getCurrentPosition(function(position){document.getElementById(\"" + ExternalInterface.objectID + "\").jsResponseHandler(position)})");
```

It looks complex initially, but it's actually all a single-line ActionScript **String**, which contains a multiline JavaScript method call and nested functions.

The complete code for this recipe should look like this:

```
override public function facebookReady():void {
    if (ExternalInterface.available) {
        ExternalInterface.addCallback("jsResponseHandler",
geolocationResponseHandler);
        ExternalInterface.call( "navigator.geolocation.getCur
rentPosition(function(position){document.getElementById(\"" +
ExternalInterface.objectID + "\").jsResponseHandler(position)})");
    } else {
        trace("ExternalInterface unavailable.");
    }
}


function geolocationResponseHandler(position:Object):void {
    var location:LatLng = new LatLng(position.coords.latitude,
position.coords.longitude);
    map.setCenter(location, map.getMaxZoomLevel(map.
getCurrentMapType(), location));
}
```

When we run this application, the user will be asked if they want to allow the current HTML page to access location data, with a message such as this one, from Firefox 4:

Once the user has confirmed and allowed access to Geolocation data, the view should re-center itself on the user's current location.

With our location successfully determined, we can now execute the existing `mapClickHandler` function, and retrieve and display information about the nearby Facebook Places.

How it works...

The techniques we've used in this recipe essentially tunnel through the external JavaScript interfaces to interact directly with the browser's geolocation support, working with the geolocation APIs specified by the W3C, which are available online at:

```
http://www.w3.org/TR/geolocation-API/
```

The resulting object we receive from JavaScript will look like this:

```
{
    "timestamp": 1302348134416,
    "coords": {
        "longitude": -0.7245695,
        "accuracy": 42,
        "altitudeAccuracy": 0,
        "altitude": 0,
        "heading": null,
        "speed": null,
        "latitude": 52.5956211
    }
}
```

The `ExternalInterface` class is normally used for interacting with existing functions in the containing HTML page, but that's not ideal for making our code standalone. Instead we follow a similar approach to that used in the `FacebookJSBridge` ActionScript class, using script-injection techniques to bypass the requirement for specific functions to be present in the containing page.

 The `FacebookJSBridge` class is available in the source code of the Facebook ActionScript 3 SDK, under the `com.facebook.graph.core` package, if you're interested to see how this technique is applied on a much larger scale in this library.

There's more...

Of course, what we haven't yet looked at is handling unsuccessful location requests, such as when a user refuses access to their location.

Dealing with Geolocation errors

To handle an error from the Geolocation API, we need to add a second parameter to our initial `navigator.geolocation.getCurrentPosition` request. Following the same response-forwarding technique as the rest of this recipe, our ActionScript code should look like this:

```
override public function facebookReady():void {
    if (ExternalInterface.available) {
        ExternalInterface.addCallback("jsResponseHandler",
geolocationResponseHandler);
        ExternalInterface.addCallback("jsResponseError",
geolocationError);
        ExternalInterface.call( "navigator.geolocation.getCur
rentPosition(function(position){document.getElementById(\"" +
ExternalInterface.objectID + "\").jsResponseHandler(position)},functi
on(error){document.getElementById(\"" + ExternalInterface.objectID +
"\").jsResponseError(error)})");
    } else {
        trace("ExternalInterface unavailable.");
    }
}


function geolocationError(error:Object):void {
    if (error.code == 1) {
        trace("Permission denied");
    } else if (error.code == 2) {
        trace("Geolocation unavailable");
    } else if (error.code == 3) {
        trace("Geolocation timeout");
    }
}
```

If a user refuses to share geolocation information with our application, this `geolocationError` function will be executed, and the response object it returns conforms to the Geolocation API's `PositionError` interface, consisting of an error `code` parameter and an optional `message` parameter.

A sample error response for the user refusing access to Geolocation data looks like this:

```
{
    "TIMEOUT": 3,
    "POSITION_UNAVAILABLE": 2,
    "PERMISSION_DENIED": 1,
    "code": 1
}
```

Using an overlay to represent geolocation accuracy

One of the most common ways to represent the accuracy of geolocation coordinates is to display a circular overlay with a diameter equal to the accuracy, as illustrated in the following image:

We can add these overlays to our Google Maps component with the assistance of the following function, which creates a circular Polygon object:

```
function drawCircle(lat:Number, lng:Number, radius:Number,
                    strokeColor:Number = 0xff0000,
                    strokeWidth:Number = 2,
                    strokeOpacity:Number = 0.5,
                    fillColor:Number = 0xff0000,
                    fillOpacity:Number = 0.3):void {
    var d2r:Number = Math.PI / 180;
    var r2d:Number = 180 / Math.PI;

    // Convert statute miles into degrees latitude
    var circleLat:Number = radius * 0.014483;
    var circleLng:Number = circleLat / Math.cos(lat * d2r);
    var circleLatLngs:Array = new Array();
    for (var i:Number = 0; i < 33; i++) {
        var theta:Number = Math.PI * (i / 16);
        var vertexLat:Number = lat + (circleLat * Math.sin(theta));
        var vertexLng:Number = lng + (circleLng * Math.cos(theta));
        var latLng:LatLng = new LatLng(vertexLat, vertexLng);
        circleLatLngs.push(latLng);
    }

    var polygonOptions:PolygonOptions = new PolygonOptions();
    var fillStyle:FillStyle = new FillStyle();
    fillStyle.alpha = fillOpacity;
    fillStyle.color = fillColor;
    polygonOptions.fillStyle = fillStyle;

    var strokeStyle:StrokeStyle = new StrokeStyle();
    strokeStyle.alpha = strokeOpacity;
    strokeStyle.color = strokeColor;
    strokeStyle.thickness = strokeWidth;
    polygonOptions.strokeStyle = strokeStyle

    var polygon:Polygon = new Polygon(circleLatLngs, polygonOptions);
    map.addOverlay(polygon);
}
```

 I can't take any credit for this function—it is in fact a slightly modified version of the code found within the Official Google Maps demo application, a live example of which is available at the URL:

```
http://gmaps-samples-flash.googlecode.com/svn/trunk/
demos/CircleDemo/CircleDemo.html
```

To use this function in our own example, we can add the following code to our
`geolocationResponseHandler` handler function:

```
function geolocationResponseHandler(position:Object):void {
    var location:LatLng = new LatLng(position.coords.latitude,
position.coords.longitude);
    map.setCenter(location, map.getMaxZoomLevel(map.
getCurrentMapType(), location));
    map.addOverlay(new Marker(location));
    drawCircle(location.latitude, location.longitude, (position.
coords.accuracy / 2) / 1609.344);
}
```

This additional code passes in the latitude and longitude parameters for the location,
along with the desired radius of the circle overlay. To obtain the overlay's radius, we convert
our Geolocation accuracy value (which is measured in meters) into a value in units of miles
(which is what the drawCircle function expects) by first dividing the accuracy value in half
(diameter→ radius) and then by 1,609.344 (meters → miles).

Working with the native Flash Platform Geolocation capabilities

Native Flash Platform support for device sensors such as GPS or Geolocation data is available
in the AIR 2+ runtime for mobile devices. It is not, unfortunately, supported for AIR for Desktop
or basic in-browser Flash Platform applications (yet).

The ActionScript 3 Geolocation class comes as part of the AIR runtime libraries. To check
whether Geolocation information is available for the current device we can use using the
Geolocation.isSupported method.

If data is available, we create a new instance of the Geolocation class, set an update
interval for that instance, and register listeners to look for those update Events. The code
that we'd need to use to do this should look like this:

```
if (Geolocation.isSupported) {
    var location:Geolocation = new Geolocation();
    location.setRequestedUpdateInterval(100);
    location.addEventListener(GeolocationEvent.UPDATE,
locationUpdateHandler);
}
```

The event that comes through to this handler function is of type **GeoLocationEvent**,
containing the latest latitude and longitude information. To take this data and use it
to change the focal point of our map component, we could use the following function:

```
function geolocationUpdateHandler(e:GeolocationEvent):void {
    var location:LatLng = new LatLng(e.latitude, e.longitude);
    map.setCenter(location, map.getMaxZoomLevel( map.
getCurrentMapType(), location));
}
```

The **GeolocationEvent** returns an object with properties for `altitude`, `heading`, `horizontalAccuracy`, `latitude`, `longitude`, `speed`, `timestamp`, and `verticalAccuracy`—depending slightly on the capabilities of the device, of course.

Geolocation updates are asynchronous—meaning that we won't get an immediate location update when we instantiate the `Geolocation` class. Instead we specify a desired frequency of updates, using the `setRequestedUpdateInterval` method, and the `locationUpdateHandler` function that we associated with the `update` event will receive this information as-and-when the device passes that information into our application.

The update frequency for these events depends on the device itself. Some devices, like the first generation iPhones, don't have proper GPS capabilities, but instead identify their location via cell-towers and suchlike. As a result the accuracy of their locations is much lower, and the frequency with which they update is also much lower.

Official documentation for the `Geolocation` class is available from `http://help.adobe.com/en_US/FlashPlatform/reference/actionscript/3/flash/sensors/Geolocation.html`

See also

▶ *Finding Facebook Places near a specific location*

Creating new Checkins at an existing Facebook Place

We may not be able to create new Facebook Places through the Graph API, but with the correct Extended Permissions for the current user, we can create new Checkins at existing Facebook Places.

In this recipe, we're going to build an interface which allows us to browse for, and check into, an existing location on the user's behalf.

The first step for our application would be to retrieve a list of the eligible locations for the current user to check in at. Our interface itself will allow the user to browse around a Map containing Markers representing the nearby Facebook Places. Clicking on a Marker will select it, and once a Marker is selected, the user can click a **Check in here** button to check in at that location.

Our finished application should look something like this:

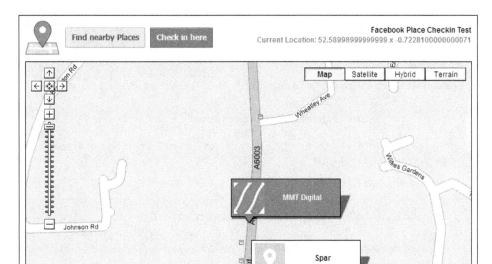

Getting ready

To create a Checkin on the user's behalf, our application will require the `publish_checkins` Extended Permission from the logged in user. To simplify the authentication process, the base class of our application should be the `ApplicationBase` class, detailed in the recipe _Creating the ApplicationBase class_ from _Chapter 11_.

In our application interface, we will need three main components: two **Button** components, with **id**s of `nearby_places_btn` and `checkin_here_btn`, which will be used to initiate a nearby Places search and create a new Checkin respectively, along with a Google Maps component (called `map`) to display the Places themselves.

1. Building on our earlier recipes, we can use the following ActionScript function to retrieve Place locations near to the current center of our map component:

```
function findNearbyPlaces(e:Event = null):void {
    var location:LatLng = map.getCenter();
    var options:Object = new Object();
    options.type = "place";
```

```
        options.center = location.lat() + "," + location.lng();
        Facebook.api("search", nearbyPlacesResponseHandler, options);
    }
```

2. We can link this function in as the click handler of the `nearby_places_btn` using the following MXML:

```
<s:Button id="nearby_places_btn"
        label="Find nearby Places"
        click="findNearbyPlaces(event)" />
```

3. Once we have retrieved these Place details, we can plot them on our Map component with the following code:

```
var currentMarkers:Array;

function nearbyPlacesResponseHandler(success:Object,
                                     fail:Object):void {
    var results:Array = success as Array;
    if (success && results) {
        removeMarkers();
        for (var i:int = 0; i < results.length; i++) {
            var place:FacebookPage = FacebookPage.
fromJSON(results[i]);
            var latlng:LatLng = new LatLng(place.location.
latitude, place.location.longitude);
            var markerOptions:MarkerOptions = new MarkerOptions();
            var markerComponent:PlaceSummaryMarker = new
PlaceSummaryMarker();
            markerComponent.data = place;
            markerOptions.icon = markerComponent;
            markerOptions.iconOffset = new Point(-30, -69);
            var marker:Marker = new Marker(latlng, markerOptions);
            map.addOverlay(marker);
            currentMarkers.push(marker);
        }
    }
}

function removeMarkers():void {
    if (currentMarkers) {
        for (var i:int = 0; i < currentMarkers.length; i++) {
            map.removeOverlay(currentMarkers[i]);
        }
    }
    currentMarkers = new Array();
}
```

This ActionScript code also uses a custom marker component—an instance of the `PlaceSummaryMarker` class—that we created as part of our previous recipe, *Finding Facebook Places near a specific location*.

How to do it...

With our setup so far, we've already got an interface which can retrieve nearby Places and plot them on a map, so the next step for this recipe is to make it possible to visually select one of those Places to check into.

We're going to make the map markers, each of which is an instance of our custom map marker class (`PlaceSummaryMarker`), selectable by the user through mouse click events. Only one Marker should be selectable at a single time, as only one Place can be checked into at any time.

1. To make our map markers modally-selectable, we would need to add the following ActionScript code to our application, which manages the visual selection styles and modal-selection behavior of all of the map markers:

```
var selectedMarker:PlaceSummaryMarker;
var currentMarkers:Array;

function nearbyPlacesResponseHandler(success:Object,
                                     fail:Object):void {
    var results:Array = success as Array;
    if (success && results) {
        removeMarkers();
        for (var i:int = 0; i < results.length; i++) {
            var place:FacebookPlace =
            FacebookPlace.fromJSON(results[i]);
            var latlng:LatLng = new LatLng(place.location.
            latitude, place.location.longitude);
            var markerOptions:MarkerOptions = new MarkerOptions();
            var markerComponent:PlaceSummaryMarker =
            new PlaceSummaryMarker();
            markerComponent.setPlace(place);
            markerOptions.icon = markerComponent;
            markerOptions.iconOffset = new Point(-30, -69);
            var marker:Marker = new Marker(latlng, markerOptions);
            marker.addEventListener(MapMouseEvent.CLICK,
            markerClickHandler);
            map.addOverlay(marker);
            currentMarkers.push(marker);
        }
    }
}
```

```
function markerClickHandler(e:MapMouseEvent):void {
    deselectMarkers();
    var marker:Marker = e.currentTarget as Marker;
    var icon:PlaceSummaryMarker = marker.getOptions().icon as
PlaceSummaryMarker;
    map.panTo(e.latLng);
    selectedMarker = icon;
    selectedMarker.currentState = "selected";
}


function removeMarkers():void {
    if (currentMarkers) {
        for (var i:int = 0; i < currentMarkers.length; i++) {
            map.removeOverlay(currentMarkers[i]);
            currentMarkers[i].removeEventListener( MapMouseEvent.
CLICK, markerClickHandler );
        }
    }
    currentMarkers = new Array();
    deselectMarkers();
}


function deselectMarkers():void {
    if (selectedMarker) {
        selectedMarker.currentState = "normal";
    }
}
```

2. Our custom marker class—`PlaceSummaryMarker`—already keeps track of the `FacebookPlace` instance it represents, so our next task is to add a click event handler to each of these Markers, and then in that event handler function extract that value of into the `currentPlace` parameter:

```
var currentPlace:FacebookPlace;


function markerClickHandler(e:MapMouseEvent):void {
    deselectMarkers();
    var marker:Marker = e.currentTarget as Marker;
    var icon:PlaceSummaryMarker = marker.getOptions().icon as
PlaceSummaryMarker;
    map.panTo(e.latLng);
    currentPlace = icon.data;
    selectedMarker = icon;
}
```

With a reference to a specific `FacebookPlace` instance stored in this `currentPlace` variable, we now have enough information to create a Checkin on the user's behalf. A request to create a new Checkin requires two parameters—the Facebook Place `id` and `coordinates` of the current user (or the Place itself).

3. To create a Checkin on the user's behalf, we can create a new function, `createCheckin`, and it should look like this:

```
function createCheckin(e:Event = null):void {
    var coords:Object = new Object();
    coords.latitude = currentPlace.location.latitude;
    coords.longitude = currentPlace.location.longitude;

    var options:Object = new Object();
    options.place = currentPlace.id;
    options.coordinates = JSON.encode(coords);
    Facebook.api("me/checkins", checkinReponseHandler,
    options, "post");
}
```

4. Finally, we should attach this function to our `Button` component with following MXML property:

```
<s:Button id="checkin_here_btn" label="Check in here"
        click="createCheckin(event)" />
```

With this request, we've now created a Checkin on the user's behalf at that Place. Add a final response handler for that request and our application should be complete.

How it works...

We create a new Checkin by issuing a `POST` request to the user's own `/checkins` connection, supplying, at the very least, the `id` of an existing Facebook Place under the parameter `place`, and the user's current location, under the parameter `coordinates`.

Beyond this, there are no checks as to the validity of the Checkin, so it's quite possible that we could intentionally spoof Checkin locations, such as creating Checkins to places like 'Area 51' (id: `147429241944882`).

 We can create a Checkin on a user's behalf at any existing Facebook Place but, unfortunately, we can't create our own Place from scratch—at least, not yet; it remains to be seen when and whether this capability will be opened up to developers working with the Graph API.

There's more...

In addition to simply checking the current user in at a location, the Graph API also supports
two additional properties: `message` and `tags`.

Adding a message to a Checkin

We can add a message to each Checkin simply by supplying a `message` parameter when we
post a new Checkin to the Graph API, like this:

```
var coords:Object = new Object();
coords.latitude = currentPlace.location.latitude;
coords.longitude = currentPlace.location.longitude;

var options:Object = new Object();
options.place = currentPlace.id;
options.coordinates = JSON.encode(coords);
options.message = "My awesome checkin status.";
Facebook.api("me/checkins", checkinReponseHandler, options, "post");
```

This message is simple plain-text String, much like we use when we create a status update for
the user—meaning that there's no support for complex text formatting or file upload support
(such as a Photo) with a Checkin.

"Tagging" other users to include them in a Checkin

As well as creating a Checkin for the current user, we can also create a Checkin on our friend's
behalf, by adding an Array of their user IDs to the request, under the `tags` parameter of our
new Checkin, like this:

```
var coords:Object = new Object();
coords.latitude = currentPlace.location.latitude;
coords.longitude = currentPlace.location.longitude;

var options:Object = new Object();
options.place = currentPlace.id;
options.coordinates = JSON.encode(coords);
options.tags = new Array("10000192832487", "10000192832488");
Facebook.api("me/checkins", checkinReponseHandler, options, "post");
```

With this request, the user IDs in the `tags` parameter will also be checked into the location
you've specified, under the same Facebook Checkin object.

See also

- ► *Finding Facebook Places near a specific location*
- ► *Chapter 4: Creating, Editing and Deleting Graph API objects*

11
Bridging the Flash and Application Gap

In this chapter, we will cover:

- ▶ Launching Facebook.com UI dialogs from ActionScript 3
- ▶ Imitating the Facebook.com UI in Flex
- ▶ Displaying a Facebook-style progress indicator
- ▶ Creating the ApplicationBase class

Introduction

In this chapter, we'll explore in further detail some of the ways through which we can achieve tighter integration between the Facebook.com website and our Flash Platform application.

By *tighter integration*, we're talking about making the switch between the official Facebook. com content and our own Facebook Canvas application as seamless as possible.

One way to do this is visually: making the components and animations visually indistinguishable from the official ones. Another effective method is to reuse existing data from the official Facebook.com SDKs and APIs—such as using the official Facebook.com dialog windows provided by the JavaScript SDK—instead of recreating the wheel and re-building dialogs from the ground-up each time.

Of course, the extent to which our application needs to integrate with Facebook depends largely on the type of application we're building, its visual style, and the actions that it needs to perform.

Bridging the Flash and Application Gap

For example, we could be building an application which seamlessly integrates with the Facebook.com website user interface, in which case the recipes *Imitating the Facebook. com UI [...]* and *Displaying a Facebook-style loading indicator* are likely to be useful. But for a completely custom interface, such as that of a game, these recipes won't be as useful as the recipe *Launching Facebook UI dialogs from ActionScript 3*.

Launching Facebook UI dialogs from ActionScript 3

In addition to the functionality provided to our application by the Graph API, there are also a few key dialog windows from Facebook that we can launch, which are described as thus:

> *Dialogs provide a simple, consistent interface to display dialogs to users. Dialogs do not require special user permissions because they require user interaction. Dialogs can be used in any type of application, whether on Facebook.com, a website, or a mobile application.*

 The key feature of these Facebook UI dialogs is that they don't require any Extended Permissions to launch and create status messages, because the pop ups are provided by Facebook, and they always require explicit user interaction before they perform any actions.

In this recipe, we're going to create an application which prompts the **Feed Dialog**, which can publish items to any of the user's feeds.

Getting ready

The Feed Dialog produces more or less the same output as posting a link or a status message through the Facebook.com website, and accordingly we need to be able to supply the same information for our dialog-created Post as we would for a wholly Flash Player-created Post.

To that end, our Flash application should contain the same or similar interface elements as in our recipe *Posting a Link with ActionScript* in *Chapter 6, Facebook News Feeds and Status Updates*. This interface should include `TextInput` components to supply a link's `message`, `name`, `caption`, and `description` along with components to supply the URLs for the `picture`, and the `link` itself. Unlike our other recipe, using Facebook UI dialogs to create Posts requires no Extended Permissions, so we can build our application directly on top of the standard MXML Application class.

The layout of our application itself need not be complex—it could simply be a stack of components, like this:

Publish a new feed item	
Message:	My pre-populated message…
Name:	Link name
Link URL:	http://facebook.psyked.co.uk/packt
Picture URL:	http://facebook.psyked.co.uk/packt/images/fb_app.png
Caption:	Link caption
Description:	Link description…
	Publish to news feed

How to do it...

To launch one of the built-in UI dialogs from the Facebook ActionScript 3 SDK, we would use code of a similar format to this:

```
Facebook.ui('feed', options, callback, mode);
```

As with the creation of Posts wholly through ActionScript (which requires Extended Permissions from the current user), the exact type of object that is created—be it a **Status message** update or a new **Link**—is dependent on the parameters that are supplied in the request.

1. Assuming that we have a `TextInput` component with an ID of `message_txt` in our application, the function that we could use to launch a dialog window could look like this:

```
function publishButtonClickHandler(e:Event):void {
    var options:Object = new Object();
    options.message = message_txt.text;

    Facebook.ui('feed', options, callbackFunction);
}
```

2. With additional similar components with IDs of `name_txt`, `caption_txt`, `description_txt`, `picture_txt`, and `link_txt`, the code needed to post a Link on Facebook would look like this:

```
function publishButtonClickHandler(e:Event):void {
    var options:Object = new Object();
    options.message = message_txt.text;
    options.caption = caption_txt.text;
    options.description = description_txt.text;
    options.name = name_txt.text;
    options.link = link_txt.text;
    options.picture = picture_txt.text;

    Facebook.ui('feed', options, callbackFunction);
}
```

The `callbackFunction` function we've specified for these two requests should both expect the same kind of a response from the Graph API—if the request is successful, it will return an object with the ID of the newly created Post object. If the request is not successful, there may be an error message from Facebook. Otherwise, if the dialog is cancelled, the response object will be a null, rather than a response object.

A successful response from the API should look like this:

```
{
    "post_id":"100001828360986_198446033525950"
}
```

And if the user cancels the dialog window manually, or there's a client-side error publishing the news item, the callback function will simply receive a value of **null**.

3. A simple response handler function which could parse this response might look like this:

```
function callbackFunction(response:Object):void {
    if(response && response.post_id) {
        // post was successfully created on Facebook.com
    } else if (response) {
        // post was made, but returned an error
    } else {
        // dialog was cancelled by the user
    }
}
```

How it works...

'Under the hood', as it were, what the Facebook ActionScript 3 SDK is doing is providing us with a shortcut method to the Facebook JavaScript SDK's FB.ui methods, the documentation for which can be found online at:

http://developers.facebook.com/docs/reference/javascript/FB.ui/

The function—both in JavaScript and ActionScript—accepts four parameters, which are:

1. The code name for the type of pop up to open, such as 'feed' or 'friends'.

2. The options for that pop up; such as the pre-populated fields, and these vary, depending on the pop up's type.

3. The call-back function, which is executed when the pop up has submitted data to Facebook and received a response.

4. And finally, the display mode of the dialog—whether the pop up should appear as an overlaid iframe, browser pop-up window, or redirect to another HTML page.

The first two of these parameters are required, with the latter two being optional. If the third parameter is omitted from the request, our Flash Player application will not receive a notification of the success or failure of the request. If the fourth parameter is omitted, the default display mode of iframe is used.

Facebook UI dialogs require an additional user interaction before they actually perform the action specified, and this interaction is not part of our Flash application, so it can be the case that the callback function takes a long time before it is executed—we should always be sure to plan accordingly, and especially to not lock the user out of our application in the meantime!

There's more...

The most common type of dialogs to use are probably the **Feed** or **Requests** dialogs—which post items to the user's news feed or invite the user's friends to use our application, respectively.

 A complete list of the other dialogs available from Facebook are listed online, along with the parameters required for those dialogs, available at:

`http://developers.facebook.com/docs/reference/dialogs/`

The display mode: Launching dialogs as inline iframes or new browser windows

There are in truth three modes of dialog windows available to Facebook applications—page, popup, and iframe—although the only two that we're likely to need are those which don't involve a complete page refresh—namely, popup and iframe.

The default setting for requests made through the ActionScript 3 SDK is iframe, which overlays an HTML iframe element over the top of the containing HTML page's existing HTML and SWF content. This HTML element is dynamically created and added to the current page by the JavaScript SDK, and because it's an iframe element, it shouldn't ever encounter any layering issues with HTML.

The alternative setting that we can use is popup, which opens a new browser window, and is documented as being 'For use in a browser popup no bigger than 400px by 580px'.

Modify the code used in earlier recipe into this to add the missing fourth parameter, with a value of popup, and our code would look like this:

```
var options:Object = new Object();
options.message = message_txt.text;
options.caption = caption_txt.text;
options.description = description_txt.text;
options.name = name_txt.text;
options.link = link_txt.text;
options.picture = picture_txt.text;

Facebook.ui('feed', options, callbackFunction, 'popup');
```

Assuming that our Flash interface contains the values listed in the preceding image, clicking the **Publish to News feed** button in our Flash Player application would launch a new browser window, similar to this:

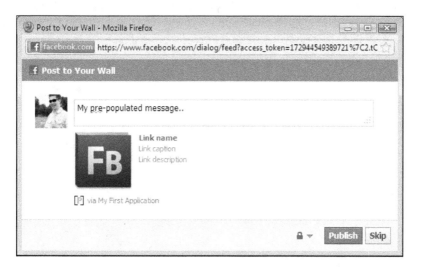

The downside to launching a new browser window is that such an action may fall foul of the browser's own pop-up blocker technologies. Generally speaking, a pop-up blocker is likely to suppress any new windows that are not triggered as a response to direct user interaction, such as a click of the mouse. Pop ups that we might try to launch purely from our own code, or those that happen as part of an asynchronous data request, will also suffer from an increased likelihood of failure against pop-up blockers. In those situations, it may be necessary to introduce further user-interaction powered steps, or simply use iframe-based dialog windows instead.

See also

▶   *Chapter 6, Posting a Link with ActionScript*

Imitating the Facebook.com UI in Flex

Facebook.com has its own unique style for interface elements, in the same way as Flex applications have their own style. In this recipe, we're going to use a Flex CSS stylesheet and Spark component skins to modify the default Flex component skins to better resemble those on the Facebook.com website.

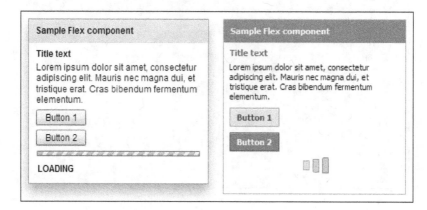

A `SparkSkin` component can be used to style our `Button` components. The first style we're going to create is the grey button—used generally for non-primary buttons, such as the Cancel button on a pop up.

The other button style used is the blue button—which is used more often for the primary buttons.

There's a wide variety of interface layouts and components that could make up our Facebook application, so we're not going to try and skin those components overly. Instead, the final component that we're going to skin is the `Panel` and `TitleWindow` components—which can be used for layout and pop-up messaging purposes, respectively.

How to do it...

Our final solution will use Flex CSS stylesheets, but before we get into creating those, we first need to create the individual component's skin classes.

1. Create a new MXML file in the skins folder, called `GreyButton`. The contents of the skin itself are simply composed from graphical `Rect` instances and `RichText` components, using the colors `0xffffff`, `0xf5f5f5`, `0xe5e5e5`, `0xe0e0e0`, `0x999999`, and `0x333333` to create the appropriate mix of fill, outline, and highlights in our components.

The complete MXML for this skin should look like this:

```
<s:SparkSkin alpha.disabled="0.5" minHeight="25" minWidth="25"
            xmlns:fb="http://ns.adobe.com/flashbuilder/2009"
            xmlns:fx="http://ns.adobe.com/mxml/2009"
            xmlns:s="library://ns.adobe.com/flex/spark">
    <fx:Metadata>
      <![CDATA[ [HostComponent("spark.components.Button")] ]]>
    </fx:Metadata>
    <s:states>
        <s:State name="up" />
        <s:State name="over" />
        <s:State name="down" />
        <s:State name="disabled" />
        <s:State name="upAndSelected" />
        <s:State name="overAndSelected" />
        <s:State name="downAndSelected" />
        <s:State name="disabledAndSelected" />
    </s:states>
    <s:Rect bottom="0" id="border" left="0" right="0" top="0">
        <s:stroke>
            <s:SolidColorStroke color="0x999999" />
        </s:stroke>
        <s:fill>
            <s:SolidColor color="0xe0e0e0"
                        color.over="0xf5f5f5" />
        </s:fill>
    </s:Rect>
    <s:Rect height="1" left="1" right="1" top="1">
        <s:fill>
            <s:SolidColor color="0xffffff"
                        color.over="0xffffff" />
        </s:fill>
    </s:Rect>
    <s:Rect bottom="-1" height="1" left="0" right="0">
        <s:fill>
```

```
                    <s:SolidColor color="0xe5e5e5" />
                </s:fill>
            </s:Rect>
            <s:RichText bottom="2" color="0x333333"
                        fontFamily="Tahoma" fontWeight="bold"
                        horizontalCenter="0" id="labelDisplay"
                        left="10" right="10" textAlign="center"
                        top="2" verticalAlign="middle"
                        verticalCenter="1">
            </s:RichText>
        </s:SparkSkin>
```

2. Create another MXML file in the skins folder, this time called `BlueButton`. The shape and construction of the button remains the same, but the colors of the button change, using instead `0xffffff`, `0x7c93c0`, `0xe5e5e5`, `0x5b74a8`, `0x29447e`, `0x8a9cc2`, and `0x9daed0`, and `0x333333`:

```
<s:SparkSkin alpha.disabled="0.5" minHeight="25" minWidth="25"
             xmlns:fb="http://ns.adobe.com/flashbuilder/2009"
             xmlns:fx="http://ns.adobe.com/mxml/2009"
             xmlns:s="library://ns.adobe.com/flex/spark">
    <fx:Metadata>
      <![CDATA[ [HostComponent("spark.components.Button")] ]]>
    </fx:Metadata>
    <s:states>
        <s:State name="up" />
        <s:State name="over" />
        <s:State name="down" />
        <s:State name="disabled" />
        <s:State name="upAndSelected" />
        <s:State name="overAndSelected" />
        <s:State name="downAndSelected" />
        <s:State name="disabledAndSelected" />
    </s:states>
    <s:Rect bottom="0" id="border" left="0" right="0" top="0">
        <s:stroke>
          <s:SolidColorStroke color="0x29447E" />
        </s:stroke>
        <s:fill>
```

```
        <s:SolidColor color="0x5B74A8"
                      color.over="0x7c93c0" />
      </s:fill>
    </s:Rect>
    <s:Rect height="1" left="1" right="1" top="1">
      <s:fill>
       <s:SolidColor color="0x8a9cc2"
                     color.over="0x9daed0" />
      </s:fill>
    </s:Rect>
    <s:Rect bottom="-1" height="1" left="0" right="0">
      <s:fill>
          <s:SolidColor color="0xe5e5e5" />
      </s:fill>
    </s:Rect>
    <s:Label bottom="2" color="0xffffff"
             fontFamily="Tahoma" fontWeight="bold"
             horizontalCenter="0" id="labelDisplay"
             left="10" maxDisplayedLines="1" right="10"
             textAlign="center" top="2"
             verticalAlign="middle" verticalCenter="1">
    </s:Label>
  </s:SparkSkin>
```

That covers the two major button styles, so now we're going to create a skin for the `Panel` and `TitleWindow` components.

3. Create a new MXML skin file in the `skins` package, called `FacebookPanelSkin`.

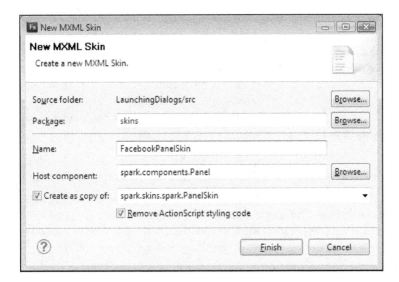

Inside this new MXML file will be all of the MXML elements needed to create the current skin's default interface. There's little problem with the default Panel skin's content area—it's just the outline color and the title bar that really needs to be modified.

4. The first step we can take is to completely remove the default dropshadow effect—just completely delete the dropShadow MXML element, which starts off looking like this:

```
<s:RectangularDropShadow id="dropShadow" blurX="20" blurY="20"
alpha="0.32" distance="11" angle="90" color="#000000" left="0"
top="0" right="0" bottom="0"/>
```

5. Next, modify the existing borderStroke element to add a fixed stroke color of 0x29447E:

```
<s:Rect bottom="0" id="border" left="0" right="0" top="0">
    <s:stroke>
    <s:SolidColorStroke color="0x29447E" id="borderStroke"
    weight="1" />
    </s:stroke>
</s:Rect>
```

6. Now we can simplify the top bar element, removing the gradients, and highlights, creating a simple 30 pixel high, flat blue bar, with bold, white text. To achieve this, modify the topGroup element, so that it looks like this:

```
<s:Group id="topGroup" mask="{topGroupMask}" minHeight="30">
    <s:Rect bottom="1" id="tbFill" left="0" right="0" top="0">
        <s:fill>
        <s:SolidColor color="0x627AAD" />
        </s:fill>
    </s:Rect>
    <s:Label bottom="0" color="#FFFFFF" fontFamily="Tahoma"
            fontSize="11" fontWeight="bold" id="titleDisplay"
            left="9" maxDisplayedLines="1" right="3"
            textAlign="start" top="1" verticalAlign="middle">
    </s:Label>
</s:Group>
```

The main content elements and control bars can remain as their default values.

Panel components are used for the interface layout, whereas TitleWindow instances are used for alerts and modal pop ups. The TitleWindow component skin is almost the same as the Panel component skin, with one exception—the border style, which is a dark grey, semi-opaque, rounded corners outline.

7. Create a new component in the `skins` package, called `FacebookTitleWindowSkin`, and have it extend the `FacebookPanelSkin` we created earlier.

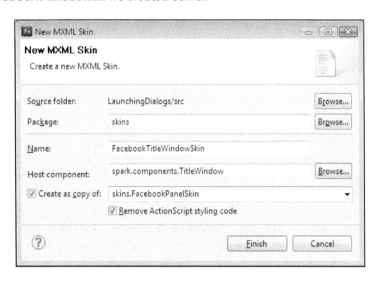

In doing this, our new component will inherit all of the customization we added to that previous skin, saving us from having to duplicate those tasks.

8. Add the following MXML element to the beginning of the skin file, which will create the semi-transparent thick grey outline:

```
<s:Rect bottom="0" left="0" radiusX="10" radiusY="10"
      right="0" top="0">
   <s:fill>
     <s:SolidColor alpha="0.7" color="0x828282" />
   </s:fill>
</s:Rect>
```

9. In order for this outline to show, we need to adjust the boundaries of the title bar and content inwards by 10 pixels. Modify the properties of the `Group` instance, encapsulating the `topGroupMask` instance, so that the `top`, `left`, `bottom`, and `right` values are equal to 10:

```
<s:Group bottom="10" left="10" right="10" top="10">
   <s:Group bottom="1" id="topGroupMask" left="1" right="1"
            top="1">
   [...]
```

When applied to the components, those components should look like this:

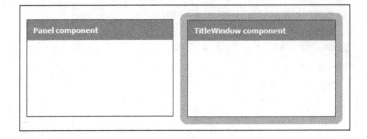

With Spark skins for grey and blue `Buttons`, `Panel`, and `TitleWindow` components, we can now create our stylesheet, which will automatically apply these skins as defaults for those components, as well as setting the default fonts and styles for the rest of our application.

10. Create a new CSS stylesheet, named `FacebookStyle.css`, and add the following code, which sets the default font and font sizes for the text-based Flex components and applies our custom Spark skins for the Button and Panel components:

```
@namespace s "library://ns.adobe.com/flex/spark";
@namespace mx "library://ns.adobe.com/flex/mx";
* {
  font-family: Tahoma;
  font-size: 11;
   modal-transparency-color:#FFFFFF;
  modal-transparency-blur:0;
  modal-transparency:0.3;
}

s|Panel {
  skinClass:ClassReference("skins.FacebookPanelSkin");
}

s|TitleWindow {
  skinClass:ClassReference("skins.FacebookTitleWindowSkin");
}

s|Button {
  skinClass:ClassReference("skins.FacebookGreyButton");
}

s|Button.blueButton {
  skinClass:ClassReference("skins.FacebookBlueButton");
}
```

11. Finally, to apply this stylesheet to our application, we need to add a stylesheet declaration to our MXML file, with the following MXML tag:

```
<fx:Style source="styles/FacebookStyle.css" />
```

How it works...

The Flex framework does not use CSS stylesheets in the same manner as might be expected, coming from a HTML background. Instead of this CSS file being a separate file that is loaded alongside pages, Flex CSS stylesheets are compiled with, and embedded into, the final SWF file of our application. The end result remains the same however, and it also allows us to use basic CSS syntax and concepts such as wildcards, classes, and individual component IDs.

In this recipe, we've used the * wildcard selector to override the default font family and font size in Flex, bringing it into line with the Facebook.com website. For our major components we've changed their default Spark skin, by specifying the `skinClass` property.

There are of course, two separate classes for the button skin—the grey and the blue button. In this recipe, we've specified that grey is the default button color, but by using the selector `s|Button.blueButton`, we've declared that—in much the same fashion as CSS—Button components with a class of `blueButton` should use a different skin. To apply a class in MXML, the property we would want to change is called `styleName`, which we'd set to `blueButton`, like so:

```
<s:Button label="Blue Button"
    styleName="blueButton" />
```

There's more...

Of course, there are more possible layouts and styles for components than can be accounted for with a generic CSS file, meaning that our applications will inevitably require more than we've created here—this is simply a starting point.

In our next recipe we will look at adding an activity indicator in the style of the Facebook.com website.

Displaying a Facebook-style loading indicator

Loading data from Facebook takes time—it's the same deal as loading any data from any other server. You request the data, and you wait for the response.

The Facebook ActionScript 3 SDK has a class, called `Distractor`, which is specifically created to replicate the appearance and animation of the loaders that you see on the Facebook.com website. It doesn't track progress—there's no real way to achieve that—but rather it signals the fact that *something* is happening, with an 'indeterminate' activity animation.

The class itself doesn't actually have any logic and that means it's magically able to know when things are loading from Facebook—all it does is displays a continually looping animation. So to make it do what we want it to, we have to add the traditional event listeners to our data requests, and show and hide an instance of the `Distractor` class.

When developing for a remote system like Facebook, we should always be sure to add an activity indicator whenever we're waiting for a response from the server—including processes like authentication, retrieving, and transmitting data, however large or small our requests may be. We can never truly anticipate when connection problems might occur, and it's better to have the user realize that a hang-up in the application is due to a connection issue, rather than having them blame our application!

In this recipe, we're only interested in demonstrating the loading animation itself, so we will build an interface which allows us to show and hide a modal pop-over version of the loading animation that comes in the Facebook ActionScript 3 SDK.

Getting ready

This recipe needs interaction or authentication with the Facebook APIs, so the starting point is to create a new MXML Application, add a **Button** component, and create a simple click-handler function for that button.

How to do it...

The `Distractor` class, which displays the Facebook-style loading animation, is an extension of the ActionScript 3 `Sprite` class, rather than any of the Flex framework components.

1. To display an instance of this `Distractor` class in our Flex application, we would first need to add a `UIComponent` instance, which in turn allows us to add plain ActionScript 3 class instances to the stage. Create this `UIComponent` within the Declarations tag of our application, using the following MXML:

```
<fx:Declarations>
    <mx:UIComponent id="distractor_component" />
</fx:Declarations>
```

2. We can't declare an instance of the `Distractor` with MXML tags, so instead we'll have to use some ActionScript code to create an instance of that class and add it to the `distractor_component`'s display list. Ideally, we should do this as soon as the application starts up, with the following function:

```
function applicationCompleteHandler(e:Event):void {
    var loadingAnimation:Distractor = new Distractor();
    distractor_component.addChild(loadingAnimation);
}
```

The dimensions of the `Distractor` class itself change during the animation's progression, but the minimum dimensions of the class are 40 pixels (width) by 25 pixels (height).

3. To ensure that the position and appearance of the components appears correctly, we should set the `distractor_component` component's `minWidth` and `minHeight` properties:

```
<mx:UIComponent id="distractor_component" minHeight="25"
                minWidth="40" />
```

In addition to this, the `Distractor` class (when it doesn't have its text property set) has a 10 pixel left margin.

4. To counter this offset, and ensure that our `Distractor` is added to our `UIComponent` in the correct position, we should make the following (highlighted) changes to our initialization function:

```
function applicationCompleteHandler(e:Event):void {
    var loadingAnimation:Distractor = new Distractor();
    loadingAnimation.x = -10;
    loadingAnimation.text = "";
    distractor_component.addChild(loadingAnimation);
}
```

5. Now that the component is established, we can use the Flex `PopupManager` class to display the animation in a modal overlay, using the following ActionScript function:

```
function showLoader():void {
    PopUpManager.addPopUp(distractor_component, this, true);
    PopUpManager.centerPopUp(distractor_component);
}
```

6. And to hide this overlay, we'd use a similar, opposing function:

```
function hideLoader():void {
    PopUpManager.removePopUp(distractor_component);
}
```

Now, whenever we're making an asynchronous request to the Facebook APIs (one that requires us to set a response handler function) we can call the `showLoader` function, and when that response is received, we call the `hideLoader` function.

The example for this is as follows:

```
function loadMyFriends():void
{
    Facebook.api("me/friends", gotFriendsHandler);
    showLoader();
}

function gotFriendsHandler(success:Object, fail:Object):void
{
    hideLoader();
    var feed:Array = success as Array;
    if (success && feed) {
        ...
    }
}
```

How it works...

For the purposes of this recipe, and consistency with the other recipes in this cookbook, we're displaying the `Distractor` class in the Flex framework. The `Distractor` class is built so it can be used in ActionScript 3 only projects, which means it's built on top of the Sprite base class rather than the `UIComponent` base class.

If we should add the `Distractor` class to the screen and make it visible, without linking it to the load progress of a request, we'll see that it's actually a looping animation. All we're doing with the code in this recipe is making that animation display in the correct place at the correct time.

There's more...

Displaying load progress for our applications should now be as simple as calling the `showLoader` and `hideLoader` functions at the appropriate times. It still has to be manually added in to our ActionScript code for each example, however.

Adding a text message to the loading animation

A message can be added to the `Distractor` class through use of its built-in text property, which will add a message to the left-hand side of the loading animation, with the resulting animation looking like this:

The ActionScript code we'd need to achieve this display could simply look like this:

```
distractor.text = "Loading animation message."
```

The existing functions could be modified to accept an optional message parameter, which is in turn applied the to the `Distractor` class instance, with the following modifications:

```
function hideLoader():void {
    loadingAnimation.text = "";
    PopUpManager.removePopUp(distractor_component);
}

    function showLoader(message:String = null):void {
    if (message) {
    loadingAnimation.text = message;
    distractor_component.width = loadingAnimation.width;
    }
    PopUpManager.addPopUp(distractor_component, this, true);
    PopUpManager.centerPopUp(distractor_component);
}
```

To be able to reference the `loadingAnimation` instance in this way, and not just show and hide the `distractor_component` **UIComponent** instance, we'd have to also make the following slight adjustments to the application initialization, which shifts the `loadingAnimation` declaration into the application-level scope, rather than the function-level scope:

```
var loadingAnimation:Distractor;

    function applicationCompleteHandler(e:Event):void {
    loadingAnimation = new Distractor();
```

```
            loadingAnimation.x = -10;
            loadingAnimation.text = "";
            distractor_component.addChild(loadingAnimation);
    }
```

Creating the ApplicationBase class

For the majority of other recipes in this cookbook, we need to authenticate our Flash Player application as a specific Facebook user.

Rather than repeatedly writing the same authentication code for each recipe, we're going to build our own class to abstract all of the authentication processes, the enforcement of the required extended permissions from Facebook, and indicate when information is being loaded from the Facebook APIs.

The class itself we'll call `ApplicationBase`, and it extends the Flex framework's `Application` class. The solution itself will be built in an MXML file, so that we can easily create custom Flex component declarations, and include ActionScript functions that can be activated in, or overridden by, the recipes which are built on top of this class.

Getting ready

1. The starting point for our new class is to extend the standard MXML Application class. From the `File` menu, select `New | MXML Application`, and name it `ApplicationBase`.

   While our application is running, it may have cause to launch two, slightly different, `TitleWindow` components—the first to notify a user that our application requires authentication with Facebook, and the second to inform the user that our application requires additional Extended Permissions granted to it.

   These two components should look like this:

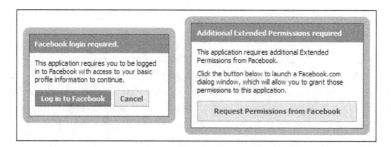

2. To create these pop ups, add the following MXML code inside the application's fx:Declarations tag, which will create the login_panel and request_panel components:

```
<s:TitleWindow height="150" id="login_panel" width="250"
               horizontalCenter="0" verticalCenter="0"
               title="Facebook login required.">
    <s:layout>
        <s:VerticalLayout paddingBottom="10" paddingLeft="10"
                          paddingRight="10" paddingTop="10"
                          gap="10" />
    </s:layout>

    <s:Label text="This application requires you to be logged
in to Facebook with access to your basic profile information to
continue." width="100%" />

    <s:HGroup width="100%" gap="5">
        <s:Button height="25"
                  id="login_panel_login_btn"
                  label="Log in to Facebook"
                  styleName="blueButton" />

        <s:Button height="25" id="login_panel_cancel_btn"
                  label="Cancel" />
    </s:HGroup>
</s:TitleWindow>

<s:TitleWindow height="186"
               id="request_panel"
               width="300"
               horizontalCenter="0"
               verticalCenter="0"
               title="Additional Extended Permissions required">
    <s:layout>
        <s:VerticalLayout paddingBottom="10"
                          paddingLeft="10"
                          paddingRight="10"
                          paddingTop="10"
                          gap="10" />
    </s:layout>

    <s:Label text="This application requires additional Extended
Permissions from Facebook." width="100%" />

    <s:Label text="Click the button below to launch a Facebook.com
dialog window, which will allow you to grant those permissions to
this application." width="100%" />
```

```
        <s:Button height="32" id="request_panel_request_btn"
                  label="Request Permissions from Facebook"
                  width="100%" />
    </s:TitleWindow>
```

When we combine this MXML with the CSS Styles from our earlier recipe *Imitating the Facebook. com UI in Flex*, we'll get two components that look like those in the preceding image.

How to do it...

After our application has started, the first thing that we want it to do is initialize the Facebook ActionScript 3 SDK, and then attempt to retrieve a valid session from the Graph API.

1. Add an event handler for the `applicationComplete` event in MXML, like so:

```
<s:Application xmlns:fx="http://ns.adobe.com/mxml/2009"
               xmlns:mx="library://ns.adobe.com/flex/mx"
               xmlns:s="library://ns.adobe.com/flex/spark"
    applicationComplete="applicationCompleteHandler(event)">
```

2. And create a new function, called `applicationCompleteHandler`:

```
function applicationCompleteHandler(e:Event):void
{
    var options:Object = new Object();
    options.appId = "[YOUR_APP_ID]";
    Facebook.setCanvasAutoResize(true);
    Facebook.init("[API_KEY]", loginStatusResponseHandler,
    options);
}
```

In this function we call the method `Facebook.init`, passing our API Key, a callback function, and an options object containing the Facebook application ID, in much the same way we covered in the recipes in Chapter 2, *Authentication with Facebook*.

 The values [YOUR_APP_ID] and [API_KEY] in the preceding code should be hardcoded and replaced with your own application's details, of course.

3. Next, we're going to create a function which will handle the response from both this `Facebook.init` method and any later, manually triggered, `Facebook.login` requests. This function should be called `loginStatusResponseHandler`, and should start out like this:

```
function loginStatusResponseHandler(success:Object,
                                    fail:Object):void
{
    if (success)
    {
```

```
            // a user is logged in
        } else
        {
            // no user is logged in
        }
    }
```

4. If there is no active Facebook session available, our first step should be to force the user to authenticate with the Graph API. To do this, we open the `login_panel` component as a modal pop up, using the following (highlighted) ActionScript code:

    ```
    import mx.managers.PopUpManager;

    function loginStatusResponseHandler(success:Object,
                                        fail:Object):void
    {
        if (success) {
            // a user is logged in
        } else {
            PopUpManager.addPopUp(login_panel, this, true);
            PopUpManager.centerPopUp(login_panel);
        }
    }
    ```

    The **Cancel** and **Log in to Facebook** buttons require their own click handler functions, which either hide the modal pop-up window, or launch the Facebook OAuth 2 login dialog, respectively.

5. To add functionality to our login `TitleWindow`, we need to add click event handlers to the Button component's MXML:

    ```
    <s:Button height="25" id="login_panel_login_btn"
            label="Log in to Facebook" styleName="blueButton"
            click="loginClickHandler(event)" />

    <s:Button height="25" id="login_panel_cancel_btn"
            label="Cancel"
            click="cancelClickHandler(event)" />
    ```

6. Next, we need to create these referenced functions in ActionScript, and have them close the pop up and call the `Facebook.login` method, as appropriate, using the following code:

    ```
    import com.facebook.graph.Facebook;

    function cancelClickHandler(e:Event):void
    {
        PopUpManager.removePopUp(login_panel);
    }
    ```

```
function loginClickHandler(e:Event):void
{
    Facebook.login(loginStatusResponseHandler);
    PopUpManager.removePopUp(login_panel);
}
```

With our code thus far, our application will prompt the user to log in to Facebook (if they're not already authenticated), and continually loop until the point that they are logged in. Assuming that this takes care of the authentication, the next step for our application should be to ensure that the current user has all of the **Extended Permissions** they're going to need in that application.

These permissions will be stored in an internal Array, with a custom getter function that initializes this Array on demand. Our recipes and other examples that use this `ApplicationBase` class can then override this getter function to specify the permissions that they will need.

7. The Array declaration and getter function that needs to be added to our application should look like this:

```
internal var _requiredPermissions:Array;

protected function get requiredPermissions():Array
{
    if (!_requiredPermissions)
    {
        _requiredPermissions = new Array();
    }
    return _requiredPermissions;
}
```

 Exactly how to use this `requiredPermissions` function to specify our recipe's **Extended Permission** requirements is explained in the upcoming *There's more...* section of this recipe.

8. Permissions should be checked after the user's authentication process is complete, so add the following (highlighted) function call to the `loginStatusResponseHandler` function:

```
function loginStatusResponseHandler(success:Object,
                                    fail:Object):void
{
    if (success)
    {
        checkPermissions();
```

```
    } else
    {
        PopUpManager.addPopUp(login_panel, this, true);
        PopUpManager.centerPopUp(login_panel);
    }
}
```

9. We need to use an FQL request to retrieve information about whether the current user has granted those permissions to our application, and we can do that with this function:

```
function checkPermissions():void
{
    if (requiredPermissions.length)
    {
        var values:Array = new Array();
        values.push(requiredPermissions.toString());
        Facebook.fqlQuery("SELECT {0} FROM permissions WHERE uid =
        me()", permissionsResponseHandler, values);
    }
}
```

The response from this FQL request will be an Array of Objects, containing two values—the name of the permission, and a Boolean as to whether the user has granted our Facebook application that permission.

In our handler function, `permissionsResponseHandler`, we loop through the results of this request, checking to see if any of the permissions we need are still missing. If any of those permissions are missing, we need to display the `request_panel` component to prompt the user to grant our application those permissions.

10. The response handler function for our Extended Permission FQL query should look like this:

```
function permissionsResponseHandler(success:Object,
                                    fail:Object):void {
    var results:Array = success as Array;
    if (success && results) {
        var requiresMorePermissions:Boolean = false;
        for (var i:int = 0; i < results.length; i++) {
            var permissions:Object = results[i] as Object;
            for (var j:int = 0; j < requiredPermissions.length;
j++) {
                if (!permissions[requiredPermissions[j]]) {
                    requiresMorePermissions = true;
                    break;
                }
            }
        }
```

```
        if (requiresMorePermissions) {
            // some of the required permissions are missing
            showPermissionsLoginbox();
        } else {
            // all of the permissions have been granted
        }
    } else {
        // there was a syntax error in the FQL
    }
}
```

11. If any of those Extended Permissions are missing, we would need to launch the `request_panel` component as a modal pop up, for which we would need the following function:

```
function showPermissionsLoginbox():void
{
    PopUpManager.addPopUp(request_panel, this, true);
    PopUpManager.centerPopUp(request_panel);
}
```

12. Requesting additional permissions is much the same process as logging in, so it makes sense to have the click handler on the button in our permissions dialog reuse the same `loginClickHandler` function.

```
<s:Button height="32" id="request_panel_request_btn"
        label="Request Permissions from Facebook"
        width="100%"
        click="loginClickHandler(event)" />
```

13. This necessitates a couple of changes to the `loginClickHandler` function, the first of which adds an options object to the `Facebook.login` method, specifying the Extended Permission details:

```
function loginClickHandler(e:Event):void
{
 var options:Object = new Object();
 options.perms = requiredPermissions.toString();
 Facebook.login(loginStatusResponseHandler, options);
 PopUpManager.removePopUp(login_panel);
}
```

14. As our `loginClickHandler` function is now responding to two separate Buttons in different components, we now need to make sure that this function always closes both the `login_panel` and `request_panel` pop ups, with the following change to our code:

```
function loginClickHandler(e:Event):void
{
```

```
    var options:Object = new Object();
    options.perms = requiredPermissions.toString();
    Facebook.login(loginStatusResponseHandler, options);
    PopUpManager.removePopUp(login_panel);
    PopUpManager.removePopUp(request_panel);
}
```

That takes care of prompting the user to log in, and requesting additional permissions. Now we're going to add some code to automatically retrieve specific details about the current user, once they're authenticated, as we otherwise have no details about them—including properties such as their name.

15. Add the following ActionScript code, which retrieves details about the currently Facebook user, and caches that information in an internally-accessible variable:

```
import com.facebook.graph.data.api.user.FacebookUser;
internal var currentUser:FacebookUser;
function getUserDetails():void
{
Facebook.api("me", userDetailsResponseHandler);
}
function userDetailsResponseHandler(success:Object,
        fail:Object):void {
    if (success)
    {
        var user:FacebookUser = FacebookUser.fromJSON(success);
        currentUser = user;
    }
}
```

16. We can have the `ApplicationBase` class load this information about the current user automatically by making our API request as soon as we've received a successful response in the `loginStatusResponseHandler` function, with the following addition to that function:

```
function loginStatusResponseHandler(success:Object,
        fail:Object):void
{
    if (success)
    {
        checkPermissions();
    getUserDetails();
    } else
    {
        PopUpManager.addPopUp(login_panel, this, true);
        PopUpManager.centerPopUp(login_panel);
    }
}
```

Finally, we can add the Facebook-style loading animations, as covered in the previous recipe, *Displaying a Facebook-style loading indicator*.

17. Add the MXML `UIComponent`, `distractor_component`, to the `fx:`
`Declarations` tag:

```
<mx:UIComponent id="distractor_component" minHeight="25"
                minWidth="40" />
```

18. Add the initialization code for the `Distractor` class to the existing
`applicationCompleteHandler` function:

```
import com.facebook.graph.controls.Distractor;

internal var loadingAnimation:Distractor;

function applicationCompleteHandler(e:Event):void
{
    loadingAnimation = new Distractor();
    loadingAnimation.x = -10;
    loadingAnimation.y = 0;
    distractor_component.addChild(loadingAnimation);

    var options:Object = new Object();
    options.appId = "[YOUR_APP_ID]";
    Facebook.setCanvasAutoResize(true);
    Facebook.init("[API_KEY]", loginStatusResponseHandler,
options);
}
```

19. Next, we should add the `hideLoader` and `showLoader` functions:

```
internal function hideLoader():void
{
    PopUpManager.removePopUp(distractor_component);
}

internal function showLoader():void {
    PopUpManager.addPopUp(distractor_component, this, true);
    PopUpManager.centerPopUp(distractor_component);
}
```

20. And finally, we should add the `facebookReady` function—the function that our
`ApplicationBase` class will execute once all of its automatic actions are complete:

```
public function facebookReady():void
{
    hideLoader();
}
```

And we want to execute this when our user details response arrives, like so:

```
function userDetailsResponseHandler(success:Object,
        fail:Object):void
{
    if (success)
    {
        var user:FacebookUser = FacebookUser.fromJSON(success);
        currentUser = user;
    }
    facebookReady();
}
```

Each of our applications which build on top of this class can override this `facebookReady` function to execute code automatically, once our application is authenticated with Facebook.

That's it—we now have a solid base class for our recipes, which abstracts the login and permissions management processes away from individual recipes. It also retrieves useful information about the current user—such as their full name (and not just their Facebook ID), and it integrates the Facebook-style loading indicator from our earlier recipes.

How it works...

The key elements that our `ApplicationBase` class provides us, which the standard Application class does not, are as follows:

1. Automatic authentication with Facebook at application startup.
2. Enforcing a minimum level of required Extended Permissions.
3. Retrieving basic information about the current user.
4. Built-in Facebook-style modal loading animations.

The key functions themselves are as follows:

- `get requiredPermissions`: Overriding the return value of the getter for `requiredPermissions` allows us to define the minimum level of Extended Permissions required from Facebook on an individual application basis.

- `facebookReady`: The `facebookReady` function is called automatically once the user has been authenticated with Facebook, had their Extended Permissions validated, and the current user's information has been retrieved.

- `showLoader`: Displays a modal Facebook-style loading animation, and should be manually executed by recipes whenever they begin an API request.

- `hideLoader`: Removes the modal Facebook-style loading animation, and should be manually executed by our recipes when they receive responses to API requests.

The specifics of how the login functionality works; how the Extended Permissions and FQL queries work are covered in more detail in other chapters, and other recipes.

Integrating the previous *Imitating the Facebook.com UI in Flex* recipe?

Unfortunately, Flex stylesheets don't inherit between MXML components, so if we added it as an MXML Declaration for our `ApplicationBase` class, it still wouldn't have an effect on those applications that we build on top of it, which makes adding integrating the two a little pointless. Each of our recipes will have to import the `FacebookStyles.css` file separately in their Declarations tag.

There's more...

Now that we have built the `ApplicationBase`, those recipes which require authentication can be built on top of this class, rather than the default `Application` class. Those recipes will then automatically inherit the functionality of this class, reducing the need for duplicate functionality.

Using the ApplicationBase class, instead of the standard Application class

This new class we've created can, and should for many of our recipes, be used in place of the default `Application` class that comes in the Flex framework.

Essentially, to use the `ApplicationBase` class rather than the default `Application` class, we simply need to turn this MXML tag:

```
<s:Application width="758" height="600"
            xmlns:fx="http://ns.adobe.com/mxml/2009"
            xmlns:mx="library://ns.adobe.com/flex/mx"
            xmlns:s="library://ns.adobe.com/flex/spark">
</s:Application>
```

Into this:

```
<local:ApplicationBase width="758" height="600"
            xmlns:local="*"
            xmlns:fx="http://ns.adobe.com/mxml/2009"
            xmlns:mx="library://ns.adobe.com/flex/mx"
            xmlns:s="library://ns.adobe.com/flex/spark">
</local:ApplicationBase>
```

This change will most likely have to be made manually, as the code-completion in Flash Builder doesn't function very well with custom component's on an Application's root level XML tag. What this code is actually doing is declaring a new XML namespace for our custom classes, and then using it in the root tag.

Specifying Extended Permission requirements in our recipes

In the recipes which extend this `ApplicationBase` class, the process for specifying Extended Permissions is actually quite simple.

What our `ApplicationBase` class does is construct an FQL request for permissions and validate the response. It constructs this request from the results of the `requiredPermissions` property, so all that we have to do in our applications that extend this class is modify that property. The property is marked as `protected`, meaning that it can be overridden by classes that extend the `ApplicationBase` class, simply by re-declaring the entire function in our application, using the `override` keyword.

For example, we could use the following code to override this property and specify the `publish_stream` permission as a requirement for our application:

```
override protected function get requiredPermissions():Array
{
    if (!_requiredPermissions)
    {
        _requiredPermissions = new Array();
        _requiredPermissions.push("publish_stream");
    }
    return _requiredPermissions;
}
```

Automatically executing code once our application is authenticated with Facebook

To execute code automatically in our applications, once its Extended Permission validation and user details retrieval requests are complete, we need to override the `facebookReady` function, like so:

```
override public function facebookReady():void
{
    super.facebookReady();
    // new code goes here
}
```

See also

▶ Chapter 2, *Authentication with the Web SDK, for Flash Player applications*

▶ Chapter 2, *Retrieving information about the current session and active Facebook user*

▶ Chapter 3, *Checking for existing Extended Permissions*

▶ Chapter 3, *Pre-emptively requesting additional Extended Permissions*

▶ Chapter 5, *Loading data with FQL*

Index

friendsArrayCollection ArrayCollection 225
friends field 184
FROM clause 132
fromJSON method 93, 239
fromJSON parsing method 230
fx$Script tag 224, 246

G

Geolocation.isSupported method 321
geolocation accuracy
  representing, overlay used 319-321
Geolocation class 321, 322
geolocationError function 318
Geolocation errors
  dealing with 318
GeolocationEvent 322
geolocationResponseHandler handler
          function 321
getCurrentPosition method 315
getImageUrl method 116
get requiredPermissions function 357
GitHub 13
Google Maps API
  downloading 298, 299
Google Maps component 298
graph_api_request_btn Button component
          102
graph_api_request_btn component 88
Graph API 27
  /[OBJECT_ID] vs. [OBJECT_ID] in requests 95
  about 85
  album, creating with 240-244
  correct URL, ensuring 219
  developer documentation, URL 168
  errors, detecting 94
  me shortcut, using to reference current users
          95
  object, loading from Facebook 91, 93
  search capabilities, using 119-122
  test console, building 86-89
  usernames, URLs 94
  vanity URLs 94
Graph API connections
  loading 100-104
  mixed result content types, responses han-
          dling with 105, 106

Graph API object
  comments, adding 204, 206
  comments, loading for 198-203
  creating 122-124
  deleting 122-124
  editing 122-124
  like, adding 211, 212
  like, removing 212, 213
  likes, retrieving for 209, 210
  specific data fields, loading 96-99
  undocumented fringes 99
GreyButton 336
group_members component 266
Group class 260
Group Membership
  URL 267
group membership information
  retrieving 263
  retrieving, steps 264-266
  working 267
groupSearchResults ArrayCollection instance
          259

H

hard-coded permission names 63
hasJSEventListener function 54
hideLoader function 346, 347, 356, 357
higher() function 165
horizontalAlign properties 235
HTML5 geolocation capabilities
  integrating with 313-317
HTML5 Geolocation specification
  URL 314
human-readable JSON string
  getting, from API 90, 91

I

iconOffset parameter 313
iconOffset property 313
ID parameter 182
IFacebookGraphObject interface 93
iframe 334
IF statement 272
image_preview component 233, 240, 246
image_preview components 245

Image component **117, 198, 223, 232, 246, 257, 260**
ImageSnapshot Flex class **253**
image URLs
  getting, from graph API objects 118
IN clause **138**
indicator_lbl component **113**
initialize_btn Button component **35, 36**
init method **43**
ItemRenderer class **201**
Item Renderer component **198**
itemRendererFunction **175**
itemRendererFunction property **174, 175**
itemRenderer property **172**

J

JavaScript events **51-53**
JavaScript SDK
  working with 29
JavaScript SDK's FB.init method documentation
  URL 42
jsLoginHandler function **54**
JSON.encode method **91**

L

Label component **34, 43, 177, 300, 312**
large data sets
  loading, with FQL multiquery 148-151
latitude parameters **321**
LatLngBounds.extend method **304**
LatLngBounds class **304, 311**
LatLngBounds instance **304, 311**
LatLng class **314**
LatLng class instance **303, 309, 314**
like_btn component **211**
likes
  about 197
  adding, to Graph API object 211, 212
  count, specifying for specified URL 214
  removing, from Graph API object 212, 213
  retrieving, for Graph API object 209, 210
  URL statistics, retrieving with FQL 215, 217
  URL statistics, retrieving with Graph API 214, 215

likes data field **212**
LIMIT key word **161**
limit parameter **111, 305**
link
  internal links, publishing to canvas application 188
  posting, with ActionScript 185-187
link_stat table **215**
LinkItemRenderer component **173, 189**
Link object **186**
List component **169, 170, 172, 174, 198, 227, 242, 264, 277**
listSelectionChangeHandler function **264**
load_button component **308, 309**
loadingAnimation instance **347**
load progress
  indicating, animation used 89, 90
locationUpdateHandler function **322**
logical operators
  using, in FQL request 143-147
login_btn component **36, 37, 80**
login_panel component **351**
login_panel popups **354**
loginClickHandler function **61, 354**
login dialog **40, 41**
loginStatusResponseHandler function **352, 355**
Log in to Facebook button **62**
logout_btn component **47**
Log out of Facebook button **46**
longitude parameters **321**
lower() FQL statement **160**
lower() function **164, 165**

M

manageSession property **43, 45**
map
  events, plotting 273-276
  integrating with 313-317
Map.setCenter method **304**
mapClickHandler function **316**
Map component **300, 303**
map component **309**
map markers
  creating, for places 312, 313

markers 236
me()
  using, to reference current user 135, 136
me() shortcut 135
me/home connection 105
me request
  using, to reference current user 95
me shortcut 118
message
  adding, to uploaded images 254
message field 204
message parameter 182, 187, 318, 328
metadata_chk component 89
multiple Graph API objects
  loading, in single request 107-110
MXML tag 169

N

name parameter 190, 193
native Flash Platform Geolocation capabilities
  working with 321, 322
navigator.geolocation.getCurrentPosition
    request 318
networks field 184
newsfeed 170
notConnected users 55
NOT IN
  used, for excluding results 148
NumericStepper component 110

O

offset parameter 111
onCommentsLoaded function 200
onFacebookLogin function 53, 67
onFacebookLogout function 53
onFQLResponse 67
onFQLResponse function 68, 69, 82
onPostStatusCallback function 75
onSelectClick function 248
options parameter 41
ORDER BY clause 159
ORDER BY keyword 162
ORDER BY statement 159
OR operator 145

overlapping results
  finding, by cross-comparing data sets 153-157
override keyword 359

P

paging results
  limiting 110-114
Panel component 336
Panel component skin 340
permissions
  about 57
  at login, requesting 59-63
  extended permissions 58, 59
permissionsRequestCallback function 76
perms property 60
photo_tag table 141
photoComments ArrayCollection instance
    200
photo information
  photos loading, without selecting album 230, 231
  photo tags, displaying 231-239
  photo tags, loading 231-239
  retrieving, from facebook 222-230
photos
  loading, without selecting album 230, 231
  uploading, on Facebook 244-253
photos_list 223
photos_list component 227, 232, 233
photosArrayCollection instance 227
photo tags
  displaying 231-239
  loading 231-239
places 297
placeSearchResponseHandler function 309
PlaceSummaryMarker class 325
Point class 313
popup 334
PopupManager class 346
post_btn component 82
postButtonClickHandler function 182
Post object 181
POST request 123, 124
post versions 213

pretty-printing 90
privacy property 184
privacy settings
about 183
adding 184
defining 184
publish_stream Extended Permission 122
publish_stream 241
publish_stream Extended Permission 204, 208
publish_stream extended permission 181
publish_stream permission 67, 359
Publish to News feed button 335

Q

query_display component 129

R

RadioButton components 245
rawResult.images property 230
read_stream Extended Permission 211
read_stream permission 168
RegExp.replace method 178
RegExp ActionScript 3 class 179
removeJSEventListener function 54
removeMakers 309
request_panel component 353, 354
request_panel components 349
request_panel popups 354
requestCallback function 88, 113
requestCallback handler function 98
requestClickHandler function 89, 97, 121
request lengths
limiting 110-114
requestPermissionsInfo function 82
requiredPermissions function 352
requiredPermissions property 359
resetInterface function 244, 251
responseHandler function 182
results_display component 129
results_txt component 96
RichEditableText component 178, 204
RichText component 128, 269, 336

S

Script tag 26, 35
SDK
AIR version 13, 14
Flash Player version 13, 14
search_inpt component 258
search_results_list component 259, 270
search_results_list List component 259
search capabilities
of Graph API, using 119-122
searchClickHandler function 258
Security Sandbox Error 27
select_btn components 245
SELECT clause 130
selectedEventChangeHandler function 279
selected property 213
setCenter method 311
setRequestedUpdateInterval method 322
showLoader function 346, 347, 356, 357
showLoader method 225
since option 114
single request
multiple Graph API objects, loading in 107
Site Domain property 25, 28
Site URL property 25
skinClass property 343
skins package 339, 341
source parameter 229
source property 227
SparkSkin component 336
specific data fields
loading, for Graph API object 96-99
Sprite class 344
Sprite instance 235
status_lbl component 47
StatusMessageItemRenderer component 188
status message updates
loading 168, 169
status update
and privacy settings 183
creating, with ActionScript 180-182
deleting, with ActionScript 188-191
posting, to users walls 183
String.indexOf method 165

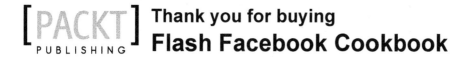

About Packt Publishing

Packt, pronounced 'packed', published its first book "*Mastering phpMyAdmin for Effective MySQL Management*" in April 2004 and subsequently continued to specialize in publishing highly focused books on specific technologies and solutions.

Our books and publications share the experiences of your fellow IT professionals in adapting and customizing today's systems, applications, and frameworks. Our solution based books give you the knowledge and power to customize the software and technologies you're using to get the job done. Packt books are more specific and less general than the IT books you have seen in the past. Our unique business model allows us to bring you more focused information, giving you more of what you need to know, and less of what you don't.

Packt is a modern, yet unique publishing company, which focuses on producing quality, cutting-edge books for communities of developers, administrators, and newbies alike. For more information, please visit our website: www.packtpub.com.

Writing for Packt

We welcome all inquiries from people who are interested in authoring. Book proposals should be sent to author@packtpub.com. If your book idea is still at an early stage and you would like to discuss it first before writing a formal book proposal, contact us; one of our commissioning editors will get in touch with you.

We're not just looking for published authors; if you have strong technical skills but no writing experience, our experienced editors can help you develop a writing career, or simply get some additional reward for your expertise.

Facebook Graph API Development with Flash

ISBN: 978-1-849690-74-4   Paperback: 324 pages

Build social Flash applications fully integrated with the Facebook Graph API

1. Build your own interactive applications and games that integrate with Facebook

2. Add social features to your AS3 projects without having to build a new social network from scratch

3. Learn how to retrieve information from Facebook's database

4. A hands-on guide with step-by-step instructions and clear explanation that encourages experimentation and play

Flash Game Development by Example

ISBN: 978-1-849690-90-4   Paperback: 328 pages

Build 10 classic Flash games and learn game development along the way

1. Build 10 classic games in Flash. Learn the essential skills for Flash game development

2. Start developing games straight away. Build your first game in the first chapter

3. Fun and fast paced. Ideal for readers with no Flash or game programming experience.Topic

4. The most popular games in the world are built in Flash

Please check **www.PacktPub.com** for information on our titles

Flash Development for Android Cookbook

ISBN: 978-1-849691-42-0   Paperback: 372 pages

Over 90 recipes to build exciting Android applications with Flash, Flex, and AIR

1. The quickest way to solve your problems with building Flash applications for Android

2. Contains a variety of recipes to demonstrate mobile Android concepts and provide a solid foundation for your ideas to grow

3. Learn from a practical set of examples how to take advantage of multitouch, geolocation, the accelerometer, and more

4. Optimize and configure your application for worldwide distribution through the Android Market

Flash 10 Multiplayer Game Essentials

ISBN: 978-1-847196-60-6   Paperback: 336 pages

Create exciting real-time multiplayer games using Flash

1. A complete end-to-end guide for creating fully featured multiplayer games

2. The author's experience in the gaming industry enables him to share insights on multiplayer game development

3. Walk-though several real-time multiplayer game implementations

4. Packed with illustrations and code snippets with supporting explanations for ease of understanding

Please check **www.PacktPub.com** for information on our titles

www.ingramcontent.com/pod-product-compliance
Lightning Source LLC
LaVergne TN
LVHW062302060326
832902LV00013B/2011